Thermal Design
of **Buildings**

UNDERSTANDING HEATING, COOLING
AND DECARBONIZATION

Phillip Jones

Thermal Design of Buildings

UNDERSTANDING HEATING, COOLING AND DECARBONIZATION

THE CROWOOD PRESS

First published in 2021 by
The Crowood Press Ltd
Ramsbury, Marlborough
Wiltshire SN8 2HR

enquiries@crowood.com
www.crowood.com

British Library Cataloguing-in-Publication Data
A catalogue record for this book is available from the British Library.

ISBN 978 1 78500 898 6

Cover design: Sergey Tsvetkov

All images are by the author P. Jones unless otherwise attributed.

Typeset by Simon and Sons
Printed and bound in India by Replika Press Pvt. Ltd.

Contents

Chapter One

Introduction

THE BUILT ENVIRONMENT IS AT ONE LEVEL a necessity for providing shelter and security for people and their communities, while on another level it can promote a more positive feeling of delight. The challenge for thermal design is to produce technical solutions that lead to an overall improvement in the comfort, health and quality of life for all people, with the efficient use of energy and aiming towards zero carbon dioxide emissions.

Many aspects of heating and cooling are as dependent on architectural solutions, such as the form and fabric of a building, as they are on the engineering of mechanical systems. This is especially the case in relation to our need to reduce energy use and produce buildings that are affordable to operate, as well as comfortable and healthy to occupy. Close working between the architect and the engineer is essential for a successful solution. Heating and cooling systems should not be simply 'bolted on' once the architecture has been designed, but, rather, they should be fully integrated as part of a 'whole building' solution, whether we are dealing with a new building or retrofitting an existing one. As the building fabric becomes more efficient in reducing energy demand, the systems must be designed to respond to the reduced demand. Of course, throughout the thermal design process we must keep in mind the role of people, as end users, builders and regulators, and the need for them to be aware of what is possible.

The use of fossil fuel energy to construct and operate buildings is a major cause of climate change. Building integrated renewable energy generation is increasingly being used to supply a building's energy needs, both for electrical power and heat. At the same time our energy supply grids are being decarbonized. Achieving an appropriate balance between building integrated renewable energy and grid-based renewable energy is therefore a major consideration in the drive towards energy-efficient zero carbon design. Sustainable design means that our buildings should be pleasing, and robust against a range of usage, rather than be dependent on control, constraint and enforced behavioural change.

Buildings do not exist independently of their surroundings. They will interact with neighbouring buildings and landscapes, creating local microclimates, which will affect energy use, and internal and external comfort. The supporting infrastructures for energy, water and sewage, waste, transport and information connectivity all have implications for energy use and sustainability.

Fig. 1.1 summarizes the main stages to thermal design, through an understanding of comfort needs; how the building interacts with climate; the heating, cooling and ventilation systems, renewable energy and energy storage; and finally within the context of the surrounding buildings and infrastructures.

Fig. 1.2 summarizes the main elements of thermal design, beginning with climate and ending with environment and comfort. The passive design elements relate to the site location, the building's form and mass, and its fabric and glazing. The active elements relate to the environmental services for heating, cooling, ventilation and lighting. Whereas passive solutions may use 'free' energy from the sun and the wind, active solutions rely on heating and cooling equipment that use 'delivered' energy.

There are various ways energy links to thermal design. The free energy is the energy gained from natural sources as part of the passive design process. The delivered energy is the energy used to power the components of active systems, such as heaters,

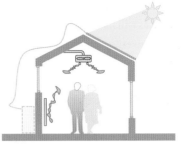

Environmental conditions for all spaces should be clearly defined in relation to space use and people's activities, and processes.

Buildings benefit from 'passive design', where the envelope of the building is used to 'filter' or 'modify' the external climate, minimising the need for mechanical 'active' heating and cooling, and reducing delivered energy.

'Active' systems for heating, cooling and ventilation respond to passive design providing comfortable healthy environments. They should operate efficiently, be low energy, using renewable energy generation and storage.

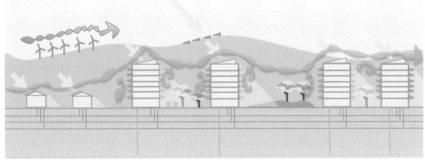

Buildings interact with their surroundings through shading and breezeways, which together with landscape features, can create microclimates. Energy can be a mix of local and grid based renewables.

Fig. 1.1 Thermal design.

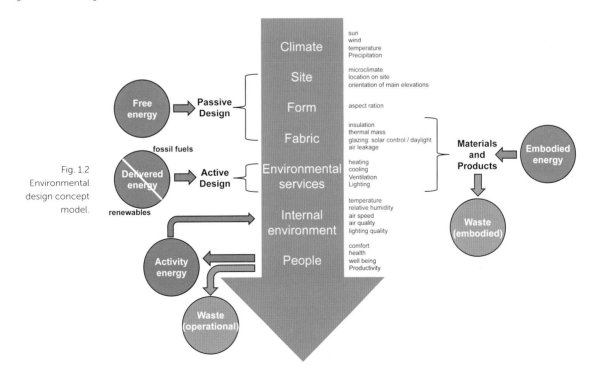

Fig. 1.2 Environmental design concept model.

chillers, fans and pumps. Delivered energy from fossil fuel sources will have associated carbon dioxide emissions. The eventual aim is to replace fossil fuels with renewable zero carbon energy. The activity energy is released within the building from activities and processes related to occupancy. It includes the heat from electric lighting and appliances, and the metabolic heat generated by people. These may result in a significant heat gain, which may be useful for space heating or, more often these days, may need to be exhausted by mechanical cooling to avoid overheating. The embodied energy is associated with the materials and products used during a building's construction and fit-out, and subsequent renovations. As the delivered energy is increasingly reduced through energy-efficient design, the embodied energy becomes a greater proportion of the overall energy balance.

There are a range of underlying topics and issues that are connected to thermal design. Globally, everything is changing, including climate, our energy systems, and people's aspirations. The rate of construction is increasing, while our dependence on fossil fuel must cease. Recent pandemics have also challenged our vision of the future, and the role our built environment plays in the spread of infectious disease.

If we are to meet the challenge of creating a more sustainable zero carbon built environment, original thinking is needed with innovative solutions. This is often not the case in everyday building design, where there are cost and time constraints, all within a conservative construction industry that tends to resist change and an architectural profession that is often seduced by external aesthetics rather than internal functionality and in-use performance. Solutions need not be that complex, but they do need to be informed by a thorough understanding of building physics: the role of the building physicist needs to have a higher profile in the design process.

This book aims to provide an insight into current thinking in thermal design, with reference to its historical context, as well as signposting future developments. There will be no single solution for all building types and locations. The development of new technologies for reducing energy use and sourcing renewable energy means that today's solutions may soon be overtaken by better ones in the near future. Therefore, the aim of this book is not to provide ready-made off-the-shelf recipes, but, rather, to provide an understanding of the subject of thermal design, and an awareness of what is possible, from which future innovative solutions can be developed.

Chapter Two

The Built Environment: Sustainability, Energy and Climate Change

What Is the Built Environment?

Let us begin by discussing what we mean by the built environment. The built environment spans from basic shelter to vast megacities, from rural to urban. It is the purpose-built physical space in which we live, work and play, as well as the 'awkward' intersections of developments and leftover space, for which people often find unforeseen solutions[2.1]. The built environment comprises many building types and urban forms. And it is more than just buildings; it includes their supporting infrastructures of energy, water and sewage, waste, transport and communications. This total physical space facilitates the social and business interactions that make up our cities and communities. The buildings themselves are not the end products; they are part of the organizational processes that form the basis for society as a whole. We need to renovate and retrofit our existing buildings, as well as designing new ones. Much of the technology we develop for new buildings can be applied to retrofitting existing buildings, albeit with more challenges and generally higher costs. When new, buildings need to achieve specific performance standards for energy use and comfort, and they need to do this in a way that supports the range of activities that take place within them. A new building quickly becomes an existing building, constantly adjusting to meet the ever-changing needs of its occupants. A successful building will not only be zero energy, but will also bring multiple benefits of comfort, health, productivity, amenity and affordability, all of which depend on a successful thermal design.

New Build

New buildings allow us to pioneer our ideas and innovative technologies, especially in relation to energy-efficient design and the use of renewable energy generation.

They provide the opportunity to respond to the immediate problems of climate change. A building's energy use and greenhouse gas emissions are determined, firstly, by the embodied energy from sourcing materials and components, and during construction, renovation and eventual disposal; and, secondly, by the operational energy used by services for heating and cooling, ventilation, lighting and appliance loads, computers, and equipment associated with the building's function. Within the current context of climate change, all new buildings should strive to be zero energy, and even energy positive in their design. This means high levels of energy efficiency combined with renewable energy generation and energy storage. We often use the term 'systems approach' (see Fig. 2.1), which integrates across all elements of construction and operation, balancing across reduced energy demand, efficient services, and renewable energy generation. The terms zero energy and zero carbon are often interchanged. A zero energy building will usually exchange energy with the supply grid, with energy imported from the grid, offset by energy exported to the grid from the building's renewable energy generation; so it will be energy neutral over a year. It may have energy storage within the building, in order to maximize the use of renewable energy generated by the building. A true zero carbon building will have no carbon dioxide emissions

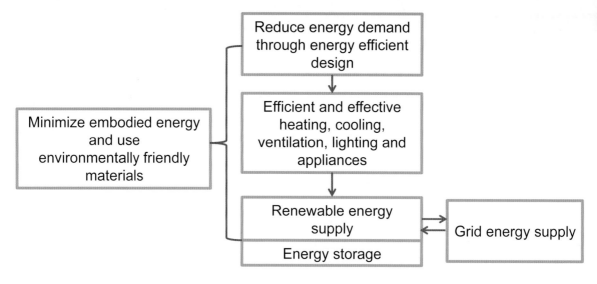

Fig. 2.1 A 'systems approach' to low and zero energy design.

associated with it, will operate 'off-grid', and will need a higher level of on-site generation and energy storage, or it may simply purchase green energy from the grid.

In spite of increasing government commitments to the zero carbon agenda, there has been a slow take-up by the construction industry, which is generally risk-averse to trying out new ideas, usually blaming high costs and lack of market demand. This is contrary to many products that are marketed on their use of the latest technology! So, opportunities to advance sustainable design are compromised. Sustainability is often regarded as an 'inconvenient distraction' from getting the job done. The person who will have to live with the building remains conveniently unaware! Nine times out of ten, the architect will do what they are told by the developer.

The rate of new build varies from country to country. In developed countries, it is relatively slow at around 1 per cent per annum. However, in developing countries it may be much higher, typically around 3 to 4 per cent, often involving fast-track construction, which means less time to change to a more sustainable approach. The total worldwide building floor area in 2016 was 235 billion m², which is projected to double by 2060. Future growth in Europe, North America and the Middle East over the next forty years will be fairly constant (*see* Fig. 2.2)[2.2], with China slowing down after 2030. India and Africa increases up to 2060, where 80 to 90 per cent new build will be residential, compared to 50 to 60 per cent in Europe and North America. So it is crucial that these countries adopt a sustainable energy-efficient approach now. They often suffer greater extremes of climate, so the benefits of energy-efficient design are potentially greater. However, globally, nearly two-thirds of countries do not have mandatory building regulations (*see* Fig. 2.3)[2.3]. What will drive these countries to transition to zero energy design?

The projected lifetime of new buildings varies from country to country. In developed countries a building will typically last sixty years plus, with many buildings over 100 years old. In developing countries, projected lifetimes may be around thirty years. Often it seems a building's lifetime, and indeed usefulness, is secondary to the need for growth and providing investment opportunities. The fast-track nature of development programmes and the shortage of skilled workers makes innovation and achieving good quality difficult. The first rule for sustainable building design should be 'do we really need this building?'

Even with the general lack of innovation, and repeating the same solutions, new buildings are

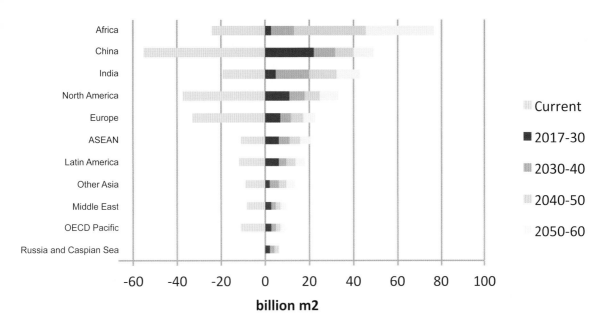

Current

■ 2017-30

2030-40

2040-50

2050-60

Fig. 2.2 Projected global figures for new construction to 2060[22].

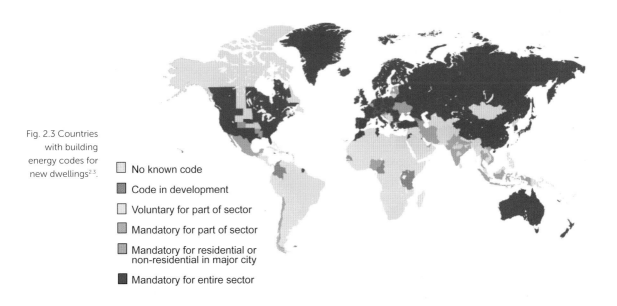

Fig. 2.3 Countries with building energy codes for new dwellings[23].

No known code

Code in development

Voluntary for part of sector

Mandatory for part of sector

Mandatory for residential or non-residential in major city

Mandatory for entire sector

riddled with performance issues. One major issue is the 'energy performance gap', between 'as-designed' and 'as-built' energy use[24]. A building may use up to 50 per cent more energy than predicted, due to a range of design, workmanship and operation failures. This may be reduced by adopting a manufacturing off-site approach to construction, using factory-made components, which are then assembled on site in a relatively short time. Off-site construction methods should lead to higher quality, better thermal and energy performance, less waste, and faster construction. They have been used in Japan for many years; however, in western countries, there has been little market penetration. Although governments promote off-site construction, there are issues of acceptability by house buyers and mortgage companies. Lower costs are predicted over time, but this has yet to be validated in practice, probably due to the initial investment needed to set up manufacturing facilities. Without a ready market this is a risky proposition.

The cost of new buildings has a huge influence on the transition to zero energy performance. However, there are two aspects to costs: the initial capital cost and the annual running costs, including energy. On a life cycle cost basis, energy savings alone should exceed any additional design and construction costs associated with improved energy performance, within an acceptable payback period. There are also added benefits, including improved comfort, health and productivity, which, in overall cost-benefit terms, may be an order of magnitude greater than energy savings. However, the construction industry has resisted a life cycle approach to costing buildings, probably because the capital and running costs are generally separated between the developer and the end user. Lowest cost construction still rules the day.

The additional cost of constructing a more sustainable building is usually based on a 'bolt-on' approach, which simply adds 'green' elements to an existing design, with additional costs easily identified as bolt-on items of construction or equipment. The cost will always be greater. Using a holistic integrative design approach, the cost of additional green technologies may be offset by reducing costs in other areas; for example, the increased cost of a high-performance façade, with high levels of thermal insulation and solar control, may be offset by lower costs for (lower capacity) heating and cooling equipment. A green feature may be simultaneously used as a traditional building element; for example, when a photovoltaic (PV) solar panel 'doubles up' as a shading device. By adopting this integrative holistic design approach, additional costs can be reduced to an affordable level, and potentially to a level comparable with standard new build costs. In addition to energy savings, operations and maintenance costs can be reduced through the use of less complex heating, cooling and ventilation systems. The current cost of a green building should be within around 12.5 per cent of existing costs, and this will come down with scaling up, eventually becoming the standard cost[2.5].

Buildings with sustainability credentials are future-proofed against changing regulations, enjoying increased marketability and increased asset value. Future regulations will likely place greater emphasis on reducing carbon dioxide emissions of existing buildings. Tenant requirements and investor risk screening may also affect the value of buildings that do not have green credentials, and in markets where green is becoming more mainstream. 'Brown discounts' are emerging, where non-green buildings may be considered high-risk and rent or sell for less. New zero energy buildings may be more attractive to tenants and command higher rents and resale prices, and offer a greater overall yield on investment.

The impact of sustainable new buildings scales up to national and global levels, with energy cost savings at building scale leading to lower carbon dioxide emissions at a global scale. Improvements in comfort, health and productivity provide multiple benefits that are both quantitative and qualitative. However, although these benefits have been identified for some time, they have yet to make a marked impact on building construction and operation. The assessment of green building benefits is still generally based on cost of energy-saving measures versus energy cost savings, usually to be realized in a relatively short payback period. We must change this 'lowest cost', 'low risk' culture! In our drive to decarbonize the built environment, every project that does not achieve a zero energy performance is a future liability. Zero energy is already possible for many building types, using available technology.

Existing Buildings

Reducing carbon dioxide emissions in our existing building stock, while providing affordable comfort and healthy living for people, is a major challenge. We have a legacy of poorly performing buildings (*see* Fig. 2.4),

(a)

(b)

Fig. 2.4 (a) Terraced housing in the Welsh valleys; (b) high-density housing in Chongqing.

in terms of their energy use and environmental conditions. We need to energy retrofit our older buildings, and we will also soon need to retrofit many of the substandard buildings that we continue to build today. There are opportunities. Heating, cooling and ventilation systems have an optimal lifetime of around fifteen years, and need frequent replacement over a building's lifetime. Likewise, some building components may also be replaced, such as windows, roofs, and wall cladding systems. Insulation may be added to external walls, roofs, and to floors. Some 35 per cent of the European Union's buildings are currently over fifty years old, and almost 75 per cent are energy inefficient, with only around 1 per cent or less undergoing renovation improvements each year[2.6].

For developed countries, some 80 per cent of buildings that will exist in 2050 are already built. We need a range of solutions that relate to a building's age and type. Retrofit measures can be elemental, such as a single measure applied widely, for example, changing to low energy lighting in offices, or applying external wall insulation across housing estates. Retrofit measures can also be 'whole building', involving a package of energy-saving measures tailored to an individual building, including reducing energy demand through better insulation and reducing draughts; improvement or renewal of heating, ventilation and air conditioning (HVAC) systems; and installing renewable

energy supply and energy storage, such as solar photovoltaic (PV) and batteries. Taking housing as an example, the return on investment will be different for elemental and whole house approaches (*see* Fig. 2.5)[2.7]. An elemental approach usually involves applying the most cost-effective measures, often at scale, which may be attractive for social housing, where funding needs to be spread across a large number of beneficiaries, achieving carbon dioxide savings typically up to 30 per cent. However, a further retrofit will probably be needed in future to apply additional measures. A whole building approach has the advantage of a one-time package applied, typically achieving up to 70 per cent energy and carbon dioxide savings. Upgrading existing buildings may be carried out as part of a targeted energy retrofit programme or as part of a major renovation, for example, when there is a change of use. Many of the low carbon technologies used in new build can be transferred to retrofitting existing buildings. Of course, improving thermal comfort should be central to any energy retrofitting exercise, as affordable warmth and energy efficiency go hand in hand.

Housing is a major focus for future retrofit programmes. Many houses will have already received improvements in roof insulation, double glazing and new heating systems. If this had not been carried out, our built environment energy use would be

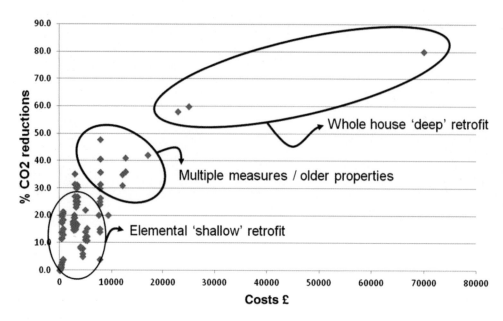

Fig. 2.5 Elemental and whole house retrofit: carbon dioxide reductions versus cost of measures. Based on a series of retrofits for Welsh housing.

considerably higher. Based on UK experience, the cost of a whole house retrofit is around £25,000 or more, depending on the age of the house and the package of measures applied. Payback time in energy cost savings may be relatively long, between twenty-five and fifty years[2.8]. However, there will also be improved comfort, through affordable warmth, and reduced fuel (energy) poverty, which will lead to multiple benefits relating to health and wellbeing. Retrofit programmes can also create economic benefits through new jobs and supply chains, such that energy retrofits yield a considerable overall societal benefit in addition to energy savings. These multiple benefits need to be considered in our cost modelling, which needs to recognize different types and tenure of building. A retrofit industry is needed that can provide a professional approach for ensuring that the most cost-effective package of measures is applied, and quality is assured.

Whereas the energy performance of new buildings is covered by building regulations, existing buildings are more difficult to regulate. In Europe, retrofit is tackled to some extent by 'consequential improvements'[2.9], whereby if general renovation occurs, an investment in energy efficiency is required. In future it may be necessary to introduce regulations that address energy performance over a building's lifetime with regular energy performance checks, similar to annual checks for motor vehicles.

For the existing built environment, there is a question over the lifetime of buildings and their services, and whether to demolish and rebuild, or renovate. The embodied energy of materials in our existing buildings plays a crucial role in this equation. By demolishing buildings we lose much of this embodied energy. Usually it is more sustainable to renovate than to renew, which also allows us to retain communities and the cultural value of the existing built environment.

Cities (Urban Scale)

The population of our cities is rapidly growing, with around half the population of the planet living in cities, and predicted to rise to 75 per cent by 2050. In the developing world, cities are growing through economic development, rural migration, and expansion into peri-urban areas, often encroaching onto arable land. The speed of this development is often very fast (see Fig. 2.6). In the developed world, more people are attracted to live in cities to engage with city life and culture, and avoid long commuting times.

Fig. 2.6 Dubai, Sheik Zayed Road in (a) 1989 and (b) 2005, showing the rapid development of the city with its growing economy in a relatively short period of time. There is little evidence of sustainability. ((a): Wikipedia)

Cities, through their buildings, together with their associated transport, water, sewage, waste and communication systems, already globally account for some 78 per cent of energy use and 70 per cent of greenhouse emissions, and yet they occupy less than 2 per cent of the earth's land area[2.10]. Consequently, they become potential hotspots of poor air quality, infectious disease, pollution and urban 'heat islands', which will be further compounded by climate change. Our cooling demands may increase in future cities, and buildings that are only heated now may also need to be cooled in future. The density of development and the high-rise nature of modern cities, results in buildings being strongly affected by their surroundings, whether other buildings or green space. Can we open windows, is traffic noise and pollution an issue; do we overlook green space; are we overshadowed by other buildings? These all impact on thermal design and affect our decisions on how we can heat, cool and ventilate, and the associated energy costs.

On the other hand, our cities may not continue to expand at today's rate. There may be a rebound, with a growth of rural living, in towns and villages, as people seek to escape from pollution, disease and congestion and the high cost of city living. Our future built environment may have a growing rural element, with groups of towns combining to provide a network of city-like facilities: one for government, one for industry, one for leisure, and so on. These will likely

to be lower density and lower rise than current city developments, providing the opportunity for a more sustainable approach, with local infrastructures, for energy, mobility, water, waste and sewage.

Outside Space

Outside spaces are an important feature of the built environment, and people need to be comfortable outdoors as well as indoors. The streets, parks, rivers and bridges are often a more memorable experience of a successful city than the buildings themselves, and they should provide shelter and comfort in order to maximize their use. It is often the smaller outside spaces that provide more useful everyday social space for city dwellers than fancy parks and squares. The 'pocket park' in the high-density Sai Ying Pun district of Hong Kong (see Fig. 2.7) is shaded and sheltered by the overhead roadway, and sea breezes are channelled from the harbour close by. There is a lot of thermal design going on here. These integrated outside spaces greatly enhance our experience of the built environment.

Green areas in the city create relatively cooler places, with a break from the anthropogenic heat gains from traffic and the exhaust of heat from building cooling systems (see Fig. 2.8). Buildings that are located adjacent to such areas enjoy reduced cooling

Fig. 2.7 Pocket park in Hong Kong's Sai Ying Pun district, which is a popular spot to meet, especially for the elderly, who sit chatting and playing board games.

loads, and windows can be opened without suffering poor air quality and noise.

Transitional Space

In between inside spaces and outside spaces, we have 'transitional' spaces, such as malls, entrances, arcades, and transport stations, which are spaces that people move through to get from outside to inside, or vice versa, and if conducive, people may stop, sit, wait, have a coffee, before they move on. These transitional spaces also need to provide shelter and comfort, but people's expectations for these spaces are not so demanding, as they can choose to spend time there or not. They are often enclosed and air-conditioned with a high energy cost; but they need not be. They can be designed to be a little cooler than outside in hot weather, and a little warmer than outside in cold weather, providing an intermediate 'transitional comfort' condition. In warm humid climates they avoid the thermal shock of going directly from a warm moist outdoors to a chilled indoor space. They may include nature-based solutions, using plants and

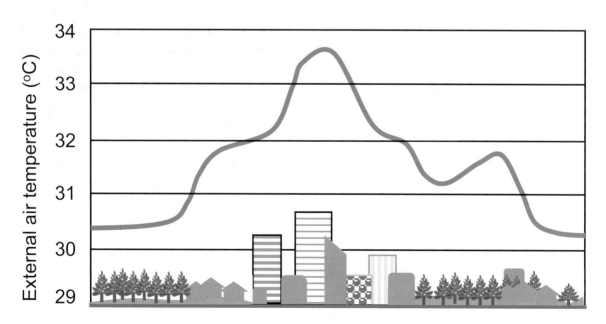

Fig. 2.8 Urban temperatures reduced by green space, which can also provide a sink for pollutants.

Fig. 2.9 Transitional spaces: (a) Brickell Centre, Miami. (Shutterstock); (b) Parkview Green, Beijing.

water features, to help create a microclimate that enhances our thermal experience.

Fig. 2.9 presents two examples. The Brickell Centre in Miami, which has a warm humid climate, has an unconditioned mall (*see* Fig. 2.9(a)). A 'solar ribbon' shades the mall, which is cooled by plants and is open to the natural breezes; the mall also benefits from spillage of cool air from the shops. Beijing's Parkview Green (*see* Fig. 2.9(b)) comprises a shopping mall, office and hotel, all enclosed within a translucent structure. The main open space is not fully air-conditioned, but has some localized floor heating and spot cooling at ground level. Both the Brickell Centre and Parkview Green contain air-conditioned shops and offices like other modern malls, although in Parkview Green the office workers can choose to open windows and naturally ventilate into the mall. Transitional spaces therefore offer a great opportunity for energy savings, by designing out high energy heating and cooling systems.

Infrastructures

The built environment also includes supporting infrastructures for energy supply, water and sewage, waste, transport, and internet broadband connectivity, all of which use energy; our internet system already uses as much energy as the aviation sector[2.11]. As with buildings and their mechanical systems, our infrastructures also have limited lifetimes and require maintenance and renewal. In future there may be a greater mix of centralized and localized infrastructures emerging, and this will impact on building design. Our future energy infrastructure may be more decentralized with greater integration into local renewable energy generation, while at the same time our central energy grids are being decarbonized. The management of energy supply and demand may require thermal and electrical energy storage in the building or community, with access to energy available from the grid or local renewables when it is needed. This works best if energy demand is reduced, reducing the pressure on energy supply systems.

For all our infrastructures, the first aim is to reduce demand, and then to look at efficient supply and operation. For example, reducing the production of waste should take priority over waste recycling. A waste recycling industry that is based on the availability of large amounts of waste is not sustainable. For transport, we should reduce the need for mobility through greater accessibility to services and leisure, and then provide efficient and effective transport systems. We may interconnect infrastructures more in future, with energy from waste and solar PV supplying vehicle batteries. Battery storage in vehicles may be used to meet peak energy demand in the building or linked to the grid. Our future energy system is therefore likely to be more integrated and more interactive. Even though our built environment infrastructures may seem at first separate from thermal design, in future they are likely to be part of the same energy system.

Sustainability and the Built Environment

Sustainability Matrix

The built environment is a key aspect of sustainability, especially related to the thermal performance and energy use of buildings. Generally, sustainable design has three targets: (i) to provide a good quality of life for people, (ii) to minimize (and eventually eliminate) the use of non-renewable resources, and (iii) to minimize (and eventually eliminate) ecological damage. Sustainability is open to many interpretations, so it needs to be qualified in operational terms and, specifically, what it means when we design and operate our built environment. We need to prioritize a zero carbon approach to the built environment as a first step, otherwise all other aspects of sustainability become insurmountable in the event of drastic climate change. We should therefore lead with zero carbon, drawing in economic and social aspects of sustainability as appropriate.

Sustainability in the built environment may be summarized in a sustainability matrix (*see* Fig. 2.10). We have already discussed the built environment in relation to new build, existing buildings and supporting infrastructures. The wider aspects of sustainability are commonly referred to as the 'triple bottom line', which includes environmental, social and economic factors. The built environment has negative impacts at global, local and indoor scales; energy use and greenhouse gas emissions have a global impact, air pollution from burning fossil fuels has a local impact, and issues of environmental comfort and health have an indoor impact.

Just as the built environment is part of a continually changing process that enables society to develop, sustainability is not itself an end product; it is also part of a process, relating to 'top-down' activities associated with policy and governance, and 'bottom-up' activities, driven by real projects. We may lead with the zero carbon agenda and technical solutions for thermal design and efficient energy use, but we also need to include socio-economic factors. A bottom-up approach to sustainability that engages with users' needs on a specific building can result in multiple benefits[2.12]. Reducing a building's energy demand can lead to affordable warmth, alleviate fuel poverty, improve health, and reduce local air pollution. Socio-economic benefits include creating jobs, improving productivity, and generating local industries and supply chains. This bottom-up project-based approach follows the up-cycling concept of 'more good'[2.13]. Top-down approaches follow the 'less bad' concept, and are generally applied at scale, such as minimum standards applied through building regulations. Sustainability is therefore not

Built environment	Triple bottom line	Impact	Activity level
New build	Environment	Global	Top-down
Existing buildings	Society	Local	Middle-out
Infra-structure	Economics	Indoor	Bottom-up

Fig. 2.10 Sustainability matrix.

just about avoiding problems, but also about promoting a better quality of life by fully engaging with the people's needs.

The concept of 'regenerative sustainability' is inherently based on a bottom-up approach, with an overall net-positive sustainability gain. Cole[2.14] argues that our response to complex environmental problems has been led by a negative approach, focussing on scarcity and sacrifice, making things 'less bad', with little attention to social dimensions, and rarely recognizing cultural, political and other processes. Regenerative sustainability is systems-based and place-based, considering the interconnections within and between ecological, social and economic systems at various scales, but with an emphasis on local thinking, experience and delivery.

Systems thinking integrates technologies and architecture from a people perspective, including both the designers and the users of the built environment, while also linking to government regulations and industry needs, spinning out bottom-up activities through the so-called knowledge triangle of research, industry and government. A systems-based bottom-up approach communicates a positive 'multiple benefits' message, and people may more readily adopt actions that lead to a clean, healthy, productive built environment than the less tangible goal

of 'saving the planet'. There is a need to change the emphasis from reducing harm to creating net-positive outcomes, in both environmental and human terms, and at the building, neighbourhood and city scale.

Energy Demand

A major portion of global energy consumption is used for the construction and operation of the built environment. Energy is used by our HVAC systems for heating, ventilating and air conditioning our buildings, and in relation to a buildings' function, for lighting, appliances, and operational processes. Energy is also used to construct buildings, including supplying materials and components; and to operate the built environment infrastructures, for transport, water, sewage, waste, and internet connectivity. Globally, buildings and their construction account for some 36 per cent of final energy use, and 39 per cent of energy-related carbon dioxide emissions (*see* Fig. 2.11), with some 6 per cent of energy use associated with construction, including materials such as steel and cement[2.15]. Transport and other sectors have strong links with the built environment, so the built environment is central to overall energy consumption.

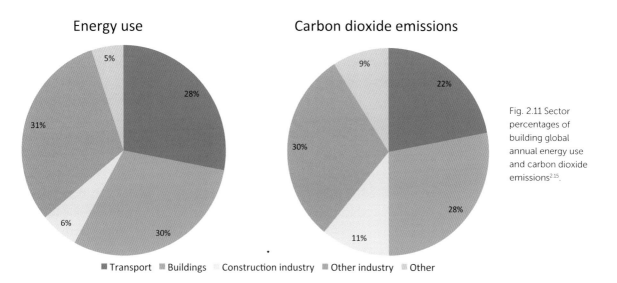

Energy use

Carbon dioxide emissions

Fig. 2.11 Sector percentages of building global annual energy use and carbon dioxide emissions[2.15].

■ Transport ■ Buildings ■ Construction industry ■ Other industry ■ Other

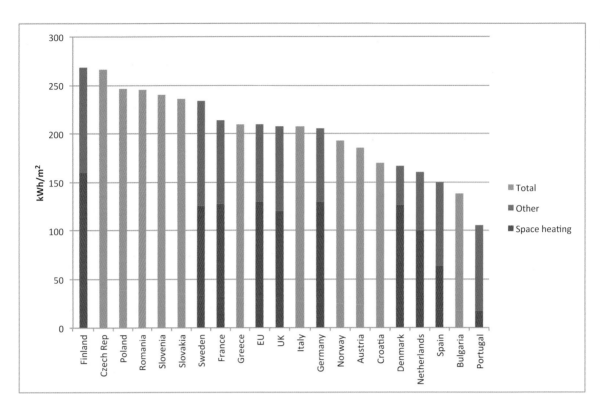

Fig. 2.12 Annual energy consumption in buildings across EU countries (kWh/m²) broken down between space heating and other, where data is available[2.16].

The profile of energy use in buildings will vary with building type, operation and location. In Europe, buildings are responsible for approximately 40 per cent of energy consumption and 36 per cent of carbon dioxide emissions[2.16]. Energy use is usually stated in kilowatt hours per square metre per year (kWh/m²/year), or kWh/year for a whole building. Space heating is generally the main energy use across countries (*see* Fig. 2.12), with colder countries consuming around double that of warmer countries.

Dwellings are the main building type, and in cooler climates, heating is the main energy load, although this does vary with age, with modern housing being relatively energy efficient (*see* Fig. 2.13), and with electricity demand from the grid reduced by using solar PV. New housing can achieve a 'zero energy', 'carbon neutral' performance and may even be 'energy positive'.

For air-conditioned office buildings, the energy load is spread across heating, cooling, fans and pumps, lighting and office equipment[2.17] (*see* Fig. 2.14). Other building types have their own specific energy use characteristics depending on their occupant density, hours of use, and any specific features, such as swimming pools, shops, kitchens, and IT rooms. Larger buildings may have lifts and escalators, ATM machines, vending machines, air curtains around entrances, all of which contribute to the whole building energy load. Indeed, as the overall heating, cooling, and ventilation loads are reduced through energy-efficient design, these additional loads become a larger proportion of the total building load, and are often overlooked, resulting in a building using considerably more energy than assumed at the design stage.

There are a range of terminologies that classify buildings in relation to their energy use and carbon dioxide emissions, including low energy, zero energy, nearly zero energy, low carbon, zero carbon, and energy positive. Generally, all these approaches begin

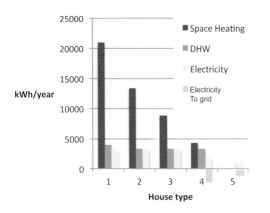

		House type			
	1	2	3	4	5
Thermal properties	Typical 1950's	Improved Insulation, glazing and boiler	Current standards	Best practice	Zero energy
U-values					
External wall (W/m².K)	1.7	0.5	0.3	0.15	0.15
Ground floor (W/m².K)	1.2	1.2	0.2	0.12	0.12
Loft (W/m².K)	0.4	0.2	0.2	0.15	0.15
Glazing (W/m².K)	4.8	2.8	2.0	0.85	0.85
Air permeability (m³/h/m² at 50Pa)	10	10	10	5	1
Gas boiler efficiency	75%	90%	90%	90%	
ASHP					X
Solar PV				X	X
LED lights				X	X
Battery					X
MVHR					X

Fig. 2.13 Summary of energy use in housing for a range of existing and new build (the domestic hot water (DHW) and electricity consumption has been assumed to be the same for all house types). It shows a reduction in space heating with improvements in thermal insulation, reduced air leakage and improvements in gas boiler efficiency (house types 1 to 4). The DHW load also improves with increasing boiler efficiency. Solar PV is introduced in house types 4 and 5, which reduces electricity use from the grid. House type 5 is all-electric and has battery storage, and is carbon neutral. Because more of the renewable energy is used in the house, through the use of battery storage, it both imports and exports less to the grid in comparison with house type 4. This analysis has been carried out using the dynamic building thermal model HTB2 (see page 50).

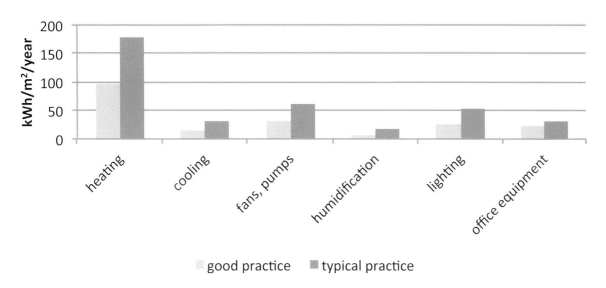

Fig. 2.14 Breakdown of annual energy use for a typical UK air-conditioned office[2.17].

with reducing energy demand, then installing efficient mechanical systems for heating, ventilating and cooling, and finally introducing renewable energy supply and energy storage, depending on how far we go down the 'low', 'zero', 'nearly zero', and 'positive' energy route. Often these terms are quite vague, allowing some degree of flexibility in their application. For example, at the time of writing, the European Energy Performance of Buildings Directive[2.18] specifies nearly zero energy as a very low energy demand for which a considerable amount is generated by renewable energy located either on or nearby the buildings. The description of 'very low', 'considerable amount' and 'on or nearby' are then left to countries to interpret appropriately.

The energy we use for thermal and electrical power in buildings is supplied from a range of fuel types. Heating buildings has traditionally enjoyed a diversity of fuel types, including gas, oil, coal, biomass and electricity. Over time, the dominant fuel for heating has changed from wood to coal to oil to gas, and in the near future probably to electricity, which will be generated from renewable systems, either on or local to the building, or through the central electricity grid.

In the UK, the main building energy supply to buildings is gas and electricity. Electrical power demand is fairly consistent throughout the year, but heating energy demand can vary considerably both seasonally and daily[2.19, 2.20]. Heat dominates (*see* Fig. 2.15(a)), and is mainly supplied by gas. Heat demand is around six times higher in winter than in summer, and daily variations can fluctuate quickly, and by large amounts, typically increasing by around 40GW per hour during the early winter morning period as heating systems are turned on (*see* Fig. 2.15(b)), which is equivalent to more than four times the UK's nuclear capacity. The advantage of using gas for heating is that it can meet the overall peak demand and respond to the rapid minute-by-minute demand fluctuations,

(a)

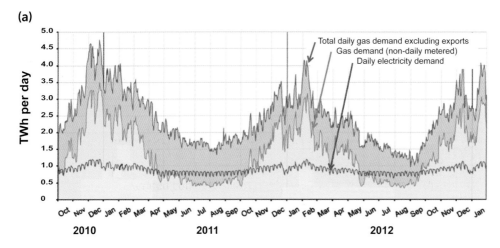

(b)

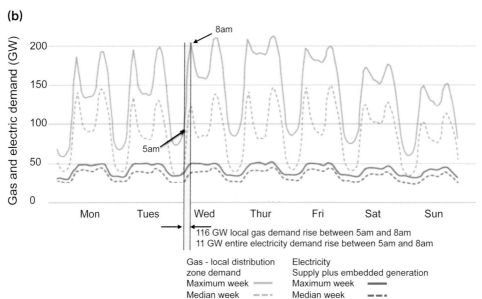

Fig. 2.15 (a) Annual daily variation in gas and electricity use for the UK[2.19]; (b) typical winter hourly variations over a week, showing rapid changes in demand[2.20].

with the gas system providing both storage and distribution. The electricity grid could not currently deal with either the peak heating demand, nor the rapid fluctuations. A recent report from the UK's Climate Change Commission[2.21] has recommended that from 2025, new housing should not be connected to the gas supply. It may be possible for new build to move to electricity for heating, because of its relatively low demand, but the existing building stock will rely on gas for the immediate future. If our future heating is to convert totally to electricity, then the heating demand of our existing buildings must be reduced, and we will also need considerable energy storage to respond to peak loads.

Gas currently dominates for both power generation and heating (*see* Fig. 2.16), especially in the domestic sector[2.22]. Petroleum is also a dominant fuel, mainly for transport. Coal is now a relatively small part of our energy system, with renewables from wind, solar and bioenergy increasing. Losses are a major problem of central grid systems. Delivering 750TWh of electricity to the end user incurs 52 per cent losses (392TWh), in conversion, transmission and distribution. There is also 10 per cent distribution losses associated with the gas grid. Energy generation and supply is shifting from centralized energy grid-based systems to building integrated and local renewable generation[2.23] with considerably lower losses. At the same time we are decarbonizing the electricity grid through large-scale renewable energy generation. Our future energy systems are therefore likely to be a combination of building, local and central energy generation, and energy storage. There will be more integration across the energy space with smart decision-making at all levels. The concept of 'consumer as king' with end users becoming 'prosumers', both producers and consumers of energy, will place more emphasis on buildings as part of the

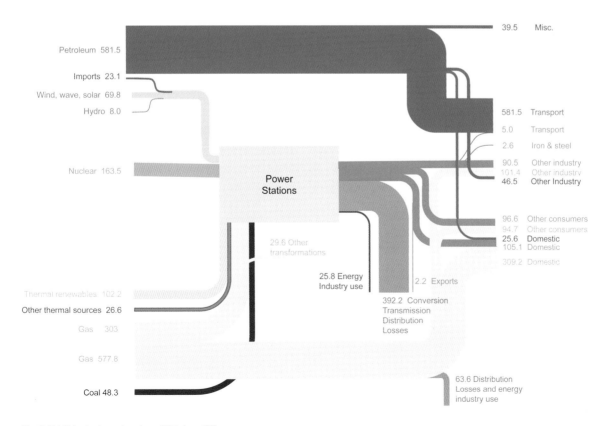

Fig. 2.16 UK fuel mix and end use (TWh/year)[2.22].

future national energy system. This will determine how energy is used over time, matching the availability of local renewable energy and energy from the grid in the most sustainable and cost-effective way. The systems approach to thermal design and energy use will therefore expand, with the building being an active part of a much larger national, and probably international, energy system, with smart energy flows in all directions.

Primary Energy and Carbon Emission Factors

Different fossil fuels are more or less carbon intensive and have an associated primary energy value (*see* Table 2.1). Primary energy is a term used to account for the total energy content of a fossil fuel. This includes the energy associated with extracting and delivering the fossil fuel from its natural source, and the conversion and transmission into a secondary energy form that is delivered to the end user, for example, gas to electricity. After it has been delivered, there will be further energy losses in converting it to useful work or heat.

In the UK, the primary energy to deliver 1kWh of gas is 1.13kWh/kWh. Grid electricity involves a mix of fuels, including nuclear and renewables that are low or zero carbon. The primary energy for electricity changes as the fuel mix changes. Current values are 1.501kWh/kWh, which is considerably reduced from the 2014 value of 2.47kWh/kWh, due to the increased proportion of renewable energy generation supplied to the grid. Renewables have a primary energy of 1.0, with no conversion inefficiencies applied. Although the energy generated by solar PV has conversion efficiency around 20 per cent, and there will be distribution losses for grid-based systems, these are not considered; solar energy is an infinite resource compared to the finite nature of fossil fuels. Renewable energy generated at the building has the lowest losses. The primary energy of different fuels will vary from country to country. In Europe, each member state can select its own method of calculating primary energy, which over time will be subject to changes as the share of renewables and efficiency of delivery increases.

Fuels also have different carbon dioxide emission factors, which is the amount of carbon dioxide released into the atmosphere due to the fuel use (*see* Table 2.1). Renewable energy has a carbon dioxide emission factor of 0. In the UK, as with primary energy factors, the carbon dioxide emission factor for electricity has also been reduced, from $0.56kgCO_2/kWh$ in 2014 to $0.136kgCO_2/kWh$ in 2019, due to the increasing proportion of renewable zero carbon energy supplied to the grid. Grid electricity now has a carbon emission factor less than mains gas. However, electricity is still more expensive than gas, currently around 17p/kWh compared to 4p/kWh (2020). If more electricity is used, based on its current relatively low emission factor, then it could place increased

Table 2.1 Primary energy and carbon emission factors for the main fuel types for the UK in 2019 (2014 value in brackets for electricity, for comparison).

Fuel type	Primary energy (kWh/kWh)	Carbon dioxide emission factor (kgCO$_2$/kWh)	Price (p/kWh)
Grid electricity	1.501 (2.47)	0.136 (0.56)	17.56
Mains gas	1.130	0.210	3.93
Heating oil	1.180	0.298	4.35
Coal	1.064	0.395	4.18

pressure on the grid, which may lead to more fossil fuel being used, which in turn would raise the carbon dioxide emission factor. It is therefore important that any increase in electricity demand is matched by an increase in grid renewable generation. Even so, the current electricity factors indicate the rapid rate at which the grid is being decarbonized, which may point the way to a greater emphasis on electricity in future.

Other countries will have different carbon emission factors, depending on their fuel mix (*see* Fig. 2.17), ranging from $0kgCO_2/kWh$, for a total renewable electricity grid, to $1.01kgCO_2/kWh$, for a coal-dominated electricity grid. The contribution from nuclear also reduces the carbon intensity of the electricity grid.

Health Impacts of Fossil Fuel

Burning fossil fuel is now a major cause of global deaths related to air pollution. Every year, some 4.5 million premature deaths are attributed to air pollution from carbon particles and nitrogen oxides[2.24]. It contributes up to one-third of four of the five leading causes of death, which are heart disease, cancer, stroke, and lung diseases[2.25], and puts children at risk of asthma and of delayed mental development. Another 500,000 annual deaths may be attributed to climate change, from extreme weather events, flare-ups in infectious diseases, and other disaster-related incidents. In addition, absenteeism from work, hospital visits, increased growth in healthcare and healthcare costs, and increased insurance premiums, all have a major impact on national economies. According to the US National Academy of Sciences, the annual cost impact of burning fossil fuels is $120 billion, in relation to health damages primarily from air pollution associated with electricity generation and motor vehicle transportation[2.26]. Linked to our reliance on fossil fuel use in the built environment is the 1.35 million road traffic deaths, with some 50 million injured or disabled every year[2.27]. In comparison, the built environment

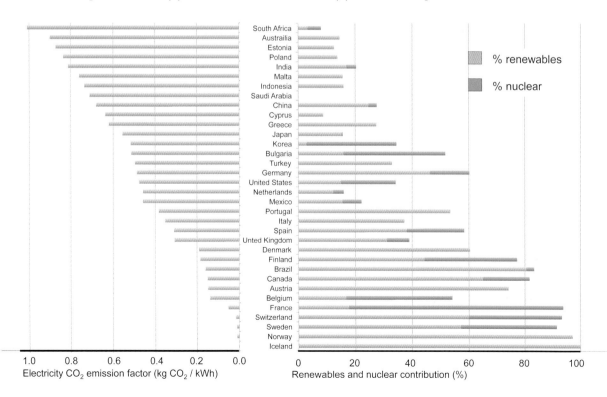

Fig. 2.17 CO_2 emission factors, and renewables and nuclear energy generation.

is also central to the spread of infectious disease with over 100,000 UK deaths from coronavirus (COVID-19), up to February 2021. A more sustainable built environment can make significant reductions in deaths, disease and injuries.

Buildings and Climate Change

Global Warming

Climate change is attributed to the increase of greenhouse gases in the atmosphere, which include carbon dioxide, methane, nitrous oxide and fluorinated gases. Carbon dioxide is the main greenhouse gas, accounting for some 80 per cent of all greenhouse gases, mainly arising from burning fossil fuels, industrial processes, forestry, and other land uses. Other gases, although not so abundant, have a greater impact on global warming. They include methane (10 per cent), Nitrous Oxide (7 per cent) and fluorinated gases (3 per cent). The impact of different gases is compared in Table 2.2, based on their Global Warming Potential (GWP), which relates to their ability to trap heat in the atmosphere, usually based on a 100-year period. GWP is benchmarked against carbon dioxide, so carbon dioxide has a GWP of 1.

Table 2.2 Global warming potential of greenhouse gases.

Gas	GWP
Carbon dioxide	1
Methane	25
Nitrous oxide	298
HFC-23	1,170
HFC-125	2,800
HFC-134a	1,300
HFC-152a	140
PFCs	7,850
Sulphur hexafluoride	23,900

As the sun's rays travel through the earth's atmosphere, about one-third are reflected back into space (*see* Fig. 2.18). Around half of the resulting incoming radiation is absorbed by the earth's surface, which in turn warms up, warming the air immediately above it. If it were not for greenhouse gases in the atmosphere, the earth would be uninhabitable. The earth also emits heat radiation, but at a different wavelength to the sun, because the earth is at a lower

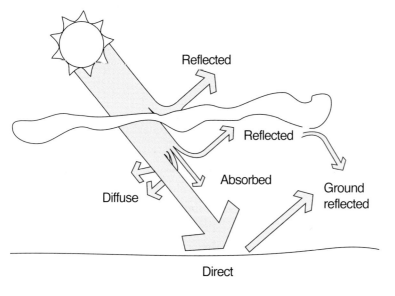

Reflected

Reflected

Diffuse

Absorbed

Ground reflected

Direct

Fig. 2.18
Greenhouse effect.

temperature. The balance of inward and outward heat radiation determines our global climate. The increase in greenhouse gases in the atmosphere increases the proportion of outward-bound heat being radiated back to the earth, which increases the average global temperature. The 'greenhouse effect' is so-called because of its similarity to the operation of a greenhouse for growing plants; like the atmosphere, glass is transparent to the sun's high-temperature radiation, but opaque to the low-temperature heat radiated from warm surfaces within the greenhouse.

Since the industrial revolution, global carbon dioxide emissions and average temperatures have risen (*see* Fig. 2.19). Predicted rises in global temperatures by the end of the century range from 1.5°C to 6°C, depending on future greenhouse gas emission scenarios. Atmospheric carbon dioxide levels have risen to 420ppm in 2019. The IPCC's (International Panel on Climate Change) advice is to reduce and eventually eliminate greenhouse gas emissions in order to maintain an end of century global temperature rise within 1.5°C, compared to 1996 levels. This is less than their previous 2°C target, largely due to the need to reduce the risk of sea level rises in relation to low-lying islands.

Impact of Changes in Weather

The built environment is vulnerable to climate change in relation to rising temperatures and more extreme weather events. Climate is the average long-term weather conditions for a location, whereas weather is the actual conditions, at a point in time, which is less predictable and varies around the average conditions; *climate is what we expect, weather is what we get!* However, with climate change, the weather is deviating from the long-term average, and generally getting warmer with more frequent heatwaves. Some areas are becoming drier, and others wetter, with increased floods. Future weather and the extremes resulting from climate change will have a major impact on the built environment, and thermal design.

Many buildings are at risk from overheating in warmer weather, especially where people are more vulnerable, including housing, schools, hospitals, and care homes. In the UK, some 2,000 people currently die prematurely each year from heat-related conditions, and the growing ageing population will place more people at risk. The number of heat-related deaths is projected to rise by 250 per cent by the 2050s[2.28]. In the UK, many new homes are at greater risk of overheating due to their lightweight

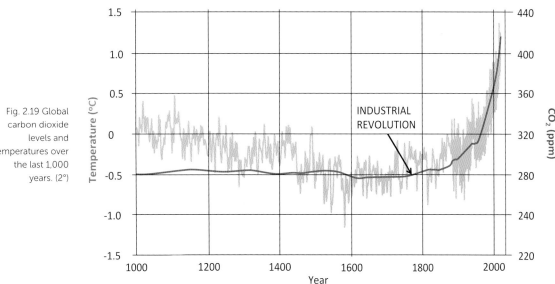

Fig. 2.19 Global carbon dioxide levels and temperatures over the last 1,000 years. (2°)

construction and reduced ventilation. Even so, the number of cold-related deaths is still greater than the number of heat-related deaths, and this is likely to continue, even with global warming. A recent long-term study across thirteen countries estimated that 7.3 per cent of all deaths were due to the cold, with just 0.4 per cent due to heat[2.29]. Results suggested more cold-related deaths in Australia than in Norway, because the thermal performance of Australian houses is worse than those in the colder climate of Norway. In the UK, cold housing is still a significant public health problem, with between 35,800 and 49,700 cold-related deaths per year (of a similar order to a COVID pandemic every year!). Even with milder average winter temperatures, this will probably persist due to the poor thermal performance of many houses, and the growing ageing population. Milder winters may reduce heating costs, but cold weather is still expected to remain a significant cause of death, and we especially need to address the poor thermal performance of housing.

Mitigation and Adaptation

Climate change is linked to the built environment through mitigation and adaptation. Mitigation relates to reducing the impact that our buildings have on climate change, mainly through reducing fossil fuel energy use. Adaptation relates to making buildings resilient to climate change. We are more familiar with mitigation measures, relating to reducing greenhouse gas emissions from fossil fuel energy used for building operation and construction.

Adaptation measures are perhaps not so familiar. Due to current levels of atmospheric carbon dioxide from the past burning of fossil fuels, climate change is unavoidable. We are already experiencing higher average global temperatures and more extreme weather events, and the balance of heating and cooling is changing. Global warming may also change the distribution of some disease vectors, such as malaria-carrying mosquitos, coming to areas previously unaffected, which may affect the design of ventilation systems, as might the increase in infectious disease.

The urban heat island (UHI) effect is already of concern in many cities that experience relatively high temperatures compared to their rural surrounds. Building roofs and pavements constitute over 60 per cent of most urban surfaces and absorb vast amounts of solar radiation, raising their temperatures and then emitting heat to the wider built environment. Changing the solar reflectance by using a light coloured roof compared to a dark roof, or planting on a roof, can reduce both the UHI effect and building cooling energy loads. Parks can also produce relatively cooler areas within our cities.

Mitigation measures may sometimes conflict with adaptation. Increasing levels of thermal insulation to reduce heat loss in winter may give rise to increased internal temperatures in summer, and so compromise solutions need to be developed. Of course, there are other socio-economic aspects of sustainable development that will need to be addressed, such that our future built environment meets not only environmental needs, but also creates places that people can afford to live and experience a good quality of life.

Chapter Three

Heat Transfer in Buildings

Introduction

The subject of thermal design is underpinned by the building physics of energy and heat transfer. Heat is a form of energy, and energy is the origin for everything that happens in the universe, in buildings and in people. Nothing happens without the exchange of energy of one form or other. Energy itself cannot be measured. It is only the exchange of energy that is measurable, and energy is exchanged through a number of processes, including thermal, electrical, mechanical, chemical, nuclear and gravitational. Thermal design in buildings is mainly associated with heat energy, which can take a number of forms. Radiant heat exchange takes place between the sun and the earth, which makes the earth habitable. Surfaces inside a building will also exchange heat by radiation, as will outside surfaces with the surfaces of other buildings and to the ground and sky. The conduction of heat through solids, from hot to cold surfaces, will determine the thermal performance of the building fabric, and its ability to insulate and store thermal energy. Heating or cooling air will generate the natural convection currents of air in a space through buoyancy forces. Forced heat convection takes place when heated or cooled air is blown into a space using fans (which use electrical energy). Evaporative heat transfer happens when there is a change of state between liquid and vapour.

Energy

Energy is the capacity to do work or to make a change. The exchange of energy is measured in joules; it takes about one joule of energy to raise an apple by one metre. Heat energy is related to the chaotic movement of atoms and molecules in solids, liquids and gases, and relates to the transfer of energy from one 'system' to another, such as from the warm air in a space to the cool surface of a window. Energy can be added or taken from a system by heat or by mechanical work. When we do work on a system, we generate heat, or heat can be used to produce work, although there will be losses at the system boundary. The first law of thermodynamics states that energy cannot be created or destroyed: energy is conserved.

Enthalpy is the thermal energy stored in a system. The terms enthalpy and heat are often interchanged, but, strictly speaking, enthalpy relates to the internal energy of a system before and after some change, whereas heat relates to the energy flow at any time during the change.

Thermal energy is mainly related to the molecular scale, which is impossible to measure directly. We can only detect energy when it is exchanged, as through heat transfer. When heat is added to a substance, its temperature will rise. If we know the temperature change, then we can calculate the heat transfer, H (joules), using:

$$H = C_p \Delta T$$

Where

C_p is the specific heat of a substance (joules/gram), which is the amount of heat required to raise the temperature of 1 gram of the substance by 1°C

ΔT is the temperature rise (°C)

If a system gains heat it is called endothermic heat, and if it loses heat this is called exothermic heat. For example, in Fig. 3.1, water, with a C_p of 4.06 joules/gram°C and an initial temperature of 10°C, is raised to a final temperature of 50°C. The heat gained by the water

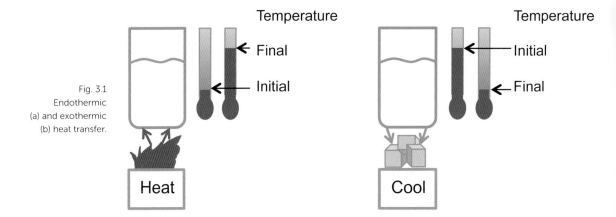

Fig. 3.1
Endothermic
(a) and exothermic
(b) heat transfer.

will be 4.06 × (50 – 10) = 162.4 joules/gram. Likewise, if the initial temperature of the water is 50°C and the final temperature is 10°C, the heat lost by the water will be 4.06 × (10 – 50) = –162.4 joules/gram. The rate of energy use is measured in Watts, where 1 Watt is equal to 1 joule/second (j/s). 1 joule is therefore equal to 1 Watt second. We often use the unit kilo-Watt hour (kWh) for energy, where there are 3.6 Mj in 1 kWh.

Solids, Liquids and Gases

To understand heat transfer we must consider the various states that a substance can exist, be it a solid, liquid or gas. At a molecular scale, there are inter-molecular forces that attract molecules to each other through the bonding of their relative positive and negative charges. There are also intra-molecular forces, which are the forces between the atoms within a molecule that hold it together; these are stronger than the inter-molecular forces that take place between molecules (see Fig. 3.2).

The kinetic energy of a substance is related to the movement of the molecules, and the potential energy is related to the molecular bonding forces between the molecules, which can be thought of as stored energy. Temperature is a measure of the average kinetic energy of molecules in a system. We normally use degrees Celsius (°C) to measure temperature, although in thermodynamics we more often use Kelvin (K = °C + 273). We often refer to temperature differences, where °C and K are the same: a rise in temperature from 0°C to 10°C is the same as a rise from 273K to 283K. At absolute zero,

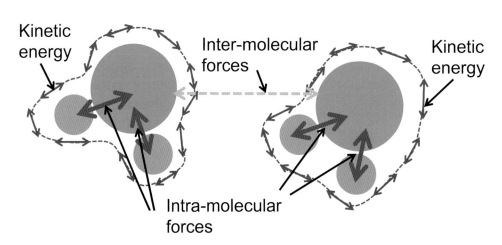

Fig. 3.2 Inter- and intra-molecular forces: the kinetic energy is related to the molecules movement.

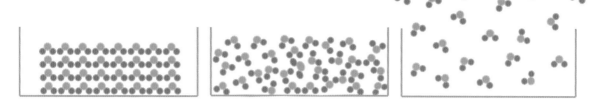

Fig. 3.3 Schematic molecular structure of a solid, liquid and gas (for water, H_2O equals two hydrogen atoms and one oxygen atom).

the kinetic energy of a substance is zero, although it will still have potential energy. In a solid, the kinetic energy of the molecules is relatively small and is in balance with the attractive forces associated with their potential energy. If heat is added, the kinetic energy is increased. Firstly, the solid will expand, and eventually the molecules will have enough kinetic energy to break out of their rigid solid structure and move more freely. The solid melts and becomes a liquid. The molecules will still remain close to their neighbours due to the inter-molecular attractive forces, although these are relatively weaker for a liquid. If heat continues to be applied, the molecules will become completely free of each other, and the liquid boils and

becomes a gas. Each change of state increases the molecular distance, which increases the potential energy of the molecules (*see* Fig. 3.3).

Sensible and Latent Heat

The amount of heat required to raise the temperature of a substance is called sensible heat. The heat required to change its state from solid to liquid and liquid to gas is called latent (or hidden) heat. This heat will separate the molecular bonding and will be stored in the molecules as potential energy. When a substance is cooled and its state changes,

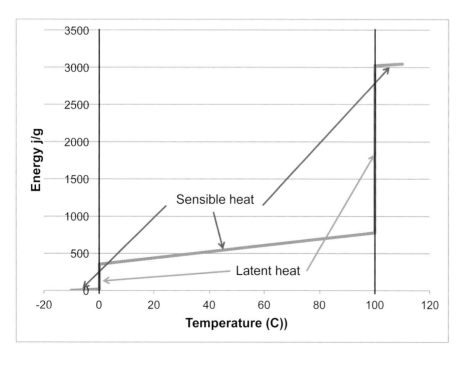

Fig. 3.4 Heat energy required to raise temperatures and change states of water, applying heat to ice at −10°C all the way up to steam at 110°C.

the molecular bonds are reformed and heat is given off. Kinetic energy and temperature do not change with a change of state. The amount of heat needed to produce a change of state is considerably greater than that needed to produce a temperature change (*see* Fig. 3.4).

The change of state will also depend on pressure. Water at a higher pressure than atmospheric pressure will not boil at 100°C. Refrigerants can be maintained as a liquid at higher pressures. If a gas is pressurized it will change state back to a liquid and in doing so will release its heat. This is the basis for heat pumps and refrigeration machines.

Entropy and Exergy

Entropy is a measure of a system's thermal energy per unit temperature that is unavailable for doing useful work, and is measured in joules/K. If energy has the opportunity to 'spread out', it will. Entropy is a measure of how much or how widely energy spreads beyond the system. For mechanical processes there will be a heat loss from the system, such as friction, which may be regarded as 'non-useful' heat. As work is obtained from ordered molecular motion, entropy is the molecular disorder, or randomness, of a system. A system that is left to itself will descend into disorder, and in an open system entropy will always increase: this is the second law of thermodynamics.

Exergy describes the quality of heat energy and how effectively it is used. Different energy forms have different qualities, with different abilities to do work. Generally speaking, the higher the temperature, the higher the energy quality, and vice versa. Exergy is the maximum amount of energy that can be transformed into useful work; the remaining part is called anergy, and this corresponds to the energy wasted. For example, in HVAC systems there is a large exergy loss as low-grade heat is lost to the atmosphere through the cooling towers.

When a system's exergy diminishes, entropy will increase. So, while exergy is a measure of the ability to produce useful work, entropy is a measure of the inability to do work. Entropy gain is equivalent to exergy loss, which in turn is equivalent to lost work.

Heat Transfer in Buildings

There are four types of heat transfer that relate to thermal design. These are radiation, conduction, convection, and evaporation (*see* Fig. 3.5).

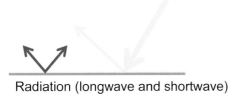

Radiation (longwave and shortwave)

Conduction

Convection

Evaporation

Fig. 3.5 Heat transfer symbols for radiation, conduction, convection, and evaporation.

Radiation

Radiation is the main source of heat to the planet; the other being the heat stored in the earth from its creation. Radiation is the direct transfer of heat from a surface radiating outwards, which is received by other surfaces, which in turn radiate heat themselves. At any surface there will be a net exchange of radiation. The air between the surfaces remains unheated, although if there are particles in the air, these may absorb heat. Solar heat radiates from the sun to the earth through the vacuum of space. This radiant heat lies in the infrared part of the electromagnetic spectrum, which is characterized by its wavelength (*see* Fig. 3.6). The hotter the emitting body, the shorter the wavelength. Below a wavelength of 3,000nm, the 'near' infrared radiation is termed short-wave, and above this, the 'far' infrared is termed long-wave. The sun emits short-wave infrared radiation with wavelengths between 290 and 3,000nm, which includes ultraviolet and visible radiation (380nm and 780nm respectively). Other relatively cooler sources of infrared radiation, such as light bulbs and fires, emit radiation of increasingly longer wavelengths, with lower

temperature building surfaces emitting long-wave radiation.

When infrared radiation meets a surface, heat energy is exchanged according to the material and its surface properties. Some radiation will be reflected to other surfaces, or be reflected into space; some will be absorbed into the material. If the material is transparent to parts of the infrared spectrum, such as glass, the radiation is transmitted through the material, with some being absorbed as it passes through.

The emissivity of a surface is the amount of radiation emitted by the surface compared to that radiated by a matt black surface (a black body) at the same temperature. The best emitters are dark matt surfaces and the worst are silvered surfaces. The emissivity varies between 0 and 1, with most common building materials, such as bricks and plaster, having an emissivity between 0.85 to 0.95. The absorptivity is the amount of radiation absorbed by a surface compared to that absorbed by a black body. The solar reflectance, or albedo, of a surface is the ratio of reflected to incident radiation. Values for emissivity, absorptivity and solar reflectance are presented in Table 3.1 for the more common material surfaces.

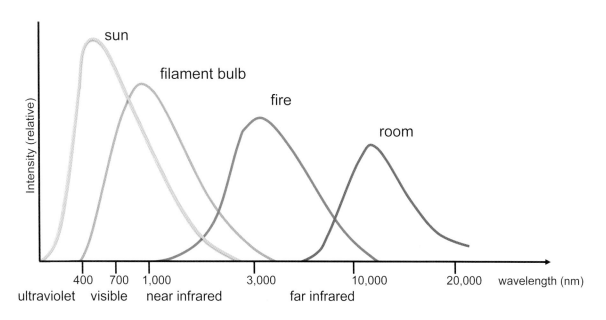

Fig. 3.6 Spectrum of long-wave (low-temperature) and short-wave (solar) radiation.

Table 3.1 Surface emissivity, absorptivity and solar reflection.

Surface finish	Emissivity	Absorptivity	Solar reflectance
Aluminium dull	0.18–0.30	0.40–0.65	
Aluminium, polished	0.03–0.06	0.10–0.40	0.61
Asbestos cement, old	0.95–0.96	0.83	
Asbestos cement, new	0.95–0.96	0.61	
Brick, dark	0.85–0.95	0.63–0.89	0.15
Brick, light	0.85–0.95	0.36–0.62	0.3
Concrete, new	0.805		0.4–0.5
Concrete, old	0.9		0.2–0.3
Galvanized iron, new	0.22–0.28	0.64–0.66	0.13
Galvanized iron, old	0.89	0.89–0.92	
White metal roof	0.85		0.67
Glass, normal	0.89	–	0.30
Limestone	0.90–0.93	0.33–0.53	0.89
Marble	0.90–0.93	0.44–0.592	
Paint (zinc)	0.95	0.30	0.8
Wood, oak	0.89–0.90	–	0.2
Stone	0.9		0.28
Slate	0.9		0.1
Tile	0.9		0.23
New asphalt	0.95		0.5
Old asphalt	0.95		0.1
Grass	0.93		0.21
Sand (desert)			0.4
Water	0.97		0.5
Snow			0.8

Source: CIBSE Guide A: Environmental Design, 2015

The rate of radiant heat emitted by a surface is related to surface temperature and emissivity according to the Stefan–Boltzmann law:

$$Q = \sigma \varepsilon T^4$$

Where

Q is the radiation emitted by the surface (m²)

σ is the Stefan–Boltzmann constant (W/m².K⁴) and equals 5.673×10^{-8}

ε is the surface emissivity

T is the surface temperature (K)

So, a surface of 20°C ($T = 273 + 20 = 293$K) and emissivity of 0.9 will emit:

$Q = 5.673 \times 10^{-8} \times 0.9 \times 293^4 = 376$W of heat.

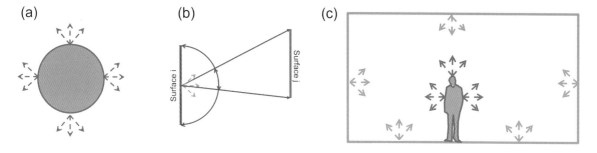

Fig. 3.7 (a) Grey body radiating to surrounding medium; (b) grey body radiating to another surface; and (c) radiation exchange between a human body and room surfaces.

This assumes that all the energy emitted by the radiating body is absorbed by the surrounding medium, and that it does not receive any radiation gain from other surfaces (*see* Fig. 3.7(a)). If there are two radiating bodies exchanging radiant energy (*see* Fig. 3.7(b)) we need to consider the radiation view factor (F) from one to the other. For a surface i, the view factor with respect to a surface j is the ratio of energy radiating from surface i which directly reaches surface j, to the total energy leaving surface i, and vice versa for surface j. The net rate of radiation exchange (Q_r) between a surface of area A_i and temperature T_i and a surface of area A_j and temperature T_j is given by:

$$Q_r = \sigma \, \varepsilon_i \, A_i \, F_{ij} \, (T_i^4 - T_j^4)$$

where:

σ is the Stefan–Boltzmann constant

ε_i is the emissivity of surface i

F_{ij} is the view factor of surface i with respect to surface j

ε_i is the emissivity of surface i

T_i and T_j are the surface temperatures of surfaces i and j (K)

If a human body of surface area 1.8m^2 and skin temperature 33°C (306K) is in a room where all the surface areas are 20°C (293K) (*see* Fig. 3.7(c)), the view factor is 1. If the emissivity of all surfaces is 0.9, the net rate of radiation exchange between the body and the room is:

$$Q_r = 5.673 \times 10^{-8} \times 0.9 \times 1.8 \times (306^4 - 293^4) = 128\,W$$

Other parameters will come into play, such as clothing, and other heat exchanges due to convection, conduction and evaporation, but this gives a general feel for the value of radiation exchange (similar to an old tungsten 100W light bulb).

Within a building the internal surfaces exchange long-wave radiation. We can simplify the heat exchange at a specific surface if we know its temperature (T_s), and assuming that the average internal air temperature (T_a) of the space is similar to the mean of the surface temperatures. We can then approximate a radiant heat transfer coefficient (h_r) for internal wall surfaces, for a typical surface emissivity ($\varepsilon >$ 0.9), using:

$$h_r = 4\sigma T_s^3$$

which gives an h_r value of 5.7 for a surface temperature of 20°C (293K). The net rate of radiation exchange at the surface is then:

$$Q_r = h_r (T_s - T_a)$$

Radiation exchange takes place outside buildings (*see* Fig. 3.8). Outside surfaces will receive direct and diffuse short-wave radiation from the sun and sky-vault respectively. External surfaces will also reflect radiation, as will surrounding surfaces, including water and snow (albedo effect).

Long-wave radiation is emitted from a building to the sky and surroundings. For clear sky conditions, the external surface of a roof may emit long-wave radiation, typically up to 75W/m^2. During the day this

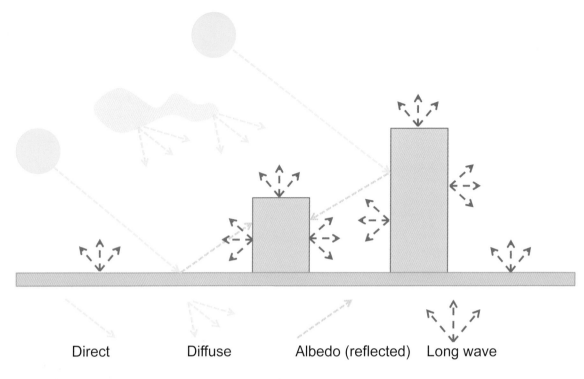

Direct   Diffuse   Albedo (reflected) Long wave

Fig. 3.8 Radiation exchange, showing solar direct, diffuse and albedo, and long-wave.

will be balanced by solar radiant gains, but at night, when there are no solar gains, the roof surface may be cooled by some 2°C to 12°C below the surrounding air. This may cause condensation to occur on the inside surface of roofs, which will need to be drained. In hot weather conditions this effect can be used to cool the building at night, using a transpired solar collector (TSC) device in reverse (*see* Fig. 3.9(left)), and then using it to collect heat on a sunny cool day (*see* Fig. 3.9(right)).

Glass is transparent to short-wave radiation while opaque to long-wave radiation. The short-wave radiation from the sun passes through glass and warms up the internal surfaces in a building, which in turn emit long-wave radiation, which is 'trapped' within the space. This is called the greenhouse effect (*see* Fig. 3.10(a)), which is important in passive solar design. The only heat loss takes place by conduction through the glass to the outside, and to the ground. A similar effect takes place in the atmosphere, which

gives rise to global warming (*see* Fig. 3.10(b)), where greenhouse gases (including carbon dioxide) act like the glass in the greenhouse. They let in the short-wave solar radiation but block the longer-wave radiation re-emitted by the earth's surface.

Not all the incident solar radiation will be transmitted through glass. Some will be reflected at the surface and some will be absorbed within the glass, depending on the angle that the sun hits the glass. By comparison, for a non-transparent material, all the radiation will be reflected or absorbed at the surface. Different glass treatments will result in different properties of transmission, reflection and absorption, which will be considered in Chapter 6.

Conduction

Conduction generally applies to heat transfer through solids. It is the transfer of heat from molecule to

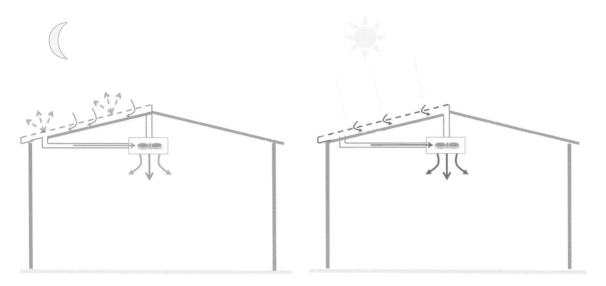

Fig. 3.9 The transpired solar collector (TSC) is a metal overcladding sheet with holes to allow air to be drawn in, which can cool at night (left) or heat during a sunny day (right).

(a)   **(b)**

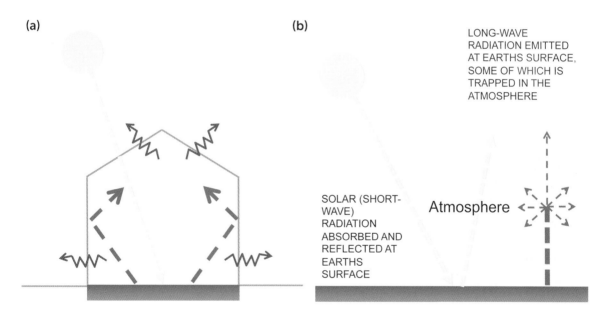

Fig. 3.10 (a) Heat transfer process in a greenhouse, which forms the basis of passive solar design; (b) solar heat travels through the atmosphere, but radiation emitted at the earth's surface is trapped.

molecule from relatively warm to cool regions. In macroscopic terms, the amount of heat transfer through a solid is dependent on its thermal conductivity, or k-value, which is loosely related to the density of the material. High-density materials, such as dense concrete and glass, have high k-values and are 'good conductors' of heat. Low-density materials, such as mineral fibre, have low k-values and are 'good thermal insulators'. Table 3.2 presents the k-values and densities of typical building construction materials.

Table 3.2 k-values and densities of typical building construction materials.

Building element	Material	k-value (W/mK)	Density (kg/m³)
Walls	Brickwork (outer leaf)	0.84	1,700
	Brickwork (inner leaf)	0.62	1,700
	Cast concrete (heavyweight)	1.70	2,000
	Cast concrete (lightweight)	0.20	620
	Concrete block (heavyweight, 300mm)	1.31	2,240
	Concrete block (medium weight, 300mm)	0.83	1,940
	Concrete block (lightweight, 300mm)	0.73	1,800
	Concrete block (insulating)	0.20	600
	Cement mortar	0.72	1,860
Surface finish	Fibre board (preformed)	0.042	240
	Plasterboard	0.16	950
	Timber	0.14	720
	Glass (solid)	1.05	2,500
	Render (moisture content 8%)	0.79	1,330
	Plaster (dense)	0.52	1,200
	Plaster (lightweight)	0.23	720
	Calcium silicate brick	1.50	2,000
Roof	Aerated concrete slab	0.16	500
	Asphalt (roofing, mastic)	1.15	2,230
	Roofing felt layer	0.19	960
	Screed	0.41	1,200
	Stone chippings	0.96	1,800
	Tile	0.84	1,900
	Wood-wool slab	0.10	500
Floor	Cast concrete	1.30	2,000
	Screed	0.46	1,200
	Timber flooring	0.13	500
Insulation	Expanded polystyrene slab	0.035	23
	Glass wool quilt	0.04	12
	Glass wool board	0.035	25
	Phenolic foam board	0.04	30
	Polyurethane board	0.023	24
	Paper (cellulose)	0.042	43
	Strawboard	0.05	310

	Material	Density (kg/m³)	k-value (W/m.K)
Construction (a) Timber, polystyrene, timber	Polystyrene Timber	23 720	0.035 0.23
Construction (b) Brick	Brick	1,700	0.84
Construction (c)	Glass	2,500	1.05
Construction (d)	Insulating block Mineral wool Brick	600 25 1,700	0.2 0.035 0.84

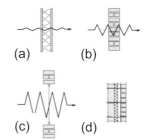

Fig. 3.11 Comparison of thermal conduction properties of different constructions (density and k-values from CIBSE Guide A (2015)).

Most wall constructions are composed of a number of material layers (*see* Fig. 3.11), with a range of densities and k-values. The thermal resistance of a material (R) is its overall ability to resist heat flow and is calculated by dividing its thickness by its k-value:

$$R = x/k$$

Where

R is the thermal resistance (m².K/W)

x is the thickness (m)

k is the thermal conductivity (W/m.K)

The resistivity (r) of a material is the inverse of its conductivity ($r = 1/k$) and so:

$$R = xr$$

The thermal performance of a construction is represented by its overall conductance or U-value. Constructions with high levels of thermal insulation have relatively low U-values, and lower rates of heat transfer. The internal surface temperatures will be higher, improving comfort and reducing the risk of internal surface condensation. Surfaces and any air gaps within the construction will also exhibit a resistance to heat flow (*see* Table 3.3).

Table 3.3 Values for surface and air space resistance.

Building element	Direction of heat flow	Surface resistance (m².K/W)			Airspace resistance,* unventilated thickness > 26mm (m².K/W)
External		Normal	Sheltered	Exposed	
Walls	Horizontal	0.04	0.06	0.02	
Roof	Upward	0.04	0.06	0.02	
Floor	Downward	0.04	0.06	0.02	
Internal					high emissivity (low emissivity in brackets)
Walls	Horizontal	0.13			0.18 (0.44)
Ceilings or floors	Upward	0.1			0.16 (0.34)
Ceilings or floors	Downward	0.17			0.19 (0.5)

Two-thirds of the heat transfer across a cavity will be by radiation. Most building materials have a high surface emissivity, unless they are lined with a low emissivity layer, such as aluminium foil.

The U-value of a wall construction can be calculated using the following procedure:

1. Calculate the resistance of the individual layers of the construction ($R = x/k$).

2. Select the appropriate values for the internal and external surface resistances (R_{si} and R_{se}) from Table 3.3.

3. Select the appropriate resistance of any air cavities (R_{cav}) from Table 3.3.

4. Calculate the total thermal resistance (R_{total}) of the wall:

$$R_{total} = R_1 + R_2 + R_3 + ... + R_{si} + R_{se} + R_{cav}$$

5. Calculate the U-value:

$$U\text{-value} = 1/R_{total}$$

The rate of fabric heat loss Q_f (W) for an area of wall A (m²) with an internal to external temperature difference ΔT (°C) is then:

$$Q_f = UA\Delta T$$

Worked Example

Table 3.4 presents the calculation of the U-value of the masonry wall construction for a normal exposure site. The rate of heat loss is calculated for 10m² of wall, for an internal air temperature of 20°C and an external air temperature of 0°C.

Table 3.4 Tabulated U-value calculation and heat loss for a wall construction.

Layer	Thickness (m)	k-value (W/m.K)	Resistance (m².K/W)	U-value (W/m².K)
Inside surface	–	–	0.13	
Plasterboard	0.006	0.16	0.04	
Block work (insulating)	0.1	0.20	0.50	
Insulation (glass wool)	0.06	0.035	1.71	
Air gap	0.05	–	0.18	
Brickwork	0.1	0.84	0.12	
Outside surface	–		0.04	
Total			2.72	0.37

For an area of 10m² and a ΔT of 20°C: $Q_f = 0.37 \times 10 \times 20 = 74$W

Sol-Air Temperature

When solar energy is absorbed by an external wall, it has a similar effect to a rise in external air temperature. The sol-air temperature is the equivalent external air temperature, which in the absence of solar radiation, would give rise to the same heat transfer through the wall (*see* Fig. 3.12).

The sol-air temperature can be calculated from:

$$T_{sol} = (\alpha I_s - \varepsilon I_l) R_{so} + T_{ao}$$

where

T_{sol} is the sol-air temperature

T_{ao} is the external air temperature

α is the solar absorptivity (*see* Table 3.1)

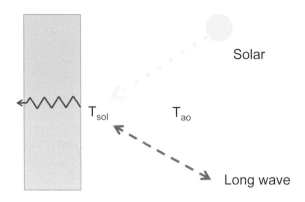

Fig. 3.12 Sol-air temperature relates to external air temperature and radiation exchange.

ε is the long-wave emissivity (*see* Table 3.1)

R_{so} is the external surface resistance (*see* Table 3.3)

I_s is the solar radiation (W/m^2)

I_l is the long-wave radiation loss (W/m^2),

$I_l = 93 - 79C$ (horizontal surfaces)

$I_l = 21 - 17C$ (vertical surfaces)

where C is the cloudiness, which varies from 0 for clear sky to 1 overcast sky

(CIBSE Guide A (2019)

The sol-air temperature for a south-facing wall in winter, when the external air temperature is 0°C and the solar radiation incident on the wall is 165 W/m^2 ($\alpha = 0.8$, $\varepsilon = 0.7$, C = 0.5, $R_{so} = 0.055$, $I_s = 165$ W/m^2, $I_l = 12.5$ W/m^2), can be calculated:

$$T'_{sol} = (0.8 \times 165 - 0.7 \times 12.5) \times 0.055 + 0 = 6.8°C$$

For a U-value of 0.28 W/m^2 K and an internal air temperature of 20°C, the heat loss will be 3.7 W/m^2 (= 0.28 × (20 − 6.8)) compared to 5.6 W/m^2 (= 0.28 × (20 − 0)) if the external air temperature of 0°C was used.

If the sol-air temperature is used in a seasonal U-value calculation, the seasonal heat loss will be less, compared to using the air temperature, especially for south-facing walls. Fig. 3.13 presents the calculated average monthly heat loss for a south-facing wall, based on UK average monthly external air temperature and solar radiation, and comparing the use of external air temperature and sol-air temperature, for walls with U-values of 1.0 and 0.2 W/m^2 K. A wall is likely to perform much better than a standard U-value calculation would predict. Poorly insulated walls may therefore perform significantly better than expected, and the impact of adding thermal insulation may not be as great as predicted. To a lesser extent this occurs on walls facing east or west.

Thermal Capacity

The thermal (heat) capacity is a measure of a material's ability to store heat. The denser a material, the greater its capacity to store heat (*see* Table 3.5). Dense masonry materials typically have around 100 times the thermal capacity of lightweight insulating materials.

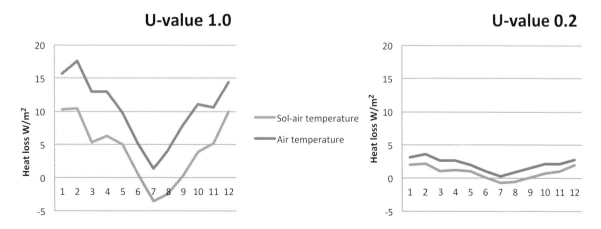

Fig. 3.13 Monthly U-value heat loss calculation for two levels of thermal insulation using sol-air temperature compared to using external air temperature.

Table 3.5 Density, specific heat capacity and thermal capacity for some common building materials.

Material	Density (kg/m³)	Specific heat capacity (J/kgK)	Thermal capacity (J/K)
Granite	2,880	840	$2,419 \times 10^3$
Brick	1,700	800	$1,360 \times 10^3$
Concrete (dense)	2,240	840	$1,882 \times 10^3$
Concrete (light)	620	840	521×10^3
Mineral fibre	12	710	9×10^3
Polystyrene board	23	1,470	34×10^3

Source: calculated from CIBSE Guide A: Environmental Design (2015)

Therefore, high-density materials, such as concrete, will store more heat than low-density materials, such as mineral wool. The thermal capacity of a material (the amount of heat stored per 1°C rise in temperature of the material) can be calculated from the formula:

thermal capacity (J/K) = volume(m³)× density(kg/m³) × specific heat capacity (J/kg K)

Fluids and gases also have a specific heat capacity: for air it is 1.0kJ/kg.K and for water it is 4.181kJ/kgK, with densities of 1.2kg/m³ and 997kg/m³ respectively, at 25°C. Water has a greater potential to store or carry heat than air, which is why hot water pipes in a building are smaller than warm air ducts.

Thermal Diffusivity

Thermal diffusivity is a measure of the ability of a material to conduct thermal energy, relative to its ability to store thermal energy, which determines the rate of transfer of heat through a material from the hot end to the cold end. The thermal diffusivity of a material is related to its k-value, density and specific heat capacity by:

thermal diffusivity (mm²/s) = thermal conductivity (W/mK) / density (kg/m³) × specific heat capacity (J/kgK)

Metals transmit thermal energy rapidly compared to wood, which is a slow transmitter. Thermal insulation materials also have low thermal diffusivity. Values of diffusivity are presented in Table 3.6.

Table 3.6 Values of diffusivity.

Material	Thermal diffusivity ($\times 10^{-6}$ mm²/s)
Aluminium	97
Steel	11.72
Glass	0.34
Brick	0.52
Wood	0.082
Concrete	0.61
Glass wool	0.023
Polystyrene	0.035
Polyurethane foam	0.023
Earth	0.52
Air	19
Water	0.143

Steady State Versus Dynamic Thermal Performance

The thermal performance of the building fabric is a time-varying phenomena, with heat transfer between the space and walls varying dynamically, in relation to both thermal conductivity and thermal capacity of the construction materials, changing direction depending on surface and space conditions, both inside and outside. A U-value calculation assumes steady state conditions both inside and outside, and so it is only an approximation of thermal performance. To obtain a more realistic estimation, computer simulation using dynamic thermal modelling is needed (*see* Fig. 3.14).

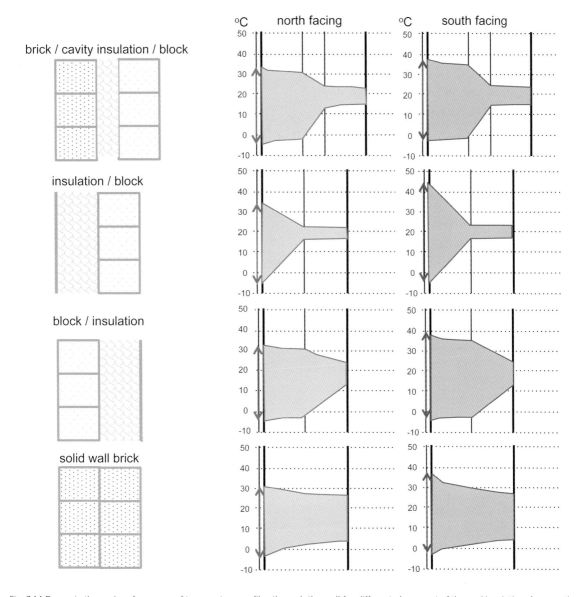

Fig. 3.14 Dynamic thermal performance of temperature profiles through the wall for different placement of thermal insulation, for a north- and south-facing wall. Internal surface temperatures vary between less extremes as the thermal mass of the inner wall layer is increased, when combined with insulation. The temperature gradient through the wall is steepest across the insulating layer. External surface temperatures are higher on the south wall in summer, especially for external insulation. The temperature simulations were obtained using the HTB2 building thermal model (*see* page 50).

Convection

Heat transfer by convection takes place in a fluid, such as air or water, where the molecules are free to move around. If a fluid comes into contact with a heated or chilled surface, heat is conducted to or from the boundary layer of the fluid, and the molecules in the fluid become either more or less energetic. If heated, the fluid becomes less dense and more buoyant, and if cooled, the fluid loses energy and becomes denser. Convection occurs when relatively warmer, more buoyant parts of the fluid rise within the whole body of fluid, and the cooler parts fall, creating convective currents and heat transfer within the fluid.

Fluids may gain heat from a warm surface, such as a room panel heater or the electric element in a hot water cylinder. Fluids may lose heat to a cool inside window surface. For a typical room, the warm and cool surfaces set up a series of interacting convective flow patterns (*see* Fig. 3.15). The convective movement of air in a room contributes to heat distribution in a space from heating and cooling systems.

The transfer of heat between a surface and a fluid is calculated using the appropriate convective heat transfer coefficient:

$$Q_c = h_c(T_a - T_s)$$

Where

Q_c is the rate of convective heat transfer (W)

T_a is the air temperature (°C)

T_s is the surface temperature (°C)

h_c is the convective heat transfer coefficient ($W/m^2 K$)

heat flow downwards from a horizontal surface: $h_c = 0.7 W/m^2.K$

heat flow upwards from a horizontal surface: $h_c = 5.0 W/m^2.K$

heat flow from a vertical surface: $h_c = 2.5 W/m^2.K$

Values of h_c are for low air speeds (< 1m/s) and for a room temperature of 21°C, although they do not vary much for typical room temperature ranges. For higher air speeds, such as for external surfaces, h_c can be approximated to $4 + v$, where v is the air speed at the surface.

The convective and radiant heat transfer coefficients can be added, to provide combined internal

(a)   **(b)**

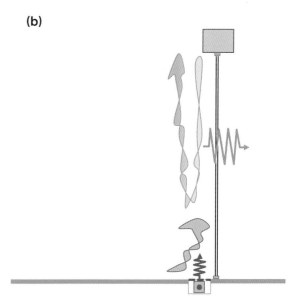

Fig. 3.15 (a) Typical convection patterns generated by relatively warm (panel heater) and cool (glazing) surfaces; and (b) trench heating to counter downdraught from large glazed areas. The warm updraught stops the cool downdraught from spreading across the floor, causing thermal discomfort.

and external surface resistances (R_{si} and R_{se}) that are presented in Table 3.3:

$$R_{si} = 1/(6/5\varepsilon h_r + h_c) \text{ and } R_{se} = 1/(\varepsilon h_r + h_c)$$

Forced convection takes place when a fluid is mechanically moved across a surface, for example, air blown across a heating or cooling coil by a fan. The heat transfer coefficients in these circumstances will vary with speed and dimensions of the coil, and whether the air movement is laminar or turbulent.

Evaporation

A phase change can be produced from energy within the system. Evaporation takes place when a liquid such as water changes state to a vapour, without the direct application of heat. Direct evaporation occurs when water is exposed to air. The water molecules will have a range of kinetic energy levels, some with sufficient energy to escape through the surface viscous forces into the air above, driven by a difference in vapour pressure. The escaping water molecules will have a higher energy content than those left behind, reducing the average heat content of the water, and its temperature. Also, the heat taken from the air to vaporize the water will reduce the air temperature. This phenomenon is called evaporative cooling. The lower the relative humidity of the air, the less will be its vapour pressure, and the greater the rate of evaporation. The rate of evaporation increases with higher airflow rates over the water or wetted surface, for example, air blown over a wetted surface will dry the surface quicker, cooling the surface. Direct evaporation also occurs when water is sprayed into the air. The water becomes a vapour and the energy for transformation is taken from the air, and the air cools. Evaporation cooling of the body takes place from the human skin through sweating and from the lungs through breathing.

Direct evaporative cooling can be used to advantage in hot countries in the form of ponds and fountains in courtyards, or in a mechanical system (*see* Fig. 3.16). Indirect evaporative cooling occurs when the cooling is separate from the air. Simply containing water in roof ponds can produce evaporative cooling, which cools the space below, or it can be produced by spraying water through a plate heat exchanger (*see* Fig. 3.17). Direct and indirect evaporative cooling can be combined in mechanical systems (*see* Fig. 3.18).

Condensation is the reverse of evaporation and takes place when air comes into contact with a relatively cooler surface. The air adjacent to the cold surface is cooled and becomes saturated, and water vapour condenses into a liquid forming droplets on

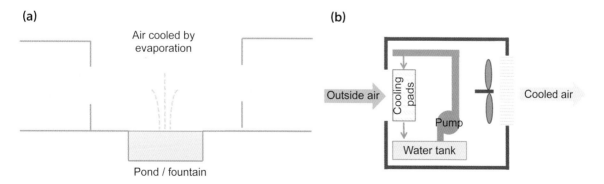

Fig. 3.16 (a) Evaporative cooling using a pond/fountain in a courtyard; (b) evaporative cooling using a mechanical system.

(a)

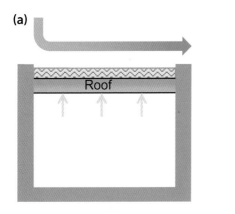

Roof pond. Direct evaporation from water cools fluid. Cool fluid cools roof and inside space, by indirect evaporation. The air also cooled by direct evaporation.

(b)

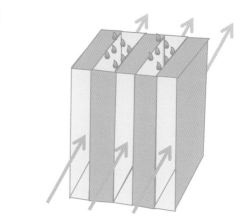

Heat exchanger: Sprayed water cools surfaces in heat exchanger, which cools the air drawn through the adjacent channels.

Fig. 3.17 Indirect evaporative cooling: (a) roof pond; (b) plate heat exchanger.

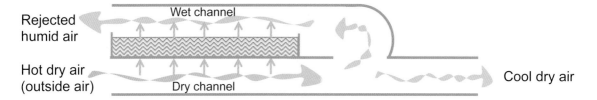

Combined direct and indirect cooling: Hot dry outside air enters and is cooled by the upper surface. Some air is directed into the wet channel where it receives direct evaporation from the water, which cools the water. This humid air is rejected. Cool air is then directed into the building.

Fig. 3.18 Combined direct and indirect evaporative cooling.

the surface. This is used to advantage in an air conditioning system, by air passing air over cooling coils to extract moisture and reduce its relative humidity. This process is called dehumidification.

The lowest temperature at which air can be cooled through evaporation is measured by its wet bulb temperature (such as that measured by enclosing the bulb of a mercury-in-glass thermometer with a wetted sock). If the air is at 100 per cent relative humidity, the wet bulb temperature is then equal to the dry bulb air temperature, which is a measure of the sensible heat, ignoring humidity. The difference between the wet and dry bulb thermometer temperature readings is a measure of the humidity of the air; the higher the difference in these temperatures, the lower the humidity. They can be related through a psychrometric chart, which can be used to explain direct and indirect evaporative cooling (*see* Fig. 3.19).

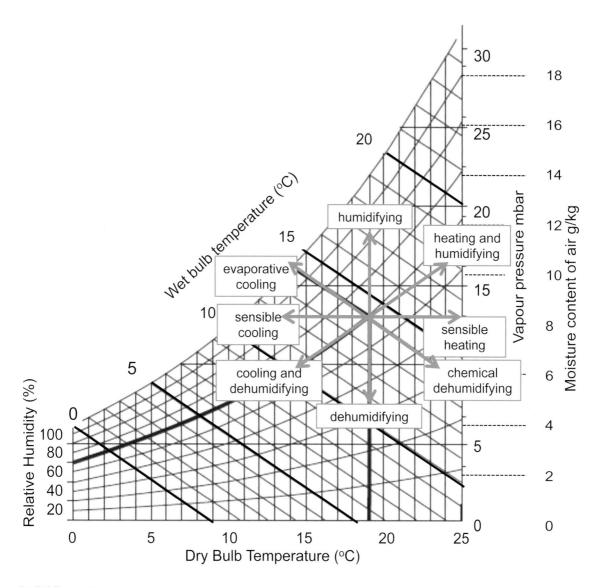

Fig. 3.19 The psychrometric chart relates dry and wet bulb temperature, humidity, vapour pressure and moisture content of air. It illustrates the various processes for heating, cooling, humidifying and dehumidifying.

Building Heat Loss

We need to be able to calculate a building's overall heat loss: to size heating equipment, referred to as the design heat loss; and to predict seasonal energy demand.

Design Heat Loss

The design heat loss of a building is its heating demand for a typical lowest external air temperature, which will vary with location. A typical value in the UK may be –1°C. The design heat loss can be estimated by adding the fabric (Q_F) and ventilation (Q_V) rates of heat loss in W/°C:

The total rate of heat loss (Q_T) in W/°C will be:

$$Q_T = Q_F + Q_V$$

$$Q_F = A_f U_f + A_w U_w + A_g U_g + A_r U_r$$

Where A and U are the areas and average U-values for the floor (f), walls (w), glazing (g) and roof (r).

$$Q_V = (AC \times V \times C_{pa})/3$$

Where AC is the design ventilation rate (ac/h), V is the space volume (m³), and C_{pa} is the volumetric specific heat of air (kJ/m³K).

If the design internal air temperature is T_i(°C), and the design external air temperature is T_e(°C), then the design rate of heat loss (Q_D) will be:

$$Q_D = Q_T \times (T_i - T_e)$$

This has units of watts (W) as it is the required power demand for the heating system. An example calculation is presented in Table 3.7.

This can be used to estimate the sizing of a heating system. It may be necessary to include an allowance for system efficiency to estimate the capacity of the system.

For sizing a cooling system, it will be necessary to estimate solar and internal heat gains to obtain a worst-case scenario, together with the peak external air temperature.

Seasonal Heating Demand

The seasonal energy use can be calculated from the design heat loss, with reference to some form of seasonal average temperature, which can be the heating season average temperature or degree days (*see* Table 3.8), and with reference to the period of time, that is, a year. If a seasonal average temperature is used, then some account of seasonal internal and solar heat gains is required. Degree days already assumes some level of useful heat gains in relation to a base temperature, which is the temperature below which heating is required. The standard base temperature

Table 3.7 Design heat loss calculation for a detached house floor area of 100m² and ceiling height 2.6m. The design inside-outside temperature difference ($T_i - T_e$) is 21°C.

	Floor	Walls	Glazing	Roof	Total
Area (m²)	50	132	15	50	
U-value (W/m².K)	0.2	0.12	1.0	0.15	
$A \times U$ (W/°C)	10	15.8	15	7.5	
Q_F (heat loss per °C (W/°C))					48.3
Air change rate (h⁻¹)					0.5
Volume (m³)					300
C_{pa} (W/m³.K)					1.2
Q_V (heat loss per °C (W/°C))					50
Q_T (W/°C)					98.3
$T_i - T_e$					21
Q_D (W)					2,064.3

for housing in the UK is 15.5°C, which takes account of the heat gain from typical incidental heat gains.

$$E = Q_T \times \text{degree days} \times 24 \times \eta$$

Where

Q_T is the total rate of heat loss (W/°C)

the degree days is taken from standard values (see Table 3.8)

24 is the hours in a day

η is the heating system efficiency

Alternatively, E can be calculated using seasonal average temperatures:

$$E = Q_T \left(T_i - T_e \right) H\eta$$

Where

T_i is the average heating season internal temperature

T_e is the average heating season external temperature (see Table 3.8)

H is the number of hours in the heating season

η is the heating system efficiency

These methods of energy prediction are approximate in that they are based on U-value calculations and average internal and external conditions. They

Table 3.8 *Seasonal average temperatures and degree days for regions in the UK.*

Region	Seasonal average temperature (°C)	Annual degree days
Thames Valley	7.5	2,033
South-eastern	6.7	2,255
Southern	7.8	2,224
South-western	8.3	1,858
Severn Valley	7.2	1,835
Midland	6.7	2,425
West Pennines	6.7	2,228
North-western	6.4	2,388
North-eastern	5.9	2,483
East Pennines	6.6	2,370
East Anglia	6.7	2,307
Borders	6.1	2,254
West Scotland	5.8	2,494
East Scotland	6.0	2,477
North-east Scotland	5.5	2,668
Wales	7.2	2,161
Northern Ireland	6.4	2,360

Source: CIBSE Guide A: Environmental Design, 2006

do not take account of the dynamic (time-varying) effects of thermal mass, weather and occupancy, and are referred to as 'steady state' models. They are the basis of simple annual energy prediction models such as UK SAP. As buildings become more thermally efficient, the time-varying effects become more dominant.

Dynamic Simulation

Dynamic building simulation can predict the detailed hourly time-varying energy and thermal performance of a building or groups of buildings, and can account for thermal mass effects. They can be used to provide predictions of internal temperatures and energy use, based on the detailed construction details, the space layout, glazing and solar gains, occupancy and weather data, for a specific building and location. Such models include Energy+, ESP-r, TRNSYS, and HTB2. HTB2, developed at the Welsh School of Architecture at Cardiff University, is typical of the more advanced numerical models[3.1]. It has been developed over a period of some forty years and has undergone extensive testing, validation, including the IEA Annex 1[3.2], IEA task 12[3.3], and the IEA BESTEST[3.4]. HTB2 has the advantages of flexibility and ease of modification, which makes it well-suited for use in the rapidly evolving field of energy efficiency and sustainable design of buildings. It has been used extensively in the thermal simulations referred to in this book. Fig. 3.20 presents a thermal analysis of the energy performance of a simple building showing the yearly and weekly variation in simulated conditions.

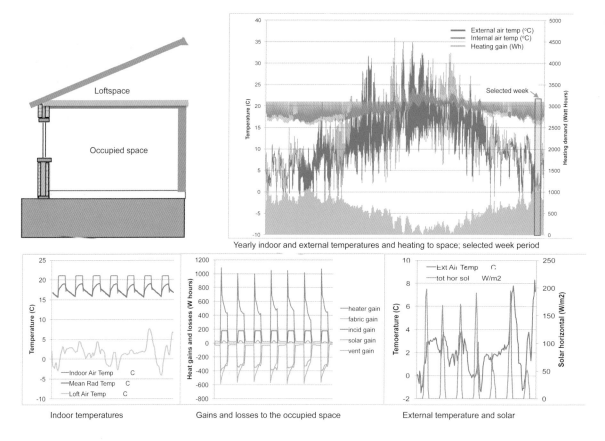

Fig. 3.20 Thermal analysis of the energy performance of a simple building.

Chapter Four

Thermal Comfort

Introduction

Comfort is the ability not to feel too warm or too cool, depending on the surrounding environment and what one is wearing and doing. People perceive their thermal environment in a number of ways, relating to the temperature of the air and the temperature of the surrounding surfaces, the movement of air, and its moisture content. All these affect the way heat is transferred between people and their surroundings, which will be modified by their clothing and activity. Health and wellbeing are related to thermal comfort, not only at the extremes of cold and hot, but also at smaller variations away from preferred conditions. These preferred conditions will vary from person to person and the situation they are in. So designing a satisfactory thermal environment is multifaceted, and how we control our heating, cooling and ventilation systems in response to varying conditions is a fundamental part of thermal design; it is not just about controlling air temperature. Buildings that have well-designed architecture and environmental systems have the potential, not only to save energy, but also to create comfortable, healthy environments where people can enjoy wellbeing and a good quality of life.

What Is Thermal Comfort?

Thermal comfort is an immediate reaction to our surrounding environment. If it is not achieved, it can cause extreme annoyance, complaints in the workplace, and may even be detrimental to health. A lack of thermal comfort is a main reason that buildings fail. We often hear complaints of too warm, too cool, too draughty, too stuffy, too humid, and too dry! The American National Standard[4.1] states that 'thermal comfort is the condition of mind that expresses satisfaction with the thermal environment and is assessed by subjective evaluation.' Fundamentally, thermal comfort is a consequence of the numerous exchanges of energy, within a person's metabolic system, between a person and their surrounds, and between the building and its natural and man-made environment. All this lies within a subjective framework relating to people's activities and expectations. Thermal design needs to recognize these complex interactions, and design for comfort spreads across a wide range of objective and subjective areas.

Most of us typically spend about 90 per cent of our time indoors, and we are constantly interacting with our indoor environment, through our heating, cooling and ventilation systems. The human body generates heat through its metabolic functions and the actions of mechanical work. It needs to continually lose this heat, but in a controlled way, in order to maintain a satisfactory level of comfort. If we lose too much heat, we feel cold; and if we do not lose enough heat, we feel warm. We control heat loss consciously, by turning our heating and cooling systems on and off, up or down, or by moving within the building to a more comfortable space, maybe to a sunny space to get warm or to a cooler space when we feel too warm. We adjust our clothing level to suit our activity within a given environment, or we may change our posture; we 'cuddle up' when we are cold and 'spread out' when we are warm. We also interact with our environment subconsciously, through our body physiologically adapting to its environment, such as shivering and goose pimples when it is cold, or sweating when it is warm.

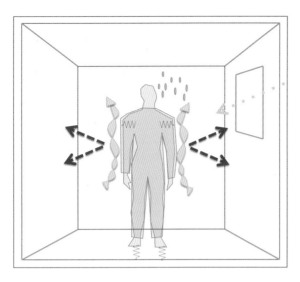

Fig. 4.1 The three thermal layers: human body, clothing, building.

parameters often combine to produce an overall sensation of cool or warmth. Purse your lips and blow against the palm of your hand and you will feel a cool draught; then open your mouth and breathe out slowly onto your palm and you will feel warmth. The air temperature is the same in both cases; it is the combination of the air temperature and air speed that changes, and changes the thermal sensation. Air temperature is generally considered as the measure of overall thermal perception, even though we sense other aspects, such as surface temperatures, air movement and moisture. Often they combine to provide an equivalent temperature that would feel like air temperature, if these other aspects were neutral. This is similar to weather forecasts, where the air temperature is adjusted to account for wind chill.

We exchange heat with our environment in a dynamic way. Coming in from the cold, we may stand in front of a fire to warm up quickly, or, in hot weather, we might seek relief from the cool draught of air from a fan. Such comfort is often pleasurable but short-lived, and continuous exposure may lead to being too hot or too cold. 'Thermal delight' is a term often used to describe this more pleasurable aspect of comfort. Lisa Heschong's excellent book *Thermal Delight in Architecture* discusses the pleasures of the thermal environment[4.2]. Heschong evokes this delight with a simple description: 'When the sun is warm on my face and the breeze is cool, I know it is good to be alive.' However, because thermal delight is often short-lived and may be experienced differently by different people, the thermal environment is usually designed to avoid thermal discomfort rather than to promote thermal delight. We may therefore think of thermal comfort on two levels: (i) the absence of discomfort, and (ii) the promotion of delight. Avoiding discomfort relies mainly on controlling air temperature, such as in air-conditioned offices. Promoting delight often relates to radiant temperature and air movement, which perhaps has its basis in the more passive features of sun and breeze.

Heating and cooling system design must respond to people's needs and behaviour, their activity and

If our physiology and clothing provide the first two intimate 'layers' of thermal comfort, the building is often regarded as the 'third skin' (*see* Fig. 4.1). The form and fabric of buildings has evolved over many centuries, in relation to a location's climate and the availability of materials, as well as responding to people's cultural needs and their use of space. Indeed, through our physiological adaptations, and with the help of clothing, buildings and heating systems, humans can survive in a wide range of external climate conditions, from –20°C in cold regions up to 50°C in hot ones, which is probably why we have populated most of the planet.

Thermal Perception

We are sensitive to the temperature of the air that surrounds us. We also feel the direct radiant heat that travels from warm surfaces, such as our heating system radiators, or from hot sources, such as the sun. When sitting close to a cold window in winter, we feel chilled as our warm bodies radiate heat to a cooler surface. We feel the movement of air across our skin, and are sensitive to its moisture content and its dryness or wetness. These physical comfort

clothing, and their expectations. Not everyone will experience optimal comfort for the same conditions, so we usually design to make most people comfortable, most of the time. We sometimes refer to a zone of 'lack of discomfort' for thermal parameters, implying that there is no optimum, long lasting comfort point, but, rather, a range of conditions where most people will not perceive discomfort. Our modern heating and cooling systems strive to achieve this, and usually for the whole building rather than individual spaces. An element of thermal delight may be added, through a sunny space or an open window, but allowing people the choice to experience it or not, as they wish.

Nowadays, we expect to be comfortable, or at least not uncomfortable, for most of the time, whether at home, at work, while shopping, at the cinema, and so forth. We take thermal comfort for granted, only to complain when we feel discomfort and cannot adapt to the situation by shedding or adding clothing, changing activity or posture, or moving to a more comfortable position. Generally, if we are not aware of the thermal environment, then its job done! No complaints.

In the UK many of our existing buildings were not built with whole building heating. In houses, coal was the main fuel, with scuttles, pokers, tongs and brushes needed, to make and control the fire, and keep the hearth clean. Keeping warm involved a lot of effort, and a lot of energy. Open fires were not efficient, with most of the heat lost up the chimney. The main warmth was the direct thermal radiation from the burning coal or logs, and the air in the room was relatively cool. Our houses were generally poorly insulated and draughty and expectations for comfort were low; health was at risk for many. Historically, an inglenook might have been used to provide a snug warm area where people could sit, with its timber surfaces warming up quickly from the fire's radiant heat (*see* Fig. 4.2). Before air conditioning, cooling was achieved by opening a window, or, in hot climates, using wind chimneys to draw air in for comfort cooling, or by constructing relatively

Fig. 4.2 The inglenook. (St Fagans Folk Museum)

dense masonry walls, which cooled down at night, and then keeping the internal spaces cool during the hot daytime. Having heating and cooling available at the flick of a switch in every room is very convenient, but also encourages excess energy use. It may also be unaffordable for an increasing number of people, who live in substandard older housing, cannot afford to pay high energy bills, and are in fuel poverty. Thermal design therefore needs to provide affordable warmth, or cooling, to achieve comfortable and healthy living conditions. The affluent may rarely perceive discomfort, but for many poorer members of society, thermal discomfort and the consequential detrimental impact on health is common.

Thermal design is generally aimed at maintaining constant thermal conditions: a state of thermal neutrality. There is a school of thought that this is a form of sensory deprivation and may give rise to stress. Humans have evolved over thousands of years to deal with variations in thermal conditions. Fluctuation of air speed, mimicking that of the natural environment, has been shown to be more pleasant compared with steady mechanical airflow [4.3,4.4]. Variations in conditions within a comfort zone may perhaps be more appropriate for the design of our future zero energy buildings. As Lisa Heschong states[4.2]: 'Uniformity is extremely unnatural and therefore requires a great deal of effort, and energy, to maintain.'

Metabolic Activity and Comfort Theory

Thermal comfort is based on our ability to control our heat loss in relation to the surrounding environment, seeking a balance between heat generation from metabolic and mechanical activities and heat lost to the surrounds via the skin and through breathing.

The heat given off by a typical human body through metabolic activity is measured in units of MET. One MET equates to a heat loss of $58.1W/m^2$ of body surface area, where the average surface area of an adult is $1.8m^2$. Clothing insulates against body heat loss and is measured in units of CLO. One CLO provides a thermal resistance of $0.155m^2\,K/W$. Values of MET and CLO for a range of clothing ensembles are given in Fig. 4.3 in relation to equivalent comfort temperatures for different activities. Heavy activities and heavy clothing ensembles require lower temperatures compared to light activities and less clothing.

Humans, like all mammals, are homeotherms, constantly regulating our heat loss in order to keep a stable core body temperature. The human body's core temperature must be maintained between 36.5°C and 37.5°C. Lower than 35°C, we suffer hypothermia;

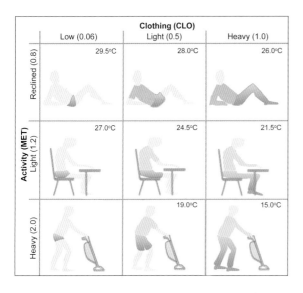

Fig. 4.3 Values of MET and CLO for a range of temperatures and activities. ASHREA 55-2017. (comfort.cbe.berkeley.edu)

higher than 38.3°C, we suffer heat stress and hyperthermia. Both can be fatal. At rest, we have to get rid of about 100W of heat generated from our internal functions, especially the liver, brain, and heart, and from the contraction of skeletal muscles. However, with our physiological mechanisms and adjustment of clothing levels, we can be reasonably comfortable over a relatively wide range of indoor thermal conditions. The primary physiological mechanism for controlling heat loss is to control the amount of blood flow in capillaries that connect the skin with the core body. These will shrink in diameter in a cold environment, known as vasoconstriction, and expand in a hot environment, known as vasodilation. Temperature-sensitive thermoreceptors are located in the skin layer and in the body core, and are analysed by the brain, which then triggers actions to control the body's heat loss. If the environment becomes too cold, then the body temperature of its extreme parts will cool down in order to maintain the core temperature (see Fig. 4.4). The body can shiver by shaking skeletal muscles in order to generate heat. In very hot environments or during exercise, our skin can sweat in order to cool through evaporation. More than any other mammal, humans are particularly good at sweating, and have the highest density of eccrine sweat glands per skin surface area of any mammal. We are the only mammal that relies on secreting water onto the skin's surface to stay cool, which is why we can endure prolonged activities in hot conditions.

The body loses heat by a combination of radiation, conduction, convection and evaporation, each varying with environmental conditions (see Fig. 4.5). At low air temperatures, radiation to surrounding surfaces is highest, with convection next. As the temperature rises, radiation and convection are reduced, and evaporation becomes more dominant, especially as temperatures approach the skin temperature of around 33°C. Evaporation takes place through respiration (breathing) and transpiration (sweating at the skin's surface). As the air temperature exceeds skin temperature, the body will need to adapt by

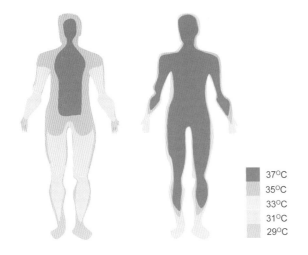

	37°C
	35°C
	33°C
	31°C
	29°C

Fig. 4.4 Body temperature in cold and warm environments.

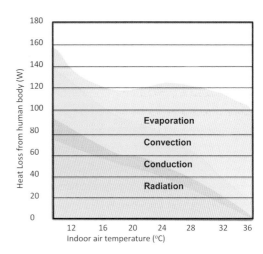

Fig. 4.5 Heat loss mechanisms with surrounding air temperature.

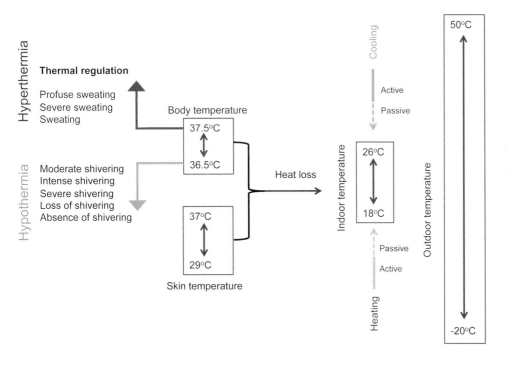

Fig. 4.6 Temperature ranges of body and skin temperature, when mechanical heating and cooling is required, and the range of outdoor temperatures that buildings experience.

reducing heat generation. Direct conduction losses, where the body is in contact with a solid, such as feet on the floor, are relatively small, although there will be conduction from the skin to clothing. These heat loss mechanisms will change in relation to air movement, moisture content and surrounding surface temperatures.

A building is designed to contribute to achieving a thermal comfort through a combination of passive design and mechanical heating and cooling systems. Fig. 4.6 summarizes the temperature ranges associated with the human body, the building and its need for heating and cooling, in relation to outdoor temperature.

Measuring the Thermal Environment

To understand and design for thermal comfort, we need to measure our physical environment in order to provide design and operational criteria, and to assess whether a building performs as designed. We can relate measurements of the thermal environment to means of heat transfer. Air temperature mainly relates to the convective exchange of heat between the body and the surrounding air. The surface temperatures relate to radiant heat transfer. Air speed relates to the rate of convective heat exchange and relative humidity relates to evaporation. The indoor thermal environment can be described by these four parameters.

Air Temperature

For normal indoor activities, people will generally be satisfied if the internal air temperature is between 19°C and 23°C in winter, and not exceeding 26°C in summer. The air temperature gradient is also important, and it should be less than 4°C, being cooler at the feet than the head. The air temperature will vary from point to point in a space, and with height due to buoyant air rising. It will also vary over time,

due to thermostatic cycling of heating and cooling systems, and in response to external weather and internal patterns of use.

Radiant Temperature

Radiant temperature is a measure of the average temperature of the internal surfaces, together with any direct radiant gains from high-temperature sources, such as the sun through a window. The mean radiant temperature (MRT) is the area-weighted average of all the surface temperatures in a room. If surfaces are at different temperatures, the distance from a person to each surface affects the MRT, with closer and larger surface areas contributing more. Comfort is affected by radiant asymmetry, and people are especially sensitive to warm ceilings. The radiant asymmetry should be less than 10°C between opposite-facing room surfaces, for example, the ceiling and floor.

'View factors' provide a measure of the relative proportion of indoor surfaces that a person 'sees' depending on their location in the room. The MRT (T_{MRT}) is a function of surface temperatures (T_s), emissivity (ε_s), and view factor (F_s) for all surfaces (s) in a room (see Fig. 4.7), and can be expressed as:

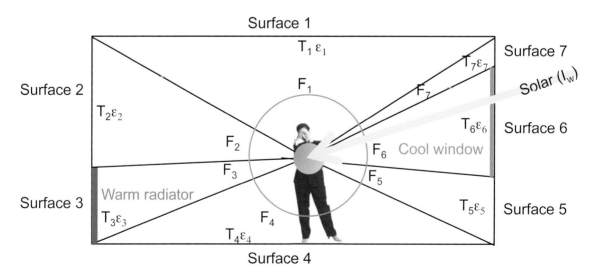

Fig. 4.7 Radiant heat view factors, including a warm radiator and cool window.

$$T_{mrt} = (\varepsilon_1 F_1 T_1^4 + \varepsilon_2 F_2 T_2^4 + ... + \varepsilon_n F_n T_n^4)^{0.25}$$

Where (for surfaces 1 to n):

ε_n is the surface emissivity (ratio of 0–1)

T_n is the surface temperature (K)

$F_{n \to \text{person}}$ is the view factor between surface and person (ratio of 0–1)

This is often simplified to:

$$T_{mrt} = \frac{(F_1 T_1 + F_2 T_2 + ... + F_n T_n)}{\text{Sum of all } F_n}$$

If there is direct solar radiation incident on a person, the MRT including the solar radiation is given by:

$$T_{mrt} = (T_{umrt}^4 + (\text{Const} f_p \, \alpha \, I_w))^{0.25}$$

Where:

T_{umrt} = MRT without solar (e.g. 20°C = 293K)

Const = $0.208.10^8 = 1/(0.97 \, \sigma)$, where σ = Stephen Boltzman constant = 5.8×10^{-8}

f_p = projected area factor (e.g. 0.26, based on a seated person)

α = absorptance (e.g. 0.9)

I_w = solar radiation incident on a person (e.g. 600W/m²)

This equation is valid when the air velocity is below 0.4m/s and when the mean radiation temperature is below 50°C.

If we calculate T_{mrt} using the assumed values in brackets above:

$$T_{mrt} = (293^4 + (0.208 \times 10^8 \times 0.26 \times 0.9 \times 600))^{0.25}$$
$$= 318K = 45°C$$

This is 25°C above the normal room MRT and can be extremely uncomfortable, especially for people in fixed locations, such as office workers.

Air Speed

Air movement can affect both convective and evaporative heat loss from the skin's surface. People begin to perceive air movement for air speeds around 0.15m/s, and air speeds greater than 0.2m/s may be perceived as

Fig. 4.8 Increased air speeds in a space from deflected air supply jets and downdraughts from a cold window surface.

a draught, especially in cooler conditions. For naturally ventilated spaces the air speed will usually be less than 0.15m/s, away from the influence of open windows, and in the absence of major downdraughts generated by cool internal surfaces. For mechanically ventilated spaces, the air speed is often greater than 0.15m/s, especially in areas close to air supply devices, or where supply air jets are deflected downwards into the occupied zone, by down (*see* Fig. 4.8). It is possible to counter draught discomfort by increasing air temperatures. In warmer and more humid conditions, such as tropical climates, a higher air speed can provide comfort cooling.

Relative Humidity

The relative humidity (RH) is the percentage of moisture in the air compared to the total amount of moisture the air can hold (its saturation point) at that temperature. The RH of a space will affect the rate of evaporation from the skin. When air temperatures are within the comfort range (say, 19°C to 23°C), the RH should be within the range 30 to 60 per cent. At higher air temperatures, approaching the skin temperature, evaporation heat loss is important to maintain comfort, and so a high RH can make it difficult to achieve thermal comfort. A wet and dry bulb thermometer is used to measure RH, with one bulb wetted using a material sock soaked in water. The dry bulb temperature sensor will exchange heat with the surrounding air by convection. The wet bulb thermometer

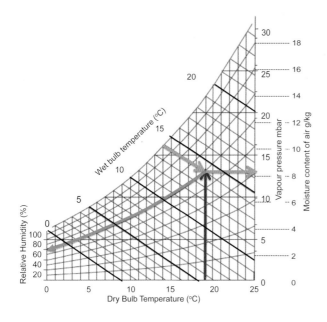

Fig. 4.9 Psychrometric chart relating dry bulb and wet bulb temperatures to RH. In this example, the dry bulb temperature (dbt) is 19°C and the wet bulb temperature (wbt) is 14°C, which combine to give an RH of 60%, indicating a room air moisture content just over 8g/kg of air.

loses additional heat by evaporation. The RH can then be obtained by referring to a psychrometric chart (*see* Fig. 4.9). The wet and dry bulbs will be the same at 100 per cent RH, which is the saturation point.

Zone of 'Lack of Discomfort'

The perception of comfort will vary with activities, clothing, thermal history and individual needs and preferences. There is no optimum combination of measures that will ensure comfort for everyone at all times. We therefore aim to provide thermal conditions that fall within a range, where most people will feel reasonably comfortable, or at least not uncomfortable. We refer to this range as the zone of 'lack of discomfort' (*see* Fig. 4.10). To avoid discomfort, air temperatures should generally be between 19°C and 23°C (up to 26°C in summer); radiant

temperatures within 4°C of air temperature; air speed below 0.2m/s; relative humidity between 30 and 60 per cent. To some extent these values can be offset by each other, for example, increased air temperature can offset higher air speed; higher relative humidity by increased air speed; lower air temperature by higher radiant temperature.

The indoor environmental conditions will vary both spatially and over time. Spatially, air temperature varies with height due to warm air rising. Radiant temperature will vary depending how far a person is from a surface, or if radiated by the sun. Increased air movement may be felt in the vicinity of air supply grilles, or an open window. There are also variations over time, due to a building heating up from cold, or the on-off cycling of controls, or when the sun is shining. When we measure the indoor environment at a point in time and space, it will not be representative of the conditions over time, a day or season, or throughout the space. We therefore need to use our knowledge of building physics to extrapolate what comfort conditions might be at other times, and points in space.

The thermal environment is also linked to other environmental parameters. Air quality is affected

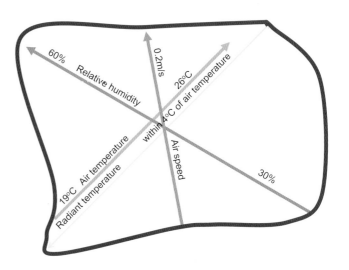

Fig. 4.10 Zone of 'lack of discomfort'.

when the supply of ventilation fresh air to a space is also used for heating or cooling. The balance of daylight and electric light gives rise to internal heat gains from electric lighting, and solar heat gains (and glare) from glazed areas. External noise is related to opening windows in naturally ventilated buildings, and fan noise may be an issue in air-conditioned buildings. Thermal comfort is therefore an integral part of overall environmental comfort.

Thermal Comfort Models

There are many models of thermal comfort, which combine the physical environmental parameters with activity and clothing levels, to provide a single value of comfort. There have been some 100 or more models developed over the last 100 years. The simplest correlate with thermal comfort is air temperature, which is the main parameter used to control heating and cooling systems. At their most basic, comfort models combine two or more thermal parameters, and at their more complex level, they are based on the physiological operation of the human body. There are also empirical models developed from surveys of people's response to their thermal environment.

The simpler models of thermal comfort use combinations of physical parameters in a compensatory way, to provide a single measure in the form of an equivalent temperature. The *resultant temperature,* sometimes referred to as *operative temperature,* combines air temperature and mean radiant temperature in a proportion comparable to the body's heat loss. At low air speeds (< 0.1m/s) the following relationship can be used:

$$T_{res} = 1/2T_{mrt} + 1/2T_{air}$$

Where:

T_{res} is the resultant temperature
T_{mrt} is the mean radiant temperature,
T_{air} is the air temperature.

The resultant temperature can be measured at the centre of a matt black globe of 100mm diameter (although globes between 25 and 150mm will give acceptable results); it is also referred to as *globe temperature.*

Corrected effective temperature (CET) combines air temperature (or globe temperature), air speed and wet bulb temperature, which can be represented in nomogram form as shown in Fig. 4.11.

Advanced models of thermal comfort account for the physiological and sometimes psychological response of people. The *predictive mean vote* (PMV) approach developed by Fanger[4,5] is based on the body's heat balance with its environment, relating mainly to perceived skin temperature and sweat evaporation rate. A complex equation, combining air temperature, mean radiant temperature, air velocity,

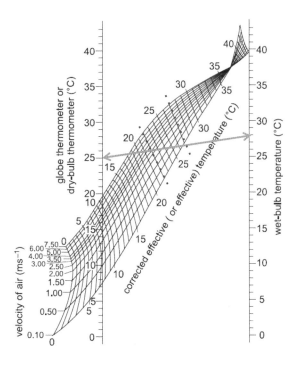

Fig. 4.11 Nomogram for calculating the corrected effective temperature (CET) with the acceptable comfort range 23°C–27°C. In the example, a globe temperature of 25°C, wet bulb temperature of 28°C and air speed of 0.5m/s provide an overall equivalent air temperature comfort sensation of 26°C.

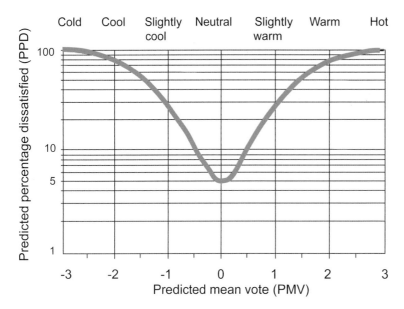

Fig. 4.12 PMV versus PPD.

relative humidity, activity, and clothing, provides a value of PMV, represented on a thermal sensation scale from –3 (cold) to +3 (hot). Another equation relates PMV to PPD, the *percentage of people dissatisfied* with their environment, which can be represented in graphical form (*see* Fig. 4.12).

Fanger's PMV model has been tested against experimental surveys collected in the laboratory and in buildings, where people are asked to assess their thermal sensation on the seven-point sensation scale. PMV is usually based on the average response from a large group of people, such as all workers in an office. As thermal comfort is subjective there will generally be a range of scores. The PPD relates to the number of people who complain of thermal discomfort in relation at each point on the PMV scale. There is no condition where everyone will experience optimum comfort conditions, and for a typical work place there will always be 5 per cent of people who report discomfort.

PMV is mainly used for air-conditioned office-type environments, where thermal conditions are relatively stable over the working day. It assumes constant conditions for the six input parameters,

and may be regarded as a steady state model over time. The PMV approach is used by ASHRAE Standard 55-2017[4.6], which requires that conditions be maintained so that at least 80 per cent of occupants are satisfied, with a PMV score between –0.5 and +0.5.

The PMV model is based on a single node representing the core temperature of the body, which exchanges heat with the environment via a fixed skin temperature of 34°C. More recent human biometeorology models involve a more detailed consideration of thermoregulatory processes and multi-node heat transfer. The physiological environmental temperature (PET) model is based on the Munich energy-balance model for individuals (MEMI). The universal thermal climate index (UTCI) uses four body cylinder layers of bone, muscle, fat, skin, and divides the body into twelve segments. Both use complex equations and can also be used for outside comfort, and they can deal with solar radiation. A tool developed specifically for outdoor comfort predictions is CityComfort+[4.7], which is based on UTCI and is able to visually present the distribution of UTCI values (°C equivalent) for an outside space (*see* Fig. 4.13)[4.8].

The adaptive comfort model, developed by Humphries, is more suited to dynamic thermal environments. It was derived from survey data of people's response to air temperature, and recognizes that occupants adapt dynamically to their environment. Adaptations may be behavioural, by people changing their clothing level, activity level, or posture. People may open windows, close blinds, turn on fans, or move to a more comfortable location. Adaptations may be physiological, through unconsciously increasing or decreasing blood flow to the skin, and through

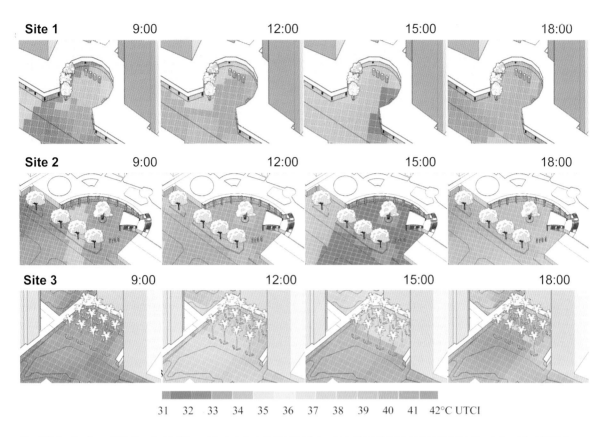

Fig. 4.13 Application of CityComfort+ Rhino software plug-in in assessing urban microclimate and pedestrian thermal comfort UTCI for the three study sites on Jun 17, 2015. Results are calculated for the 3×3m grid. (Jianxiang Huang, University of Hong Kong[4.8])

shivering or sweating. Psychological adaptation comes through a person's expectation and memory of previous experiences, and their perception of control of their environment.

A main feature of the adaptive comfort model is the relation of indoor comfort to outdoor temperature. Survey data has shown that 'occupants of naturally ventilated buildings prefer a wider range of conditions that more closely reflect outdoor climate patterns'[4.9]. When the outdoor temperature is warm, people will accept warmer indoor temperatures, so the indoor operative temperature for comfort relates to mean outdoor temperature (see Fig. 4.14). People can therefore adapt to a range of geographical climates and thermal experiences. de Dear and Brager[4.9] have proposed the following expression for an adaptive indoor comfort temperature (T_{comf}) in relation to outdoor temperature (T_{out}):

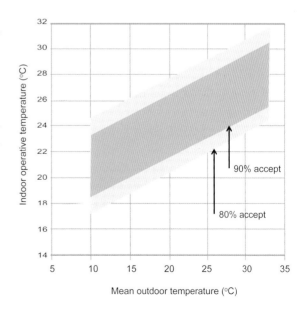

Fig. 4.14 Adaptive comfort range. (Redrawn from CBE Thermal Comfort Tool for ASHRAE-55)

$$T_{comf} = 0.31 T_{out} + 17.8$$

while Humphreys and Nicol[4.10] have proposed a similar expression for naturally ventilated buildings:

$$T_{comf} = 0.534 T_{out} + 11.9$$

The adaptive approach can also be applied to air-conditioned buildings, where less rigid temperature control may result in significant energy savings, typically of the order of 10 to 18 per cent.

Thermal comfort theories do not generally differentiate between gender and age. However, there is a growing body of work that suggests they are both important. The elderly population are considered physiologically more vulnerable under heat stress due to reduced thermoregulatory responses, such as sweating rate, skin blood flow and cardiovascular functions[4.11, 4.12]. When exposed to the same thermal conditions, older people have different comfort needs, and their means of adaptation or options of personal control may be more limited[4.13].

There are also significant gender differences in thermal comfort, temperature preference, and the use of thermostats. Females are generally less satisfied with room temperatures than males, preferring higher room temperatures than males, and feeling both uncomfortably cold and uncomfortably hot more often than males. Women have been shown to need a temperature 2.5°C warmer than men for comfort, typically between 24°C and 25°C. Although men and women have a similar core body temperature of around 37°C, our perception of comfort relates also to skin temperature, which is nearly 3°C lower for women compared to men[4.14]. Although females are more critical of their thermal environments, males tend to control the use of thermostats in households more often than females[4.15].

Even with our comprehensive understanding of thermal comfort, we still generally use air temperature as the major measure of comfort and as the main design parameter, often with a backstop approach that other comfort parameters are within an acceptable range, within the lack of discomfort zone.

Health and Comfort

The World Health Organization (WHO) defines health, not as the absence of ill-health, but as 'a state of complete physical, mental and social wellbeing', which includes physical, social and psychological aspects[4.16]. The built environment has a major role in promoting people's wellbeing and providing environments that encourage and maintain good health.

We often talk about comfortable and healthy environments, as though they were the same. Of course, extremes of low and high temperatures will be both uncomfortable and unhealthy, and both extremes can increase mortality rates. Whereas comfort in buildings may be considered an immediate perceived response to our environment, health is more affected by longer-term conditions, such as extended periods of warmth or cold, or poor air quality. Sometimes people's actions to maintain thermal comfort can be harmful to health. They may turn off air supply grilles in a mechanically ventilated space if they feel a draught, and as a consequence suffer poor air quality. As with a diet, people tend to control for a comfortable environment rather than a healthy one, perhaps similar to preferring burger and chips to salad!

Indoor Air Quality

Exposure to outdoor and indoor air pollutants increases the risk of disease. The WHO report[4.17] states that 91 per cent of the world's population lives in places where the air quality is poor, and outside WHO guideline recommendations. Air pollution is the world's largest single environmental health risk, killing more people than malaria and AIDS. Polluted air has many constituents from both outdoor and indoor sources (see Table 4.1). Often the dilemma in a building is whether to ventilate indoor pollutants to outside, or to restrict outdoor pollutants from getting in. In Hong Kong, for example, indoor radon levels

Table 4.1 Internal and external pollutants and their sources.

External source	External pollutant	Indoor source	Indoor pollutant
Man-made fuel combustion in stationary sources (e.g. power plants).	• sulphur dioxide • ozone • particulates • carbon monoxide • hydrocarbons	Construction materials and finishes.	• radon, formaldehyde • asbestos • fibreglass • organics and lead
Fuel combustion from transport.	• carbon monoxide • lead • hydrocarbons • benzene • nitrogen oxides	Heating, air conditioning, and cooking products.	• carbon monoxide, formaldehyde • nitrogen oxides • particulates microbes
Industrial and construction processes.	• particulates • nitrogen oxides	Chemicals from office machines.	• ozone and organics
Natural sources.	• volcanic dust • eroded soil particles, spores and microbes; windblown sea salt.	Occupants.	• carbon dioxide • water vapour • odours • odorants
Microorganisms (could also be internal).	• pollen • bacteria • viruses • fungal and plant spores	Activity-related substances.	• smoking (carbon monoxide, particulates, odorants) • aerosol sprays (fluorocarbons, odorants) • cleaning (organics, odorants)

may be high due to their emission from the aggregate used to make concrete. However, the outdoor air may be highly polluted from traffic emissions. Ventilation alone is not the answer, and outdoor air must be filtered.

Good quality indoor air is fundamental to people's health and wellbeing. The average person will typically require 15kg of air a day (compared with 1kg of food and 2kg of water), yet there are no clear guidelines to ensure good air quality in buildings. Comparatively little is understood about the levels and limits of pollutants in the air we breathe. The external air is used as a source of dilution by a number of sectors, including transport and industry, and although there

are emission controls on individual sources, there is no control over the accumulation of sources; as a result, the air quality in many cities is extremely poor. This air 'cocktail' finally ends up in our buildings, often naively referred to as 'fresh air'. The spread of infectious diseases, such as SARS and COVID-19, are also of particular concern in relation to ventilation rates, with densely populated spaces that are poorly ventilated at more risk of spreading disease.

Ventilation design is mainly based on the dilution and exhaust of internally generated pollutants. Recent changes in building design have led to an increasing airtightness of building envelopes (lower air leakage), smaller volume spaces (less volume for dilution), and more types of construction materials, furnishing and surface finishes (more pollutant sources). Design ventilation rates are generally based on occupancy density and not the total pollution load. Indoor air quality is considered to be acceptable if there are no known contaminants at harmful concentrations, and where 80 per cent or more occupants do not express dissatisfaction. Increasing fresh air rates brings in more outside pollutants and has a major impact on heating and cooling loads. Poor external air quality may rule out natural ventilation for some buildings, which will require mechanical ventilation systems with filtration.

Metabolic Carbon Dioxide as an Indicator of Indoor Air Quality

It is impossible in practice to measure the vast range of indoor air pollutants and how they vary over time. Indoor carbon dioxide levels can be used as a surrogate indicator of ventilation. A building's occupants generate metabolic carbon dioxide, and its concentration for a given occupancy will depend on the building's ventilation rate and the outside carbon dioxide levels. Spaces with a relatively high build-up of metabolic carbon dioxide for a given occupation level may be assumed to have a low fresh air ventilation rate.

In mechanically ventilated or air-conditioned offices, carbon dioxide levels for normal occupancy (approximately 1 person per 10m²) will typically be 600 to 700ppm. Between 800 and 1,000ppm is considered borderline satisfactory, while above 1,000ppm is unsatisfactory, and 1,500 to 2,000ppm indicates little fresh air arrives to a space's occupied zone. In naturally ventilated offices in winter, with windows closed, carbon dioxide levels could rise to 1,600ppm. In naturally ventilated school classrooms with relatively high occupation levels and windows closed, levels could rise to 2,500ppm. Naturally ventilated spaces may therefore suffer poor air quality when windows are closed in winter.

It is assumed that if carbon dioxide levels are high, other pollutant levels will also be high, and controlling for carbon dioxide levels may ensure that other pollutant levels are maintained within an acceptable range. This is a general assumption for average pollutant sources, but does not apply if there are specific high emission pollutant sources or a high risk of infectious disease. Controlling the fresh air supply by monitoring carbon dioxide levels is also used for energy efficiency, to reduce heating, cooling and fan power during periods of low occupancy.

Perceived Air Quality

Low levels of pollutants are difficult to measure with physical sensors, although they may be perceived as poor air quality by occupants. Two units, the olf and the decipol, have been developed to assess air quality. An olf is a measure of pollution emission, while the decipol is a measure of perceived air quality (see Fig. 4.15). Various pollutant sources, including people, carpets, building materials and tobacco smoke, can be assigned an olf value. The decipol is measured subjectively by panels of trained 'sniffers', who assess the air quality of a building by reference to a standard olf smell. Ventilation requirements are usually based on occupancy levels. However, people are not the only source of contamination, and other sources, such as the furnishing, surface treatment, the outdoor air, and the HVAC system itself, contribute to the total olfs in a space. Ventilation requirements can be related to perceived air quality (decipols) and the pollution source strength (olfs) by:

$$Q = \frac{10\,G}{(C_i - C_o)}$$

where

Q is the ventilation rate (l/s)

G is the pollution source strength (olf)

C_i is the perceived internal air pollution level (decipols)

C_o is the perceived outdoor air pollution level (decipols)

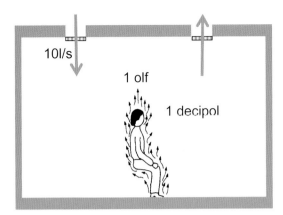

1 decipol is the perceived air quality in a room with 1 person (emitting 1 olf) and with a fresh air supply of 10l/s.

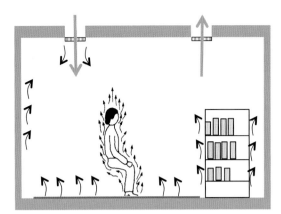

Other sources of 'olfs' include furnishing, wall finishes, carpets and the HVAC supply.

Fig. 4.15 The olf and the decipol, related to people and other sources of pollution.

For a 'low olf' office, the pollutant emissions would be about 0.2 olf/m². Therefore, to achieve an indoor air quality of 1.4 decipol (which represents an 80 per cent satisfaction level), and assuming negligible outdoor air pollution, the required ventilation rate would be 1.4l/s/m². This is somewhat higher than the requirements to satisfy existing office ventilation standards of around 1.0l/s/m². The olf approach recognizes all sources of contamination, and suggests increasing fresh air ventilation to achieve an overall satisfactory perceived indoor air quality.

Sick Building Syndrome

Sick building syndrome (SBS) is associated with a set of commonly occurring symptoms that affect people at their place of work, usually in an office-type environment, and which disappear soon after they leave work[4.18]. These symptoms include dry eyes, watery eyes, blocked nose, runny nose, headaches, lethargy, tight chest and difficulty in breathing. The shape of the profile in Fig. 4.16 is typical, with headaches and lethargy tending to be at the high end of complaints, and breathing problems at the low end, although the absolute values will vary from building to building. The personal symptom index (PSI) is used as a measure of the average number of symptoms per person; in some offices, up to 50 per cent of staff might report one or more symptoms. Office workers who report high levels of SBS also often report thermal discomfort, and may perceive the air quality as stale, dry or warm. Air-conditioned buildings tend to have a higher level of SBS than naturally ventilated ones. Possible reasons for this include cost cuts in their design, difficulties and complexities in their maintenance and operation, problems associated with hygiene and cleanliness (especially the air distribution ductwork) and poor room fresh air distribution. Also, symptoms seem to be higher in open-plan spaces compared to cellular ones, for clerical workers compared to managerial workers, women compared to men, and those in public sector buildings compared to the private sector. Reducing SBS can reduce absenteeism, as well as increasing productivity, creating a more favourable working environment.

Productivity in Relation to Comfort and Health

If people are uncomfortable or unwell, this will affect a person's ability to perform specific tasks. In the

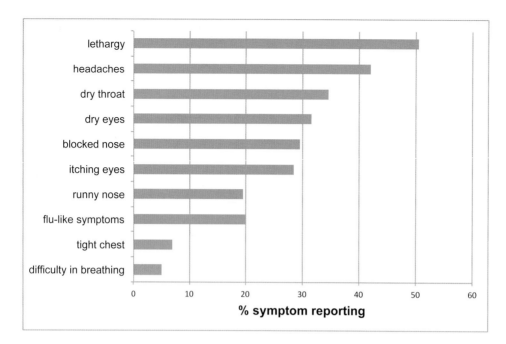

Fig. 4.16 Example of a typical level of SBS symptom reporting in an air-conditioned office.

workplace, performance may be affected both physiologically and psychologically; manual dexterity may be compromised and cognitive activities dulled. At the more extreme ends of hot or cold, sweating or shivering will affect dexterity and lessen the ability to carry out specific manual tasks. In the early part of the twentieth century, output from manual tasks in coal mining, glass, steel, tinplate and weaving industries was found to be reduced during periods of warmer working conditions. Accidents increased in munitions factories as temperatures varied from the optimum (20°C)[4.19]. In schools and offices, cognitive tasks are compromised by discomfort. The academic performance decreases by around 20 per cent for an increase in temperature over the range 20°C to 30°C[4.20]. Thermal discomfort may cause distraction and psychological strain for office workers, and speed and accuracy of tasks will suffer. An analysis of twenty-four studies of mainly office workers indicated that performance is maximized when the air temperature is around 22°C, with a decrease in performance of around 0.2 per cent for each 1°C higher and lower temperature (*see* Fig. 4.17)[4.21], with changes near the optimum temperature having less impact. Other studies have indicated increases in productivity of 4.8 per cent for green buildings with a good environment[4.22], and up to some 30 per cent suggested for Australian workforces, attributed to good indoor environmental quality[4.23]. Further studies[4.24] link individual temperature control to 3 per cent productivity gains; improved ventilation to 11 per cent gains; improved lighting to 23 per cent gains; access to the natural environment through daylight and operable windows to 18 per cent gains.

The cost of reduced productivity to a business is high. Some 90 per cent of office business costs relate to staff costs. For US LEED-certified buildings, benefits of $37 to $55 per square foot (equivalent to £280 to £420 per m²) were identified from less sick time and greater worker productivity, arising from better ventilation, lighting and general environmental improvements[4.25]. Estimated annual savings in the US through productivity gains are between $10 billion and $30 billion from reducing sick building syndrome symptoms, and between $20 billion and $60 billion from direct improvements in worker performance from non-health-related improvements[4.26]. Productivity gains may therefore be the main benefit of a sustainable building – much greater than energy savings.

However, although the benefits of a good environment on staff morale, productivity and learning in schools seem obvious, improving indoor environmental quality has not generally been a priority in building design and construction.

Comfort and Health in Zero Energy Buildings

The thermal characteristics of zero energy buildings use the passive design of the building form, construction and envelope, to reduce energy demand for heating, cooling, ventilation and lighting, which are reasonably well understood. We then need effective ways of providing comfort by means of mechanical heating, cooling and ventilating systems that meet the reduced, and often intermittent, thermal demand; this is not so well developed. The standard method of controlling air temperature within a narrow band may not be the best way to achieve comfort, and an adaptive approach might be more appropriate.

We often refer to the passive design principles of traditional or vernacular buildings and how they respond to climate, such as comfort cooling through air movement in warm humid climates and night-time cooling of thermal mass in hot desert climates. A comfortable air temperature was rarely the design intent of traditional buildings, which were often too 'leaky' for a narrow range of air temperature control. Comfort was mainly achieved through radiant heat transfer (for heating and cooling), or air movement (for cooling).

We may consider a 'modern vernacular' approach to comfort for zero energy buildings. We can use large-area chilled or heated surface systems, which provide both comfort and energy efficiency; air temperature might vary more widely, with radiant heat exchange more dominant. This is perhaps not surprising when a major part of heat transfer of the human body is through radiant exchange with the surroundings. Achieving comfort by the more traditional means of radiant heat exchange and air movement might be considered to deliver a more pleasurable thermal experience of 'thermal delight', while using a tightly controlled air temperature is more associated with 'lack of discomfort', or avoiding problems; this follows the principle of 'more good' rather than 'less bad'.

Certain features will potentially improve comfort for zero energy design, while some might compromise conditions. Reducing building heat loss in winter may result in overheating in summer, especially with the trend towards lightweight timber construction. Solar heat gains may be used to supplement space heating in winter, but they are often unwanted, resulting in the need for cooling in summer. As glazing systems become better insulated, we may place daylit spaces facing north to avoid solar overheating and glare. Thermal mass may provide temperature stability and surface temperatures that can help cool a space in summer. However, excessive thermal mass may be a problem in winter, and it may take a long time to warm up the building from cold, to achieve comfort for intermittent use or after periods of non-use. Buildings that are naturally ventilated may be difficult to control at times. If natural ventilation openings are closed to avoid draughts, then spaces may become stuffy and suffer poor air quality. Reducing a building's natural air leakage places more emphasis on ventilation control, to ensure sufficient ventilation at all times. However, once understood, all these issues can be dealt with through design, although our approach to comfort might change, to be one of a pleasant varying of conditions, rather than thermal neutrality.

We therefore need to question how we design for comfort in our future sustainable zero energy building. Can we combine 'thermal delight' with 'lack of discomfort'? Should we look at heating or cooling surfaces and providing comfort cooling through air movement, rather than subjecting people to a constant air temperature? How can we provide comfortable and healthy environments at the same time? If we are to design sustainable buildings to rediscover the response to climate through passive design, we should also consider a more interactive approach to our physical and psychological expectations for comfort; it does not make sense to have a climate-responsive building and a thermally neutral indoor environment. We need to develop innovative ways of delivering heating, cooling and ventilation; this might be regarded as a modern vernacular approach to comfort.

Chapter Five

Buildings and Climate

Introduction

Over time, buildings have gradually evolved from basic shelters to today's wide range of modern structures. Around the world we can see that traditional buildings are of a form and construction that respond to their local climate, the availability of materials and the local culture. To fully understand thermal design, we need to understand how buildings have developed over time, in relation to their interaction with sun, wind, temperature and moisture. Modern buildings have generally moved away from this climate-responsive approach, using fossil fuel energy to create internal environments, rather than taking advantage of passive solutions. The challenge is to develop an environmental approach, based on the principles of traditional passive design, but within a modern context. Just as our buildings are impacted on by their local macroclimate, they themselves create an external microclimate. They provide shade, channel breezeways or create stagnant areas, and they raise external temperatures creating urban heat islands. This chapter reviews global climate and looks at the traditional vernacular solutions that have evolved in response to climate, leading to a more detailed discussion of how buildings interact with climate (*see* Fig. 5.1).

Global Climate

Everywhere in the world the climate is different, some locations being more extreme than others. Sun, wind, temperature and precipitation all affect building design and building performance. It is therefore important that we understand the climate for a specific location when we design a building, and especially when we consider its thermal performance.

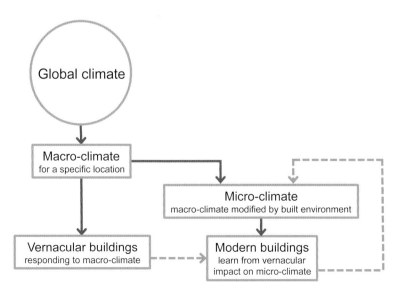

Fig. 5.1 The relationship between global climate, macroclimate and microclimate with vernacular and modern buildings.

Sun

The variation in global climate is mainly determined by the amount of sun falling on the earth at different locations. This relates to the angle at which the sun hits the earth; the more overhead the sun, the more concentrated its radiant heat. The sun's angle is relatively shallow at the poles, spreading the sun's radiation over a relatively large area, compared to when closer to the equator, where it is spread over a comparatively smaller area (*see* Fig. 5.2(b)). As the sun heats the earth, this determines the local air temperature, which is then modified by topographic factors that also affect rainfall and wind, such as whether a location is near the sea, or is in mountains, or is on plains. Oceans tend to have a moderating effect on coastal areas, producing less

extreme conditions, compared to areas far away from the sea, which generally have hotter summers and colder winters. Temperature also depends on rainfall and cloud cover, which will shadow and absorb the incoming solar radiation in the atmosphere, and dissipate temperatures through evaporation at the earth's surface. Atmospheric absorbance is greater at the poles because the solar radiation travels through more atmosphere before it hits the earth. Solar heat will be reflected at the earth's surface, which is greatest at the snow-covered poles. With climate change, there is less snow cover and therefore more solar radiation will be absorbed by the ground, resulting in warmer conditions and even less snow cover, and so on. Reduced cloud cover at night will increase the radiation emitted from the earth's warm surface to the clear cold night sky. Global air temperatures can

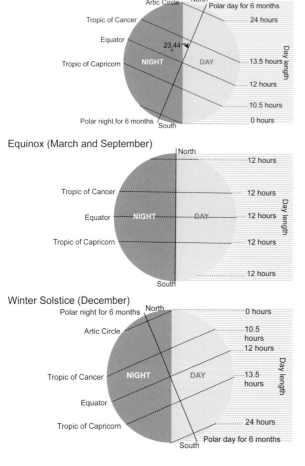

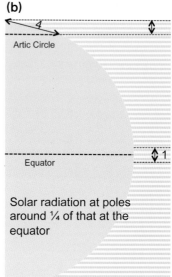

Fig. 5.2 (a) Day length at summer and winter solstices, and equinoxes; (b) comparison of average solar radiation incident at the poles compared to the equator.

vary from −60°C at the South Pole to +50°C in hot desert climates (the highest temperature of 54.4°C was recorded in Death Valley in August 2020).

The sun's angle changes with location and season, which determines the day length as well as the average solar intensity falling at a particular place (*see* Fig. 5.2(a)). The sun's angle will be highest when it is overhead at midday, which varies from directly overhead near the equator to less than zero at the poles during the polar night. Seasonal changes are determined by the earth's tilt on its axis, which slants at a 23.44 degree angle with respect to the plane of the earth's rotation around the sun. Locations tilted towards the sun receive more solar radiation. In summer, the northern hemisphere tilts towards the sun, and in winter it tilts away from the sun. Daylight hours are longer at some locations than others as the sun rises and sets at different angles. In the UK, at the summer solstice the sun will be 63.5 degrees above the horizon at midday, with sunrise at 4.45am and sunset at 9.20pm. At the winter solstice, its midday angle will be only 16.5 degrees, with sunrise at 8am and sunset at 4pm. Further north during the summer solstice, the day length gets longer, reaching twenty-four hours at the Arctic Circle.

The average direct solar radiation arriving at the top of the earth's atmosphere is $1,361W/m^2$, which

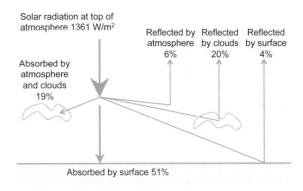

Fig. 5.3 Solar radiation and atmospheric absorption.

is $342W/m^2$ when averaged over the earth's sphere (*see* Fig. 5.3). The sun's rays are attenuated as they pass through the atmosphere, through absorption and reflection. The maximum irradiance at the earth's surface is around $1,000W/m^2$ at sea level, of which 51 per cent will be absorbed by the earth, which in turn heats the adjacent air and radiates to nearby surfaces and the atmosphere.

The average annual amount of incident solar radiation varies globally, from around $800kWh/m^2/$year towards the poles to around $2,800kWh/m^2/$year nearer to the equator, and for the UK, ranges from around $800kWh/m^2/$year in northern parts to around $1,100kWh/m^2/$year in the south (*see* Fig. 5.4).

(a)   **(b)**

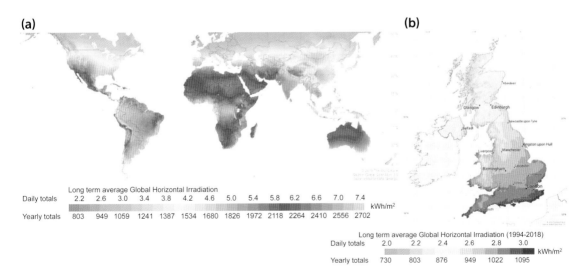

Fig. 5.4 Yearly and daily total average horizontal solar radiation: (a) global; (b) UK. (Solargis).

Wind

Global temperature differences give rise to wind currents. Warm air rising at the equator will travel towards the cooler poles via the more temperate zones creating convection flow patterns in each hemisphere (*see* Fig. 5.5).

The rotation of the earth causes the direction of the winds to bend, towards the right in the northern hemisphere, and towards the left in the southern hemisphere. The combination of thermal and rotational forces gives rise to the major global wind patterns, including the westerlies, the trade winds and the polar flows (*see* Fig. 5.6). The air circulates through the entire depth of the troposphere, which extends from the earth's surface up to between 10 and 15km high. Above them are the fast-moving global jet streams caused by the convective circulation cells and the spin of the earth, modified by land, sea, and air temperature differences. The jet streams move west to east, the strongest being the polar jets, at a height of between 9 and 12km, and the weaker subtropical jets between 10 and 16km high. Speeds range from 129km/h to more than 443km/h, which drive the changing weather fronts. Climate change affects the jet streams; the polar regions warm quicker

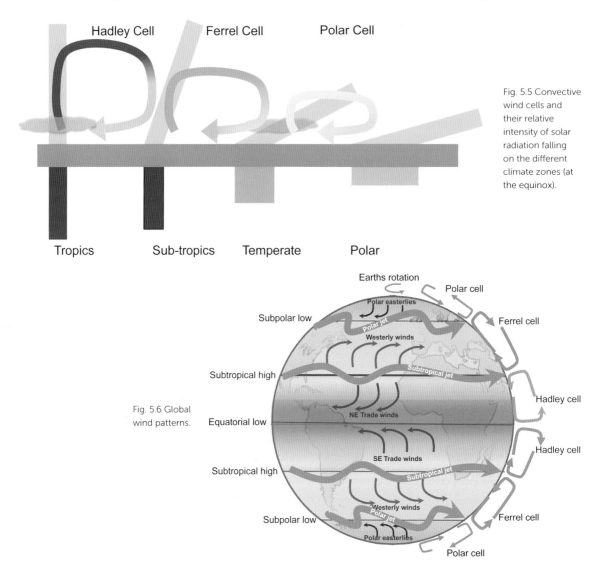

Fig. 5.5 Convective wind cells and their relative intensity of solar radiation falling on the different climate zones (at the equinox).

Fig. 5.6 Global wind patterns.

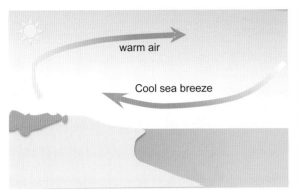 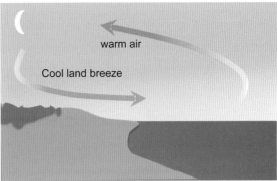

Fig. 5.7 Sea breezes.

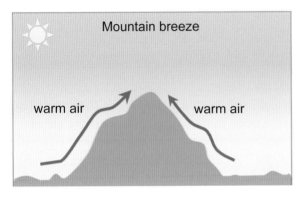 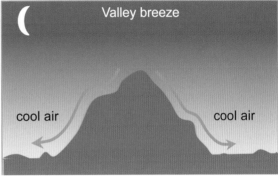

Fig. 5.8 Mountain and valley breezes.

than the rest of the world reducing the temperature contrast that drives them. Slower, weaker jet streams can lock bad weather systems into place for prolonged periods.

At a local level, sea breezes occur next to large waterbodies (*see* Fig. 5.7). The sun heats the air above the land more than the air over the water. The air over the land rises, drawing breezes from the sea to the land. At night the air above the land cools down faster than the air above the sea, and the opposite flow occurs. There are also local mountain and valley breezes (*see* Fig. 5.8). During the day, the sun heats the air over mountain slopes more than the air at the mountain base, causing a cool upward 'valley breeze', more common in summer. At night, the air at the upper slope of the mountain cools down quickly, becomes denser, resulting in a cool downward 'mountain breeze', more common in colder months.

Rain

Precipitation deposits some 505,000km³ of fresh water on the planet every year. The global average annual precipitation is 990mm/year, or 2.69mm/day, with ocean and land values of 2.89mm/day and 2.24mm/day respectively. Around 80 per cent of rain falls on the oceans, which cover 70 per cent of the earth's surface. Areas near the equator receive the highest amounts of rainfall due to converging air masses, with intense solar heat producing large-scale evaporation and rising moist air that cools with altitude, producing rain. Global annual rainfall ranges from 3,000mm/year in tropical zones to less than 200mm/year in desert and polar regions (*see* Fig. 5.9). Rainfall varies with season, with light rain falling up to 2.5mm/hour, moderate rain above 7.6mm/hour, and with rainfall above 50mm/hour causing a flood risk.

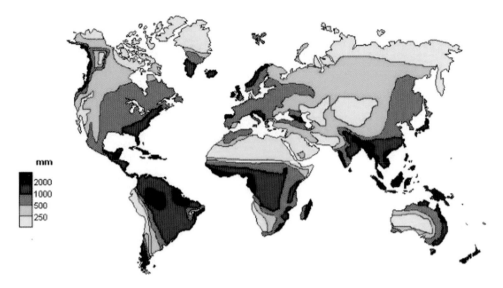

Fig. 5.9 Global rainfall. (DEFRA Information and teaching resource)

mm

2000
1000
500
250

The amount of precipitation on land is greater near oceans, where temperatures decrease rapidly with altitude in mountain areas and with advancing weather fronts (*see* Fig. 5.10).

Climate Zones

The combination of sun, wind, temperature and rain produces a range of global climate zones that circle the world. There are many classifications of climate zones; however, for the purpose of introducing buildings and climate, we can consider four main ones (*see* Fig. 5.11), which are polar, temperate, subtropical and tropical.

The polar regions are located at the earth's poles. The Arctic polar zone extends from the North Pole to 60 degrees north latitude. The Antarctic polar zone extends from the South Pole to 60 degrees south latitude. In the polar regions the sun has a relatively low angle to the ground, and the earth's tilt angle results in the greatest seasonal variation of day length. In the summer, 24-hour polar days occur, while in winter the sun remains below the horizon. The average Arctic summer temperature is 0°C, and the Antarctic is −28.2°C, with winter extreme lows of −40°C and −60°C respectively. The Arctic is relatively

warmer because it is located on the Arctic Ocean, compared with the Antarctic, which is located on land mass. In the Antarctic the temperature never rises above freezing. For a short period in the Arctic, temperatures rise above freezing and the ice can melt, supporting plants and animal life. Climate change has produced much warmer temperatures in the Arctic, causing much of the ice cap to melt. The borderline subarctic zone includes habitable areas in Greenland, Labrador, Alaska, Canada, Scandinavia and Siberia.

The temperate regions span between the tropics and the polar regions, lying between 40 and 60 degrees latitude. Temperate regions have less extremes of weather compared to the other climate zones. The sun's angle varies throughout the year, creating distinct seasons and varying day length over the year. The weather in temperate climates is the most varied and unpredictable, influenced by sea currents, prevailing wind direction, landmass and altitude. There are two main types of temperate regions, namely oceanic and continental. Oceanic temperate regions are found near the coast, where the sea and onshore winds produce more rain and relatively less temperature variation throughout the year. Some are relatively warm, with hot dry summers and milder winters, such as around the Mediterranean. Cooler regions include the British Isles, northern Europe and New Zealand,

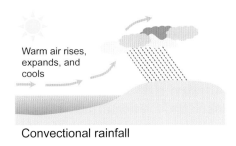

Convective rain occurs when the sun heats the ground and the layer of air above it, causing the heated air to rise, which cools down with height, condensing and causing rain; typically causing local showers with intermittent sunny periods.

Warm air rises, expands, and cools

Convectional rainfall

Fig. 5.10 Types of rain.

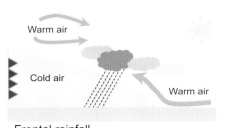

Relief rain occurs when warmer, moist ocean air flows inland, cools as it rises up mountain slopes, condensing into clouds causing rain; typically the ocean side of mountains may have a mild, wet climate, while on the other side it may be dry, as the air loses its moisture.

Warm moist air from sea rises

Rain shade area

Relief rainfall

Frontal rain occurs when a 'weather front' of cold air meets warm air and the warm air rises over the cold air, cools down, forming clouds, and rain; typically skies are overcast and there is persistent rain throughout the day.

Warm air

Cold air

Warm air

Frontal rainfall

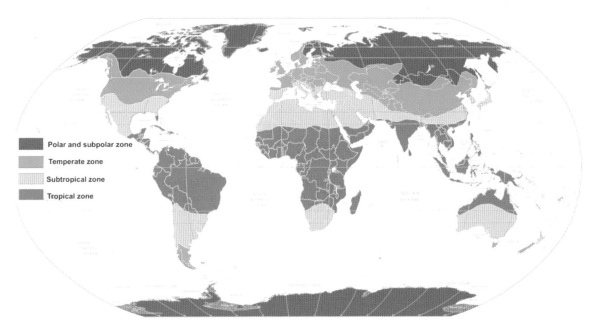

Polar and subpolar zone

Temperate zone

Subtropical zone

Tropical zone

Fig. 5.11 Four main climate zones. (meteoblue CC BY-ND)

with typically warm summers and cold winters, with short periods of snow and freezing temperatures. Continental temperate regions have more pronounced dry periods, with more extreme hot summers and cold winters, due to less moderating influence of the sea. There are deserts, such as the Gobi Desert, in areas located far inland, and grasslands, where there is not enough rainfall for forests to grow.

The subtropical regions span from 23.5 degrees to 40 degrees latitude. They receive relatively high amounts of solar radiation in summer, due to the high sun angle and thin cloud cover. These regions receive low rainfall, which increases the impact of the sun's radiation; most of the world's deserts are situated in this zone. In summer, average temperatures typically range from 20°C to 35°C, with maximum temperatures reaching over 50°C in desert areas. However, the temperature can drop significantly at night as the warm ground radiates its heat to the clear cold night sky. In winter, the sun's radiation decreases, and it can be cool and moist with temperatures falling as low as –5°C. The subtropics are divided between the north and south hemispheres, including parts of the United States and South America, South Africa, Australia, and Asia, India, China and Japan.

The tropical regions span between the equator and the subtropics, from 0 degrees to 23.5 degrees latitude. Here the solar radiation is directly overhead at midday throughout the year. It is warm with temperatures typically rising to 35°C in daytime, with little seasonal variation. The diurnal temperature difference is smaller, typically cooling down by less than 10°C at night, and retaining a high relative humidity. There is a greater amount of moisture in the tropics, resulting in frequent and dense cloud cover and high levels of rainfall, so temperatures are not as high as in the subtropics. There is rainfall throughout the year, often with distinct rainy seasons. Tropical regions include Central and South America, central Africa, India, Malaysia, Singapore and Indonesia.

People have settled across all climate zones (*see* Fig. 5.12), although temperate zones, which cover about 7 per cent of the world's land surface, are by far the most populated areas, due to the mildness of the climate, the plentiful supply of rain and fertile soils. Lowlands are more populated than higher altitudes, with 80 per cent of people living below 500m above sea level, and 60 per cent within 100km of an ocean, with coastal areas having the densest settlements. Even though temperate zones are generally preferred, there are increases in population in tropical zones, which are at most risk from climate change.

Climate Zones and Climate Change

The climate is changing and already we are seeing changes in the climate zones. The Arctic ice is shrinking, and seawater is rising by some 3.2mm per year, encroaching on land mass, and is expected to rise by at least another 20cm by the end of this century.

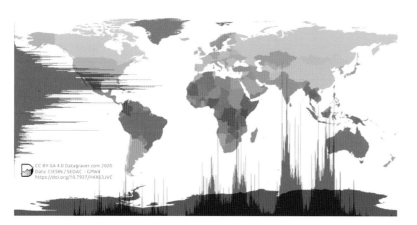

Fig. 5.12 Distribution of world population (year 2000). (Open source)

Glaciers are shrinking, reducing water flow in rivers. The tropical regions are getting drier and hotter and expanding northwards by some 30 miles per decade, and since 1920 the Sahara Desert has grown by some 10 per cent[5.1]. The so-called 100th meridian climatic transition line cutting through the US, where 'luxuriant growth of grass gives way to naked ground', has shifted 140 miles east[5.1]. The wheat belt in Australia is pushing down towards the south pole at up to 160 miles per decade[5.1]. In parts of Canada, the permafrost line has moved 80 miles north in fifty years, with ground temperatures at 20 metres depth increasing by a rapid 1°C to 2°C per decade. Tornado Alley, in the US, has moved some 500 miles to the east[5.1]. The pace of shifting climate zones increases with increasing global temperature, and by the end of this century some 20 per cent of all land could undergo significant climate change, giving species little time to adapt[5.2]. People, plants, animals and diseases are on the move, as they search for more suitable climates, as land becomes too hot, or too dry, or too flooded; changes that will reduce some countries' ability to grow food, and provide enough water. The rules applied to traditional global built forms, which have evolved in response to the climate over hundreds, if not thousands, of years, may no longer apply. Modern buildings may struggle to heat and cool as designed, and suffer increasing energy costs.

The Vernacular

Throughout history, buildings have responded to the local climate, the availability of materials and the culture of the region. Traditional buildings are sustainable both environmentally and socially, with their form and fabric incorporating what we now call 'passive design' features. Materials were sourced locally and were easily maintainable. Spatial planning reflected cultural needs, with the ability to be flexible and adapt for changes of use. There may be seasonal variations of space use with changing weather, or over time, as a family grows. These aspects have evolved rather than designed, using skills and crafts from within the community. This 'bottom-up' approach is often referred to as 'vernacular' and differs from a more purpose design, which is sometimes referred to as 'polite' design, involving ornament or stylistic features beyond their functional and cultural needs. Bernard Rudofsky was the first to use the term vernacular in this context in his book *Architecture without Architects*[5.3], and he coupled the term with anonymous, spontaneous, indigenous and rural, although it also occurs in towns. Vernacular solutions vary widely between location and climate zone (*see* Fig. 5.13), using different building forms and materials to produce relative comfort. The more extreme climates appear to have a greater influence on the built form of vernacular solutions.

Polar: Temporary igloo structure, and timber constructions with a low pitch roof to allow snow to lie, which gives more insulation.

Temperate: Need to deal with cold and warm weather, and rain. They may use lightweight timber or heavy weight masonry wall construction, depending on location.

Fig. 5.13 Basic form of vernacular buildings with climate zone.

Sub-tropical: Hot dry climates have thick stone walls to provide thermal mass that cools down at night, which then keeps the inside cool during the day. The roof is flat as there is little rain.

Tropical: Lighter materials allow the building to cool down at night. Steep thatch roofs with overhangs shade solar heat and shed heavy rainfall. Large openings provide ventilation cooling. Raised off the ground they catch the breeze and avoid flooding in monsoon seasons.

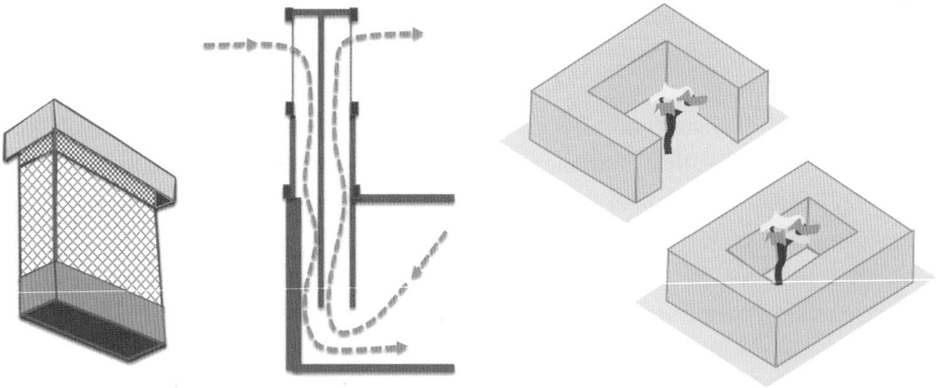

Fig. 5.14 Features including mashrabiya, wind towers, and open and closed courtyards.

Additional features were sometimes added, which define the 'architecture' of the place (*see* Fig. 5.14). Decorated carved mashrabiya in Asia provide openings for a cool breeze to enter into the building, while maintaining both a view outside and the privacy of the occupants. In the Middle East, wind chimneys and sails were used to provide ventilation cooling. Courtyards were often used to provide enclosed private outside space, facing south in colder climates for solar heat in winter and turning their back to the colder north.

Vernacular buildings used local materials, including lightweight timber or reeds, heavyweight stone or adobe earth (*see* Fig. 5.15). Thermal mass is important in relation to diurnal and seasonal changes in weather. Heavyweight materials stabilize temperatures, buffering against extremes of hot or cold, useful in hot dry climates with a higher diurnal temperature range. Lightweight materials respond quicker to changes in temperature, cooling as the outside temperature drops, which is useful in warm humid climates where

(a) (b)

(c) (d)

Fig. 5.15 (a) Lightweight timber house (Malaysia); (b) Reed house (Chongming Island, Shanghai); (c) Heavyweight stone house (native American); (d) Adobe house (China). (Photos: (a) and (c) Shutterstock)

there is a lower diurnal temperature change. Less extreme temperate climates use both heavy and lightweight materials, more in relation to material availability than the climate.

Thermal Mass

Climates that experience warm summers and cool winters can use thermal mass coupled to ventilation. Sixteenth-century houses in the Italian city of Vicenza were built on mountain slopes, channelling cool air from caves into cellars and then into the occupied spaces (*see* Fig. 5.16). This provided a steady flow of ventilation air at a temperature of around 10°C to 12°C for summer cooling. The ground thermal condition recharges, cooling in winter and warming in summer, maintaining a time average ground temperature close to the average annual outside temperature.

Ventilation is combined with thermal mass cooling in traditional houses in Malta[5.4], being constructed from stone quarried from the site of the new house, with the hole left in the ground used as a basement and a cistern for water. During the hot summer, outside air is naturally drawn into the below ground space and cooled before circulating through

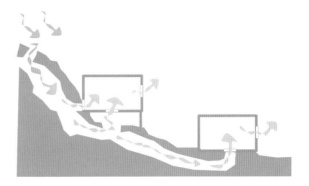

Fig. 5.16 Sixteenth-century houses in Vicenza, Italy, built on mountain slopes with caves.

the house, picking up heat, and exhausting through high-level openings (*see* Fig. 5.17).

Thermal mass and shading underpin the environmental performance of the Ancestral Pueblo cliff dwellings of Mesa Verde in southwest Colorado (*see* Fig. 5.18), which were occupied until the thirteenth century. Entire villages were constructed in the sides of cliffs, with thermal mass providing seasonal temperature stability. Rock overhangs provided shade from the high-angle summer sun, while allowing heat from the low-angle winter sun to provide warmth.

Chinese cave houses (yaodongs) dating back some 4,000 years are located in the colder areas of Shanxi,

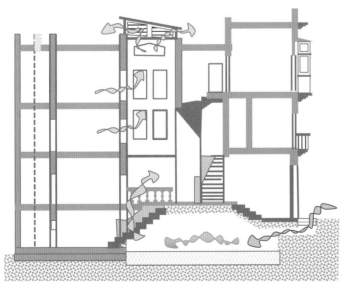

Fig. 5.17 Maltese house, indicating air exhaust devices on the roof and air supply into the basement[5.6].

Fig. 5.18 Cliff dwellings of Mesa Verde in southwest Colorado. (Photo: Rob Kroenert)

Fig. 5.19 Chinese 'yaodong' cave houses. (Photo: Shutterstock)

(a)

(b)

Fig. 5.20 (a) Rural courtyard house (photo: Prof. Jianxiang Huang); (b) earth as part of the roof construction.

which has extreme winter temperatures below −20°C, and high summer temperatures around 40°C. Excavated from a central sunken courtyard (*see* Fig. 5.19), they use the ground's thermal mass to stabilize inside conditions throughout the year. With the ground at an even temperature of around 15°C throughout the year, the temperature in the caves is maintained at 10°C to 22°C, with a relative humidity of 30 to 75 per cent. In 2006, an estimated 40 million people in northern China still lived in yaodongs[5.5].

Traditional northern Chinese courtyard houses also exhibit a range of passive features (*see* Fig. 5.20), in response to similar hot summers and cold winters. Courtyards are orientated facing south to gain winter solar heat, with the northern elevation protective against the cold. Using earth in the roof structure provides thermal mass to protect from solar gains in summer, and to insulate against heat loss in winter.

The hot desert climate of the Saudi Arabia has a diurnal temperature variation in summer, from 50°C in the day, dropping to 30°C at night. Heavyweight walls with small openings maintain a low daytime ventilation rate, when outside temperatures are high (*see* Fig. 5.21)[5.6]. The building's structure cools down at night keeping the inside relatively cool during the day.

Wind Catchers

Cairo's wind catchers were observed in the mid-nineteenth century (*see* Fig. 5.22), possibly dating

(a)

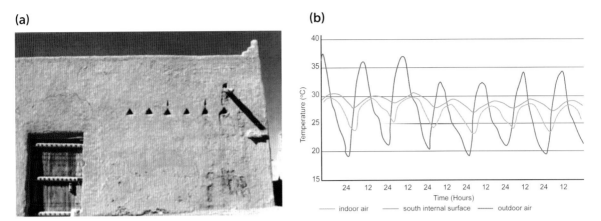

(b)

Fig. 5.21 (a) A traditional building in Saudi Arabia with heavyweight walls and small openings; (b) showing indoor air temperature, indoor surface temperature and outdoor air temperature[5.6].

Fig. 5.22 The skyline of Cairo in the mid-nineteenth century, and a close-up of a wind ventilation tower[5.7].

back to around 1300BC[5.7]. They are omni-directional, channelling the prevailing breeze to cool the indoor spaces. Similar devices were used in Hyderabad, where each room would have its own wind catcher, called a bad-gir (*see* Fig. 5.23). In the Middle East, wind catchers may date back to 4000BC. They have multi-directional ports at the top, allowing the positive windward pressure to drive air down the chimney into the living spaces, and the leeward wind pressure to draw air out (*see* Fig. 5.24). They may incorporate wetted jars at the bottom of the tower for evaporative cooling, or they may link with the water supply system drawing cool air up into the living spaces. When there

Fig. 5.23 Wind catchers of Hyderabad.

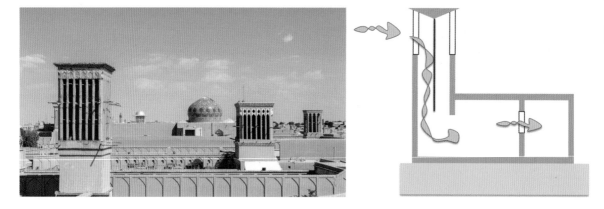

Fig. 5.24 Wind catchers in Yazd, Iran. (Photo: Shutterstock)

is no wind, they can function as a thermal chimney, exhausting the warm indoor air.

Warm Tropical Climates

In tropical climates, diurnal and seasonal air temperature variations are relatively small, and lightweight structures are the tradition. Typical daytime temperatures peak at 32°C to 35°C, reducing to around 26°C at night, with relative humidity typically varying from 70 per cent during the day to 90 per cent at night. The traditional Malaysian lightweight timber 'kampong' village house (*see* Fig. 5.25) quickly cools down at night, taking advantage of the relatively small diurnal temperature variation. It has large overhangs that shade the walls and openings, while also shedding rainwater. The thatch (atap) roof insulates the interior from high solar heat gains. Large openings allow the breeze to flow through the internal spaces for comfort cooling. The building is raised off the ground to catch the breeze, and protect from flooding and pests. These houses are still widely used, especially in rural areas of Malaysia, although the thatch roofs have usually been replaced by corrugated metal.

Village Vernacular

A vernacular approach is also used for groups of buildings in villages and towns. In hot climates, buildings are grouped together to shade each other from the intense solar heat in daytime, with covered shaded walkways for external comfort (*see* Fig. 5.26). Alleys may provide breezeways for ventilation (*see* Fig. 5.27), with houses having openings to allow the breeze to enter into their courtyards. Alleys may be located downwind of a lake, which cools the prevailing breeze.

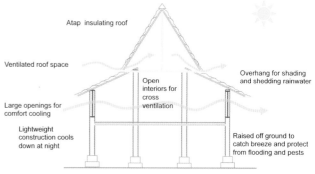

Atap insulating roof

Ventilated roof space

Large openings for comfort cooling

Open interiors for cross ventilation

Lightweight construction cools down at night

Overhang for shading and shedding rainwater

Raised off ground to catch breeze and protect from flooding and pests

Fig. 5.25 Malaysian village house and schematic of the main environmental features.

Fig. 5.26 Shaded walkways in the Middle East and Malta. (Photos: Shutterstock)

Fig. 5.27 Ventilation breezeways.

Space Use in Vernacular Buildings

The difference between inside and outside space is often not so marked in traditional buildings, with people carrying out their daily activities outside. In rural areas of China, south-facing courtyards are still in use today, providing a sunny space that extends the living space in warmer weather (*see* Fig. 5.28). The courtyard becomes a place for preparing food, growing fruit and herbs, drying corn, and various other household tasks. Covered courtyards in city houses provide a sheltered area for drying clothes, or even as a main living and cooking space (*see* Fig. 5.29), with occupants only going indoors to sleep. In hot desert climates, people may sleep outside on the roof at certain times of the year. People may occupy different spaces depending on the time of day or season, and often buildings are largely unoccupied during the day. In more temperate climates, summer conditions are generally comfortable; however, in winter, comfort is achieved by gathering around open fires to keep warm, the rest of the house remaining relatively cold.

Fig. 5.28 Rural house courtyard in North China, near Jinan.

Fig. 5.29 Sheltered courtyards in Hangzhou, China.

Vernacular Comfort

In colder climates, comfort might be achieved through warm surfaces as well as warm air, and using timber, which warms up quickly. In igloos, animal skins would be hung on walls; in more temperate European climates, decorated wall hangings were similarly used. In hot arid climates, the internal surfaces of thick stone walls would be relatively cool. In warm humid climates, air movement and shade would be the main way to keep comfortable. Fig. 5.30 shows a man sitting in the shade of an open alley in rural China, benefitting from a cooling breeze, shaded from direct sun, and next to the shaded cool surface

of a high thermal mass wall. This might be termed 'vernacular comfort'.

Design with Climate

We can learn from how traditional buildings around the world have evolved in response to climate, and take these basic principles and apply them within a modern context, with an emphasis on comfort and energy efficiency. Design with climate allows us to select the positive aspects of the prevailing weather, while rejecting the negative parts.

Sun

The sun is important when we design the form and orientation of the building, and locate the glazing systems and shading devices. It also relates to the design of atria, courtyards, transitional and external spaces, and the integration of renewable energy systems for solar thermal and solar photovoltaic (PV).

The sun tracks through the sky in a predictable way, described by the daily and seasonal variation of its altitude and azimuth angles. For the UK (*see* Fig. 5.31), the summer sun will provide direct radiation on all elevations at different times, even a small amount on the north in early morning and late afternoon; a fact often overlooked in design. However, the actual amount of solar radiation will depend on cloud cover, which is not so predictable.

Fig. 5.30 Passive design features providing thermal comfort.

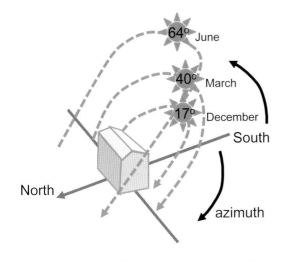

Fig. 5.31 Sun angles for the UK, indicating azimuth and peak altitude.

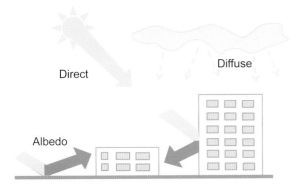

Fig. 5.32 Direct, diffuse and (albedo) reflected radiation.

There are three components of solar radiation that impact on a building (*see* Fig. 5.32):

- Direct radiation, from the position of the sun in the sky
- Diffuse radiation, from the whole of the visible sky
- Reflected radiation (albedo) from adjacent surfaces, such as other buildings, roads and paved areas, and green and water features

All three components will vary according to the time of day, time of year, cloud cover, and how much sky is 'seen' by the building, depending on neighbouring natural or man-made obstructions. The largest component of solar radiation is the direct radiation, peaking at around $1,000W/m^2$ in UK summertime, although the amount incident on the building depends on its angle with respect to the building façade and any cloud cover. Diffuse radiation can also be significant, on bright cloudy days reaching over $300W/m^2$, and up to $200W/m^2$ on bright clear days. The combination of direct and diffuse radiation are added to provide the total radiation falling on a building (*see* Fig. 5.33). Cloud cover is measured in octals, on a scale of 0 to 8, with 0 being completely cloudless and 8 being completely overcast. Cloud cover can also be measured in 1/10ths or 'cloudiness', with a scale 0 to 1.

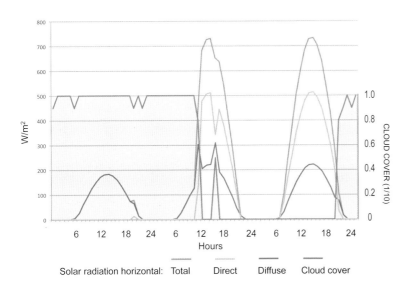

Fig. 5.33 Three-day example summer period: when there is 100 per cent cloud cover the only radiation will be diffuse, which on overcast days peaks at just under $200W/m^2$. On bright cloudy days the diffuse rises to around $300W/m^2$, while on clear days the diffuse will peak at around $200W/m^2$.

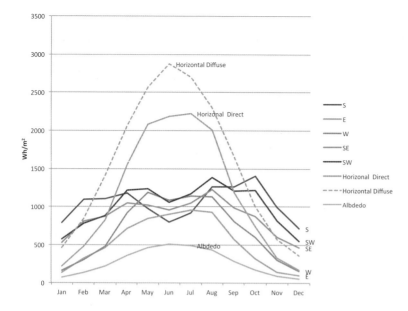

Fig. 5.34 Annual solar radiation for London: the total horizontal diffuse radiation is greater than the horizontal total direct (or beam) radiation. The direct radiation falling on façades will vary with their orientation, with the west receiving slightly more than the east elevations in the UK.

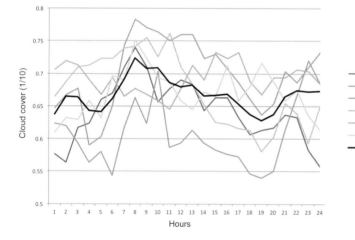

Fig. 5.35 During daytime in the summer months, there is a larger level of cloud cover in the morning (easterly sun) than the afternoon (westerly sun).

The amount of direct, diffuse and reflected radiation will vary over the year, depending on the level of cloud cover, and will be different for different façades (see Fig. 5.34). The albedo, which is generally small but can be significant, is reflected from nearby walls of neighbouring building surfaces, or from the ground and water, especially for low sun angles. During the summer months in the UK, there is generally a larger level of cloud cover in the morning (easterly sun) than the afternoon (westerly sun) (see Fig. 5.35).

Buildings can be overshadowed by other buildings, topography or landscape features (see Fig. 5.36). Sometimes this is useful in providing shade, or it

Fig. 5.36 Buildings in shade from other buildings and landscape features.

can be a problem if solar radiation is beneficial for providing heat or powering solar PV systems. The SkyDome at Cardiff University has used physical scale models to simulate both direct solar radiation and different overcast sky conditions (*see* Fig. 5.37).

A building can interact with solar energy by direct and indirect means.

Direct solar gains are used in the space they enter (*see* Fig. 5.38). Direct gains to a south-facing room may be useful in colder climates, although in well-insulated buildings, they may give rise to overheating; they often occur when the building has already been warmed up by heat gains from people, lighting and appliances. Direct gains may be absorbed and stored for later, using thermal mass. Direct gains may be collected in sunspaces, used by choice when conditions are comfortable, or in transitional spaces used for circulation. In some cases, southerly facing glazed areas may be relatively small, allowing just enough sunshine to create a sunny space when required, while larger northerly facing glazing is used for daylight.

Indirect solar gains may be delivered to a buffer space (*see* Fig. 5.39) and transferred to an occupied space for space heating, if the buffer space is warmer.

Fig. 5.37 SkyDome at Cardiff University, used to analyse shading for a high-rise, high-density urban development in Hong Kong.

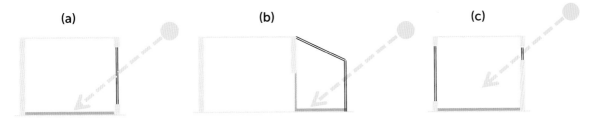

Fig. 5.38 Examples of direct solar radiation: (a) to a space, (b) to a sunspace or transitional space, and (c) reduced south glazing, with the bias of glazing for north daylight.

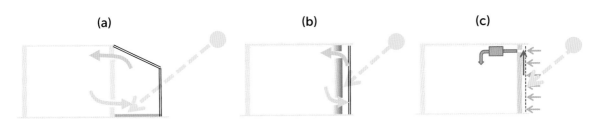

Fig. 5.39 Example of indirect solar radiation: (a) buffered, (b) using a Trombe wall, and (c) to a transpired solar (air) collector (TSC).

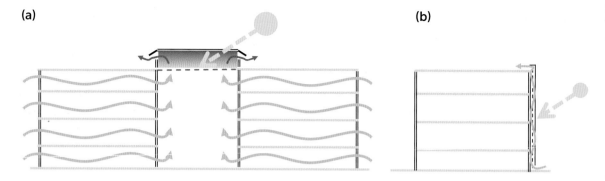

(a)

(b)

Fig. 5.40 Solar radiation driving air movement: (a) in a central atrium with solar heat contained at high level, (b) to exhaust solar heat gain from a layered façade.

A Trombe wall can collect solar heat in a glazed cavity adjacent to thermal mass storage, which may be later conducted to the occupied space, or vented directly, controlled by opening dampers. A transpired solar (air) collector (TSC) has an external metal sheet which has small holes (about 1mm) that allow air to be drawn in from outside. The air is heated by contact with either side of the metal sheet, to provide ventilation preheat for mechanical ventilation heating systems, or to supply heated air to the space directly, which then exhausts by natural leakage. It can also be used in conjunction with a heat pump to supply hot water.

For larger buildings, solar heat may be used to drive ventilation airflow through the buoyancy effect (*see* Fig. 5.40). A naturally ventilated atrium may use solar heat, contained at high level, with the heated air escaping through roof openings, drawing outside air in through perimeter openings. A double-skin façade's shading may trap solar heat, which is then ventilated to outside, with air being drawn in at a lower level.

Solar heat may be used indirectly to generate energy using solar PV or solar thermal renewable energy systems (*see* Fig. 5.41). These work best for southerly facing roofs or façades, although east- and west-facing roofs and façades can also generate useful energy.

Wind

Wind will impact on ventilation and infiltration rates, and influence the location of natural and mechanical ventilation outlet and inlet devices. The form of the building may include wind devices, such as chimneys and atria, for natural ventilation. In colder locations, we need to create shelter against the cold wind. In warmer locations, especially dense urban areas, we can design for controlled breezeways to reduce external temperature and pollution hotspots. Wind may be turbulent and accelerated by the built form, affecting outside comfort, and even pedestrian safety in extreme situations, especially in relation to entrances and pedestrian routes.

Wind speed is measured in metres per second (m/s) or knots, where 1 knot equals 0.4 m/s. The Beaufort scale relates wind speed to physical conditions (*see* Table 5.1). Wind direction is usually measured at eight compass points or in degrees clockwise from the north. Wind will tend to come from one or more prevailing directions, according to the season or time of day. Wind speed and direction can be represented by a wind rose (*see* Fig. 5.42), which indicates the

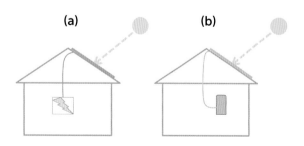

(a)   (b)

Fig. 5.41 (a) Solar PV and (b) solar thermal systems.

Table 5.1 Beaufort scale.

Wind Force	Description	km/h	m/s	knots	Description
0	**Calm**	< 1	< 0.4	< 1	Smoke rises vertically.
1	**Light air**	1–5	0.4–1.2	1–3	Direction shown by smoke drift but not by wind vanes.
2	**Light breeze**	6–11	0.16–2.8	4–6	Wind felt on face; leaves rustle; wind vane moved by wind.
3	**Gentle breeze**	12–19	3.2–4.8	7–10	Leaves and small twigs in constant motion; light flags extended.
4	**Moderate breeze**	20–28	5.2–7.2	11–16	Raises dust and loose paper; small branches moved.
5	**Fresh breeze**	29–38	7.6–9.6	17–21	Small trees in leaf begin to sway; crested wavelets form on inland waters.
6	**Strong breeze**	38–49	10.0–12.4	22–27	Large branches in motion; whistling heard in telegraph wires; umbrellas used with difficulty.
7	**Near gale**	50–61	12.8–15.2	28–33	Whole trees in motion; inconvenience felt when walking against the wind.
8	**Gale**	62–74	15.6–18.4	34–40	Twigs break off trees; generally impedes progress.
9	**Strong gale**	75–88	18.8–20.16	41–47	Slight structural damage (chimney pots and slates removed).
10	**Storm**	89–102	55–63	48–55	Seldom experienced inland; trees uprooted; considerable structural damage.

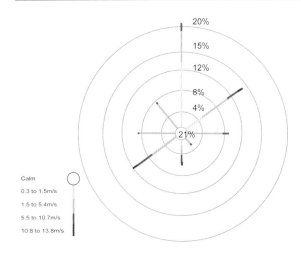

Fig. 5.42 Wind rose showing percentage of time the wind is from prevailing wind directions and the range of wind speeds for each direction.

relative frequency and speed of the wind from different directions, usually on an annual or monthly basis.

Wind speed increases with height due to frictional drag at ground level. The upward profile of wind speed with height is called the boundary layer, which will vary from in towns to open country, with relatively higher low-level wind speeds in rural areas due to less frictional drag from buildings (Fig. 5.43). The wind profile can be calculated using the equation:

$$v/v_r = \kappa(h/hr)^\alpha$$

where

v is the mean wind speed (m/s) at height h(m)

v_r is the mean wind speed (m/s) at a reference height h_r (m)

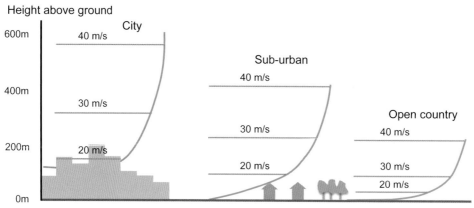

Height above ground

City

600m — 40 m/s

30 m/s

400m

20 m/s

200m

0m

Sub-urban

40 m/s

30 m/s

20 m/s

Open country

40 m/s

30 m/s

20 m/s

Wind speed ratio

Fig. 5.43 Wind boundary layer relating to different terrains.

values κ and α depend on the local terrain:

	κ	α
Open flat country	0.68	0.17
Country with scattered windbreaks	0.52	0.20
Urban	0.35	0.25
City	0.21	0.33

Total wind pressure (P_t) is the sum of the static and dynamic pressures $(P_t = P_s + P_d)$. The static wind pressure (P_s) is the free-flowing wind pressure, as shown on the isobars of a weather map, that arises from global wind flow. The dynamic pressure (P_d) is exerted when the wind comes into contact with an object such as a building. The static pressure (P_s) is generally ignored in wind-related ventilation design; our interest is with dynamic pressure differences across a building, where the static pressure is considered constant. The dynamic wind pressure in units of pascal (Pa) is related to the air density $(\rho$ kg/m$^3)$ and the square of the wind speed $(v$ m/s$)$ by:

$$P_d = 0.5\rho v^2$$

When the wind hits a building, it will exert relative positive and negative pressures over the building's external surfaces, and set up patterns of wind flow around the building that create turbulent updraughts, downdraughts and acceleration around corners (see Fig. 5.44).

The pressures will vary, depending on wind speed and direction for a given building form, and can be estimated if the pressure coefficient (C_p) at a location is known. The pressure coefficient ranges between

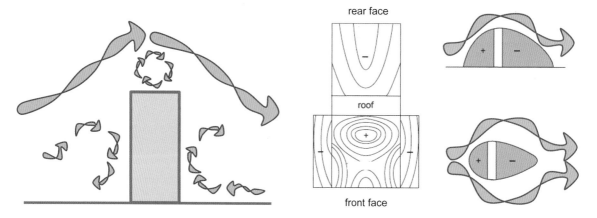

rear face

roof

front face

Fig. 5.44 Wind and pressure distribution around a building's envelope. The impact of the wind on the building form creates areas of relative positive pressure on the windward side of a building and negative pressure on the leeward sides of the building.

−1 and +1, and is a measure of how the pressure over a building's surface varies. It can be derived from computational airflow simulation, or wind tunnel measurements, from which generic tables can be produced. They relate to wind speed at a reference height (v_h). The wind pressure (Pa) at the building surface is then:

$$P_d = C_p \times 0.5\, \rho v_h^2$$

Where

v_h is the wind speed (m/s) at a reference height h (m)

ρ is the air density (kg/m³)

C_p is the pressure coefficient with reference to the wind speed at height h

Openings and 'wind wing-walls' can be located to produce 'cross ventilation' for prevailing wind conditions (see Fig. 5.45).

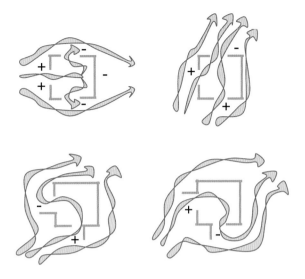

Fig. 5.45 Wind-driven cross ventilation through openings with relative positive and negative C_p values.

Case Study 5.1 UMNO Building, Penang

The UMNO building is a 21-storey office block in Penang, Malaysia, designed by T.R. Hamzah and Yeang. Although the building is air-conditioned, it was designed to provide the option for natural cross ventilation, using a wind wing-wall concept to channel the prevailing wind (see Fig. 5.46)[5.8]. The office space is open-plan and the openable windows are located on the balcony areas, which are aligned with the prevailing wind directions from the north-east and south-west.

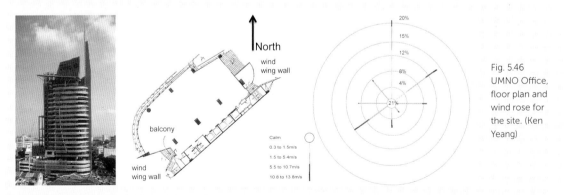

Fig. 5.46 UMNO Office, floor plan and wind rose for the site. (Ken Yeang)

CFD (computational fluid dynamic) airflow modelling was used to estimate the dynamic pressure distribution between the window openings (see Fig. 5.47(a) and (b))[5.9]. CFD was then used to simulate the internal heat and airflow distribution using the simulated external wind pressure values (see Fig. 5.47(c)).

continued

Although internal temperatures are relatively warm, the simulation demonstrates the relative cooling effect of natural ventilation, exhausting the internal heat gains, from left to right. This demonstrates how a CFD simulation model can be used as a numerical wind tunnel to estimate external dynamic pressures, which can then be used as input for a CFD simulation of indoor conditions.

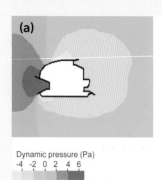

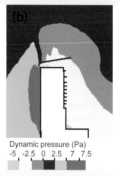

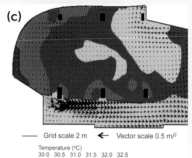

Dynamic pressure (Pa)
-4 -2 0 2 4 6

Dynamic pressure (Pa)
-5 -2.5 0 2.5 7 7.5

—— Grid scale 2 m   ← Vector scale 0.5 m/²
Temperature (°C)
30.0 30.5 31.0 31.5 32.0 32.5

Fig. 5.47 (a) and (b) CFD simulation of external dynamic pressures for a south-westerly wind direction; and (c) internal airflow and heat distribution.

The interaction of wind and the built form can produce areas of shelter. Rules of thumb can be used to estimate protection from the wind in relation to building spacing (*see* Fig. 5.48).

High wind conditions can be created by down-draughts from tall buildings, wind 'canyons', and acceleration of the wind around corners (*see* Fig. 5.49).

Typically, wind acceleration factors of three times can be experienced.

Barriers can be used to reduce wind speed and create external sheltered areas. Porous barriers are often more suitable than hard barriers as they reduce wind speed and do not induce counterwind flow areas (*see* Fig. 5.50).

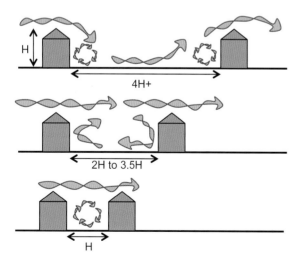

Fig. 5.48 Building spacing and provision of shelter. The distances between buildings should be less than about 3.5 times the building height in order to create shelter from the prevailing wind. These rules also apply for enclosed courtyards.

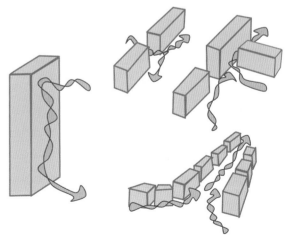

Fig. 5.49 Wind acceleration from: (left) tall buildings, (bottom right) canyon effect, and (top right) around corners.

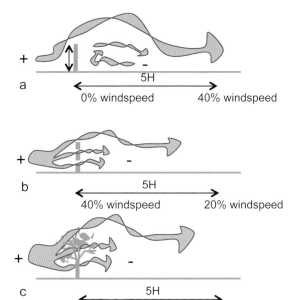

a

5H

0% windspeed   40% windspeed

b

5H

40% windspeed   20% windspeed

c

5H

90% windspeed   70% windspeed

Fig. 5.50 Barriers and their effect on wind flow, creating negative pressure areas: (a) dense, (b) medium, and (c) loose.

Case Study 5.2 Tseung Kwan O, Hong Kong

Wind tunnel analysis can provide information on external wind conditions and dynamic wind pressures on external surfaces. A wind tunnel model for a high-rise, high-density site in Hong Kong included one building fitted with pressure sensors (*see* Fig. 5.51) at a sample of window locations[5.9]. Pressure coefficients were produced that were combined with wind speed to estimate the variation of external wind pressure across the façades. CFD airflow modelling was then used to predict internal temperatures (*see* Fig. 5.52), indicating apartments on the windward side were cooler, with potential for overheating on the west apartments for natural ventilation, due to relatively high levels of solar gains.

Fig. 5.51 (a) The site and (b) the wind tunnel model; the white building has pressure sensors. This building can be moved to other positions, as all buildings are identical.

(continued)

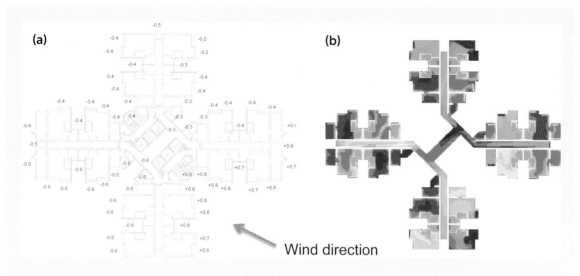

Fig. 5.52 (a) Pressure coefficients (C_p): red are negative and blue are positive; (b) CFD airflow simulation to provide temperatures: red to blue representing hot to cool.

External wind tunnel results at pedestrian level were compared to CFD simulations (*see* Fig. 5.53). Values were similar, both identifying local wind acceleration of up to three times, at corner and canyon locations, indicating that both CFD computer simulation and wind tunnel measurements are suitable for this type of analysis. In Hong Kong, all new developments require a wind analysis to indicate how the building development will affect existing breezeways.

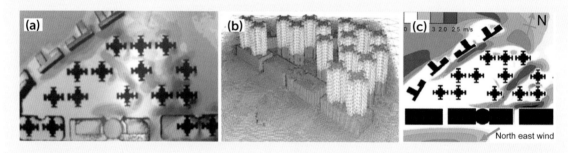

Fig. 5.53 (a) Wind tunnel analysis of external wind acceleration at pedestrian level; (b) CFD simulation grid; and (c) CFD wind simulation results. The darker areas indicate relative wind acceleration[5.11].

Microclimate

In this chapter we have discussed the global variation in climate, how buildings have evolved in response to climate, and how buildings interact with the main climate variables. The microclimate of a site is a modification of the local macroclimate. It will be affected by natural features, such as its location on a southerly facing slope, or in the shadow of a north-facing slope, whether open to the prevailing wind or sheltered, or close to greenery or water. A main feature of the modern built environment is its direct impact on the microclimate due to the physical built environment, including built form, solar reflection and absorption at building and external surfaces, and anthropogenic heat gains from traffic and air conditioning exhausts. These all combine to modify the effects of sun, wind, rain and external temperatures.

Microclimate changes can be at building scale, up to urban scale. It affects the outside environment and people's outside comfort, as well as a building's energy and environmental performance. At the same time a building will impact on its surrounding microclimate and, in doing so, affect the performance of neighbouring buildings. We can summarize the main microclimate effects as follows:

- The built form may prevent sun, daylight and wind from reaching some areas while concentrating it in others.
- Tall structures cast shadows that shade neighbouring buildings, and make some streets darker than others, and may give rise to downdraughts from wind.
- Surfaces such as pavements absorb solar energy, which then convect and radiate heat into the local environment, raising temperatures. Soft green areas can absorb sun and reduce air temperatures through evaporation.
- Anthropogenic heat gains and pollution from transport and exhausts from HVAC systems can affect outside thermal and air quality conditions.

- There may be significant differences in air quality from one neighbourhood to the next, based on proximity to pollution sources, or pollution sinks such as green space.
- The built form may be designed to encourage breezeways to take away pollution and heat, or it may accelerate the wind. Hard and soft landscaping may be used to provide shading and wind shelter.

The microclimate may be beneficial or problematic. Traditional buildings often provided some degree of microclimate such as through shading or breezeways, especially in denser settlements in hot climates. These are generally positive effects, improving external comfort and reducing the climate impact on buildings. In modern urban environments, the microclimate more often has negative implications, raising external temperatures resulting in urban heat islands (UHIs), and creating areas of high pollution.

In high-rise, high-density urban developments, such as Hong Kong (*see* Fig. 5.54), upper-floor apartments are more exposed to sunlight, daylight and the

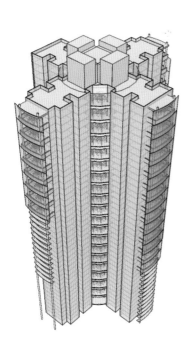

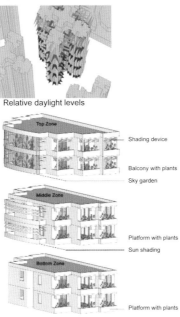

Relative daylight levels

Top Zone
— Shading device
— Balcony with plants
— Sky garden

Middle Zone
— Platform with plants
— Sun shading

Bottom Zone
— Platform with plants

Different façade treatments

Fig. 5.54 High-rise, high-density apartment blocks, typical of Hong Kong, illustrating the variation in microclimate around the building and with height. Different façade treatments can offer varying degrees of solar shading, access to daylight and protection from noise.

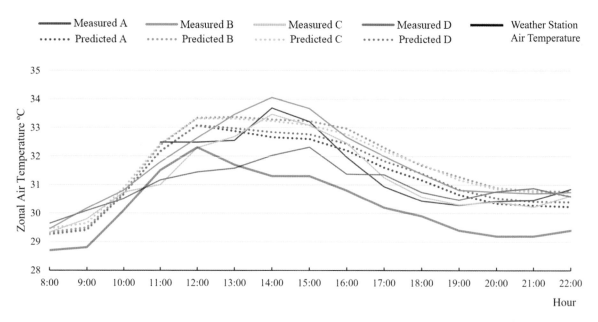

Fig. 5.55 Urban Heat Island results in increased external air temperatures in the high-rise, high-density area of Sai Ying Pun in Hong Kong, where temperatures are predicted to vary by 2°C–3°C across the site in relation to the built form's interaction with sun and local heat generation. Measurements are compared with computer simulation, taking account of the weather, and anthropogenic heat gains from traffic and building exhausts[5.10].

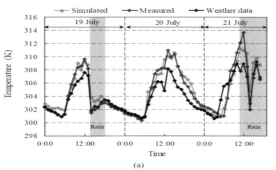

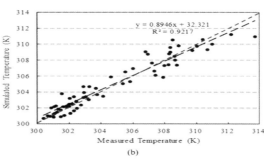

Fig. 5.56 Testing a building microclimate model for assessing street canyon air temperature of high-density cities, using city scale modelling in Guangzhou[5.11].

wind, while the lower ones are exposed to noise and pollution and receive little sun and daylight. Overheating and high cooling loads may be experienced on upper floors, with apartments unprotected against the afternoon and evening sun. Façade design rarely responds to this variation in microclimate with height and orientation. Different façade treatments relating to height and orientations could be used to better respond to the immediate microclimate.

A desktop study of the solar and wind environments can be carried out using 'rules of thumb', based on the building physics described in this chapter. We are also developing our understanding through computer modelling[5.10, 5.11], such that we can simulate the external microclimate (see Figs 5.55 and 5.56), and its impact on comfort and building energy performance.

Design with climate needs to consider inside, transitional and outside spaces (see Fig. 5.57). This will inform of the need for shading or openings for natural ventilation. Transitional spaces may interact more with the outside microclimate, selecting sun and wind to create pleasant conditions suitable for transitional comfort. External spaces have maximum contact with the microclimate and may need protection from sun and wind, especially around entrances and pedestrian routes, or they may benefit from sunny spaces with breezeways.

Fig. 5.57 Impact of sun and wind on internal, transitional and external spaces using shading and openings. The building will affect its surrounds and the ground beneath.

Chapter Six

Building Fabric

Introduction

The first stage of energy-efficient thermal design is to reduce a building's heat loss, or heat gain, which begins with the design of the building fabric (*see* Fig. 6.1); this is a major part of passive design. This 'fabric first' approach maximizes the thermal performance of the components and materials to reduce a building's energy demand, prior to the design of efficient 'active' HVAC systems. The fabric of a building generally includes the walls, roof, floor (and ground beneath) and glazed areas. The fabric heat transmission between inside and outside is reduced, mainly by increasing the level of thermal insulation. Thermal performance will also be affected by the thermal mass of the building's construction, which is a measure of its capacity to store heat. Glazing may be a major source of heat loss in colder weather, and heat gain in warmer

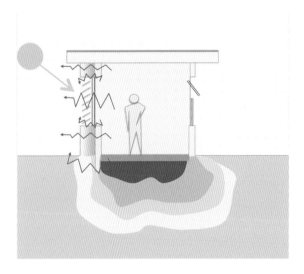

Fig. 6.1 Thermal aspects of the fabric, insulation, thermal bridging, thermal mass and glazing.

weather, while also allowing solar heat and light to enter the building. Modern glazing systems can be relatively well insulated, with solar control against excess solar heat gains and visual glare. There may be localized heat leakage, or thermal bridging, where the insulation levels are reduced, at construction details, or through poor design and workmanship. As a building becomes better insulated, thermal bridging has a proportionally larger effect, significantly increasing heat loss in colder climates or heat gain in warmer ones. Thermal bridging is a major contributor to the 'performance gap' between design and as-built performance. The fabric of a building is difficult to retrofit later, so it is important to get it right at the start.

From a sustainability perspective, we should consider the properties of construction materials in relation to insulation, thermal capacity, embodied energy, recycling and reuse, disposal at end of life, and any impact on health. Materials such as timber, stone, metal and paper can be recycled and reused. Natural materials, such as bamboo, hemp and straw, grow quickly and can be renewed. Synthetic materials such as polystyrene are difficult to dispose of. Fibrous insulation materials, such as glass and mineral wool, may cause a health hazard during installation and over their lifetime.

Fabric Construction

The building fabric is multi-functional. It provides shelter from rain and wind, and so it must be watertight and airtight. The building structure may be integral with the construction, such as in a block or brick wall construction, or the structure may be separate, as for a steel, concrete or timber-frame building. The external fabric includes windows, which allow

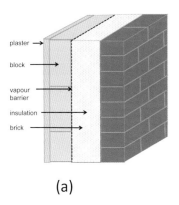
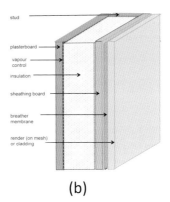
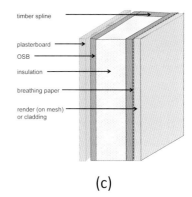

Fig. 6.2 Examples of domestic wall construction: (a) masonry; (b) timber-frame; (c) SIPs (Structurally Insulated Panel) system. Each layer performs a function, including internal surface finish, vapour control, insulation, structure and external weather protection.

the ingress of sun and daylight, offer a view to the outside, and may be opened for ventilation.

The fabric is also multi-layered, and each layer will relate to a different function (*see* Fig. 6.2). The insulation layer has the main effect on thermal performance. Vapour checks restrict the flow of moist air through construction elements, avoiding condensation and material damage. Or constructions may 'breathe', allowing the natural flow of water vapour, without incurring condensation or water ingress.

The construction process may be site assembled or modular. Traditionally, basic materials, such as bricks and timber, and components, such as windows and doors, are delivered to site and assembled on site. An increasing number of buildings are now constructed off-site from modular units (*see* Fig. 6.3). These may be in panel form, which are manufactured off-site and delivered to site as ready-made elements. Or they may be volumetric units, manufactured as whole spaces, delivered to site complete with services and internal and external finishes. Modular construction methods are potentially of better quality and incur less waste during manufacture. Although widely used in some countries, such as Japan, they are not so popular in others, the UK being one, where the demand is not sufficient to establish a modular construction

Fig. 6.3 Examples of modular construction: (a) SIPs system; (b) volumetric system. (b: Premier Modular)

industry, and because there is no such industry, the demand is not there: a chicken and egg situation.

Thermal Insulation

The insulation value of a construction element (wall, roof, floor, glazing) is measured by its thermal conductance (U-value); the lower the U-value, the lower the rate of heat transfer. A modern well-insulated wall construction might have a U-value of $0.12\,W/m^2\,K$, compared to an uninsulated cavity wall construction of $1.5\,W/m^2\,K$, and an old uninsulated solid wall construction of around $2.0\,W/m^2\,K$. Modern constructions are therefore more than ten times as efficient in reducing heat loss compared to older constructions.

Building regulations in many countries, including the UK, prescribe thermal insulation standards as the main criteria for energy-efficient design. Since the 1970s oil crises, thermal insulation standards have improved, mainly to reduce heat loss in cooler climates. Recent new buildings are generally well insulated and many older buildings have had insulation added. For new buildings, the inclusion of thermal insulation in wall, roof and floor constructions takes many forms, and can be located near the inside, the middle, or to the outside of a construction (*see* Fig. 6.4). The interaction of thermal insulation and thermal mass is important for reducing heat loss while also providing indoor temperature stability. As a general rule, thermal mass should be located towards the inside of a construction and in thermal contact with the inside space; the building then acts as a 'heavyweight' construction. Where there is little thermal mass in the construction, or the insulation is in the form of internal 'dry lining', the construction is relatively 'lightweight'. Cladding systems used in industrial buildings or in large retail and warehouses are considered lightweight (*see* Fig. 6.5). Any air cavities should be on the cold side of the insulation; otherwise the insulation may be compromised by heat short-circuiting through the cavity to outside.

Insulation Materials

Insulation materials are reliant upon their physical structure to minimize heat transfer by radiation,

a

Internal render
Structurally insulated
Panel (SIPs)
Air gap
External cladding

b
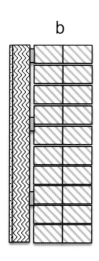

Internal render
Internal insulation
Air gap
External solid wall

c
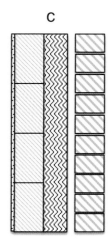

Internal render
Block
Insulation
Air gap
External brick

d
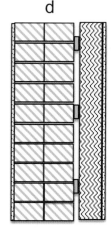

Internal render
Solid wall
Air gap
External insulation
External render

Fig. 6.4 Constructions with different locations of insulation, thermal mass and air gaps: (a) and (b) are lightweight, while (c) and (d) are heavyweight. (a) and (c) represent typical new build, while (b) and (d) represent the retrofit of existing solid wall constructions with internal dry lining wall insulation and external wall insulation (EWI).

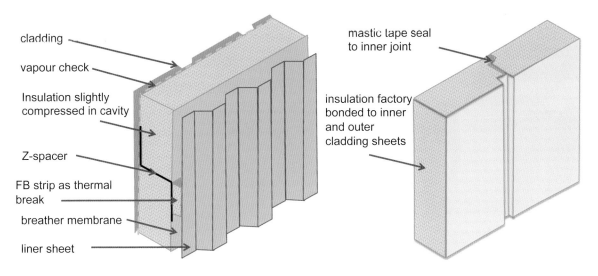

cladding

vapour check

Insulation slightly
compressed in cavity

Z-spacer

FB strip as thermal
break

breather membrane

liner sheet

mastic tape seal
to inner joint

insulation factory
bonded to inner
and outer
cladding sheets

Fig. 6.5 Lightweight cladding systems found in industrial buildings or large retail and warehouses.

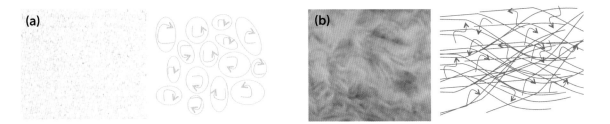

(a)

(b)

Fig. 6.6 (a) Closed cell extruded polystyrene; (b) open cell mineral wool.

convection and conduction, through the containment of small pockets of air or gases that may be either open or closed cell (*see* Fig. 6.6). Closed cell insulation, such as extruded polystyrene and chemical foam boards, have gases (blowing agents) introduced into the material during manufacture that form a dense matrix of closed cell gas bubbles, which have a thermal conductivity less than air. The bubble skin is relatively small in cross-sectional area, so conduction through the material is minimized. Open cell insulation materials, such as mineral or sheep's wool, contain naturally occurring small pockets of air between the fibres, connected by a tortuous route, such that air movement between cells is small. Closed cell materials can provide a vapour check, but are more brittle and prone to deterioration over time through cracking

and leakage of the filler gas, and are susceptible to damage by poor workmanship. Open cell insulation products breathe, and can diffuse any water vapour to the outside. Also, their flexibility enables ease of installation, potentially resulting in a better performance in use.

Insulation materials with a more dense composition will generally have a lower thermal conductivity, because they will absorb more heat before their temperature rises to transfer the heat through the material; they will have a lower diffusivity, or speed of heat transfer. A shiny foil layer may be added to the insulation surface, as a vapour barrier, which will also reduce radiant heat transfer. There is a range of insulation materials, depending on the specific application, whether for walls, roof or floor, or whether for new build or retrofit (*see* Fig. 6.7).

(a) Mineral fibre batt and roll   **(b) rigid board**

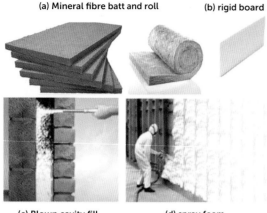

Fig. 6.7 Example of different types of thermal insulation: (a) mineral fibre, (b) rigid board, (c) blown cavity fill, (d) spray foam, and (e) insulating blocks. (Shutterstock)

(c) Blown cavity fill   **(d) spray foam**   **(e) insulating block**

Mineral fibre is generally in the form of glass or rock fibre, available as a lower-density roll or higher-density batt. The manufacturing process forces air into the glass fibres, using a binding agent that locks the composition together, and produces a 'spring loading', allowing it to regain its shape and thickness after compression. The roll form is generally used to insulate roofs, while the batt form is mainly used in walls, where its greater rigidity makes is easier for vertical fixing. Mineral fibre insulation forms a good attachment to the inner skin of the construction, leaving no air gap.

Rigid board is generally made from foamed plastic. It can be gas-filled to give a lower k-value. They can also be made from natural materials, such as wood fibre and hemp. Its attachment to adjacent materials should avoid any air gap, which will compromise its performance. Rigid board insulation is often used in composite 'factory-made' cladding systems, such as structural insulated panels (SIPs), where it is bonded between two layers of timber, metal or a composite material.

Blown insulation cavity fill includes mineral or cellulose fibres, or plastic granules, which are blown into a cavity after completion of construction. Care is needed to avoid any voids in areas where the insulation has difficulty to penetrate. This method of cavity insulation has the advantage that it can be applied to retrofitting existing constructions, although it may not be appropriate in exposed locations where a cavity is needed to avoid moisture transfer to the inner skin.

Spray foam insulation such as polyurethane (PU) foam is created by combining two liquids, isocyanate and polyol resin, during application. The foam expands in seconds to 40 to 100 times its size. It can be closed cell or open cell, with the closed cell having a slightly lower thermal conductivity. It can be applied to a roof, loft, walls, and floors. It may prove difficult to remove and off-gassing during installation may be a health hazard.

Insulating lightweight concrete blocks contribute to the overall insulation of a construction, but usually require additional insulation to achieve the required U-value performance. They can be used in a cavity wall construction, especially when the cavity cannot be completely filled with insulation in exposed locations. Other blocks, such as hemp based, may provide a more sustainable option.

The choice of insulation material for a specific application will be determined not only by its thermal conductivity (k-value), but also the type of construction. Different materials have characteristics that affect their thermal performance, health impacts and general sustainability. Design factors include, thickness, weight and moisture risk (whether the construction is breathable or not). Embodied energy should be considered, although this must be viewed on a whole-life basis; some less sustainable materials may cost more energy to produce, but save more energy during their lifetime. End-of-life disposal is another sustainability factor to consider. Health

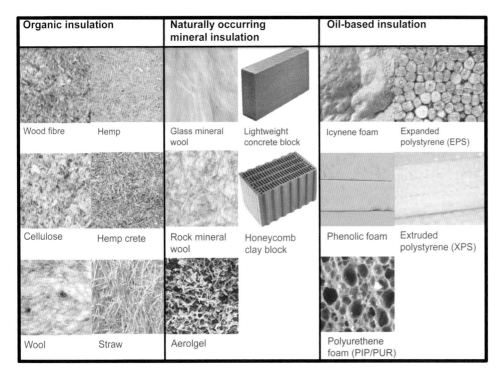

Organic insulation	Naturally occurring mineral insulation	Oil-based insulation
Wood fibre Hemp	Glass mineral wool Lightweight concrete block	Icynene foam Expanded polystyrene (EPS)
Cellulose Hemp crete	Rock mineral wool Honeycomb clay block	Phenolic foam Extruded polystyrene (XPS)
Wool Straw	Aerolgel	Polyurethene foam (PIP/PUR)

Fig. 6.8 Insulation materials.

implications, such as off-gassing of pollutants, or the emission of fine particles or fibres, also need to be considered. Generally, cost and dimensionality dominate the choice of material, which may lead to the selection of less environmentally friendly materials that achieve maximum reduction in heat loss for minimum thickness of material.

A range of insulation materials (*see* Fig. 6.8) is reviewed below and their properties are summarized in Table 6.1.

Table 6.1 Typical values of the properties of insulation materials. The information for thermal properties has been gathered from a range of sources and as these values vary somewhat, they are given as ranges[6.1, 6.2]. The values should therefore be considered as indicative and specific data should be sourced for specific product applications.

	Material	k-value (W/m.K)	Specific heat capacity (J/kg.K)	Density (kg/m³)	Embodied energy (MJ/kg)
Natural organic materials	Wood fibre	0.04–0.09	1600–2100	40–260	10.8
	Cellulose	0.035–0.048	2020	27–65	4.9–16.6
	Sheep's wool	0.038–0.045	960–1800	19–30	12–36.8
	Hemp fibres	0.039–0.044	1400–2300	25–60	10.5–33
	Hempcrete	0.06–0.07	1300–2500	330	2–5
	Straw	0.08	2000	110–130	0.91

(continued)

	Material	k-value (W/m.K)	Specific heat capacity (J/kg.K)	Density (kg/m³)	Embodied energy (MJ/kg)
Naturally occurring mineral materials	Glass mineral wool	0.035–0.047	850	10–48	28–49.6
	Rock mineral wool	0.032–0.047	850	21–250	16.8–24.4
	Aerogel	0.012–0.021	70–1150	30–60	53
	Low-density concrete blocks	0.25–0.60		650–2100	1.5
	Aircrete concrete blocks	0.09–0.2		275–750	3.6
	Honeycomb clay blocks	0.10			6.5
Oil-based materials	Phenolic foam board	0.018–0.023	1500	10.4–26.0	84
	Expanded polystyrene board and beads (EPS)	0.030–0.045	1500	10–35	108
	Extruded polystyrene board (XPS)	0.029–0.038	1500	15–48	95
	Polyurethane/polyiso-cyanu rate board and foam (PUR/PIR)	0.021–0.025	1500	30–40	101

Natural Organic Materials

These include natural materials, mainly chemical free, breathable, reusable and compostable. They tend to have relatively high k-values, typically between 0.035 and 0.080W/m².K, and a relatively high cost. Although they are natural and renewable, they may still incur a significant embodied energy in their production. Some examples are included below.

Wood fibre insulation is available as rigid or semi-rigid board, and is made from softwood timber waste, generally sourced from the manufacture of timber or timber furniture. It is recyclable and sequesters carbon during the timber growth, and is either carbon neutral or carbon negative over its lifetime, producing an overall positive carbon balance of around 600kg per tonne of material used. It can be used to retrofit external solid walls, requiring a thickness of 120mm to achieve a U-value of 0.3W/m².K.

Cellulose is usually made from recycled newspaper, which is shredded, with added inorganic salts, such as boric acid, for resistance to fire, mould, insects and vermin. It is installed either as loose-pack, blown or damp-sprayed. Its relative high density helps stabilize internal space temperatures, reducing the risk of overheating.

Sheep's wool is available in rolls and slab form and is usually a blend of 75 per cent wool combined with recycled polyester fibres. It is sourced from wool discarded as waste due to its colour or grade. It can be used in roofs, walls, lofts and floors. It is breathable and can buffer moisture by a cycle of absorption and desorption.

Hemp fibre (hemp wool) is produced from the outer fibrous skin of the hemp plant, and is available in batts and rolls, which are biodegradable and non-toxic. Hemp is fast growing, reaching heights of 4 metres within 100 to 120 days. It needs little water to grow, so does not require irrigation. It typically comprises 85 per cent hemp fibre, with a polyester binding, and 3 to 5 per cent soda for fire-proofing. It is breathable and can absorb up to 20 per cent of its weight in moisture without affecting its thermal performance, acting as a 'moisture buffer', absorbing any influx of condensation and allowing it to gradually evaporate. During growth, hemp will typically lock away $110-165 kgCO_2/m^3$ of fibre harvested, which more than displaces any fossil fuel energy used during production. At its end of life, it can be incinerated to provide heat.

Hempcrete is a mixture of hemp shives, which are the woody inner core of the cannabis sativa plant, combined with water and lime, producing a biocomposite material with a porridge-like consistency. It can be used in a loose poured form, or in precast panels and bricks. It can be used for construction and insulation, usually for walls, but can also be used to form floor slabs, ceilings, and roof insulation. It is not load-bearing so it needs a structural frame. It is breathable to water vapour, but is water resistant, and can act as a moisture buffer, absorbing and desorbing moisture, providing stable indoor humidity levels. As with hemp fibre, the hemp crop locks away carbon dioxide as it grows.

Straw is available in bales and prefabricated panel units. It is an agricultural by-product from the dry stalks of cereal plants after the grain and chaff have been removed. It requires a minimum wall thickness of between 450 and 500mm to achieve required insulation levels.

Naturally Occurring Mineral Materials

These materials are mid-range options in terms of price and performance, having k-values of between 0.03 and $0.04 W/m^2 K$, although aerogel is significantly lower. Their production process is usually energy-intense, reflected by their high embodied energy. They are typically reusable and recyclable.

Glass mineral wool is made from fibres spun from molten glass at around 1,500°C. It uses natural sand with up to 70 per cent recycled glass, with a resin binder that traps small pockets of air between the fibres. It is available in batts and rolls, and is used in walls, floors, ceilings, and attics. It is incombustible and resistant to mould and vermin. Its density can be varied through pressure and binder content. It can cause skin irritation, so care is needed during installation.

Rock (stone) mineral wool is spun from molten rock at around 1,600°C, producing fine intertwined fibres to which a binder is added. It contains up to 75 per cent recycled content. It is available in boards, batts and rolls, and is used in walls, floors, ceilings and attics. It is incombustible and resistant to mould and vermin. It can cause skin irritation, so care is needed during installation.

Aerogel is a synthetic low-density material formed by removing the liquid from a gel and replacing it with a gas under special drying conditions, creating a solid three-dimensional, low-density nanoporous structure containing 80 to 99 per cent air. It has a very low thermal conductivity. Silica aerogel is the most common type, with the material comprising only 3 per cent of its volume. It is lightweight and transparent, so it can be used for insulating windows and skylights. It is relatively expensive but useful where width is limited. Offcuts are cheaper and can be used around window reveals when retrofitting external wall insulation.

Lightweight concrete blocks can contribute to the thermal insulation of a wall, usually combined with other insulation, such as in a filled or part-filled cavity wall. The density of the aggregate is proportional to its insulation properties and structural strength, with lower density blocks having higher insulation values. Aerated concrete (or 'aircrete') blocks, made from cement, lime, sand, pulverized fuel ash and water and contain air bubbles, provide good insulation properties and are breathable. Cement manufacturing produces 5 to 7 per cent of the world's carbon dioxide emissions, with 40 per cent from the fossil fuels used to heat cement kilns, and 60 per cent from the decarbonation of limestone. The environmental impact of concrete blocks can be reduced by replacing a portion of the cement with natural or waste materials, such as granulated or foamed blast-furnace slag, expanded clay or shale, furnace bottom ash, pulverized fuel ash or, less commonly, volcanic pumice.

Honeycomb clay blocks are formed from natural clay mixed with waste paper and sawdust, which is extruded into a lattice network and then fired. It has a cellular structure of vertical perforations that reduces material quantity as well as its weight, while the combination of aerated clay plus air trapped within the lattice system gives the blocks increased insulation performance. They are breathable. They can be used as the inner leaf in cavity walls or as a single-skin external load-bearing wall. They will usually require a layer of additional insulation to achieve the required thermal performance.

Oil-Based Materials

These materials are usually the cheapest and most effective in reducing heat transfer, with k-values between 0.02 and 0.04W/m².K. They also block moisture, if a non-breathable construction is required. They are oil-based and manufactured at high temperatures. They off-gas toxins and have a relatively high embodied energy, although this may be offset by their increased insulation performance over their lifetime.

Phenolic foam has a thermally efficient closed cell structure and is used as rigid insulation boards. Its main component is phenolic resin, which has a high embodied carbon dioxide content of some $4.15kgCO_2/$ kg of material. Specific applications are where space is limited, such as plasterboard drywall lining, to minimize impact on internal room space. End-of-life options are limited to landfill or incineration.

Expanded polystyrene (EPS) is a white, tough, rigid closed cell foam plastic made from styrene, using the blowing agent pentane to form bubbles and expand the foam. Styrene and pentane are hydrocarbon compounds, obtained from petroleum and natural gas by-products. EPS is available as loose fill beads for cavity fill, or in boards, which are often used as external

wall insulation finished with a reinforced fibreglass mesh basecoat with a primer and render. Discarded polystyrene does not biodegrade for hundreds of years.

Extruded polystyrene (XPS) is a closed cell board, slightly denser and therefore slightly stronger than EPS. Its water vapour diffusion resistance is low, making it suitable for application in wetter environments. It is used for ceiling tiles, wall insulation and floors.

Polyurethane (PUR)/polyisocyanurate (PIR) boards are closed cell thermoset polymer plastic

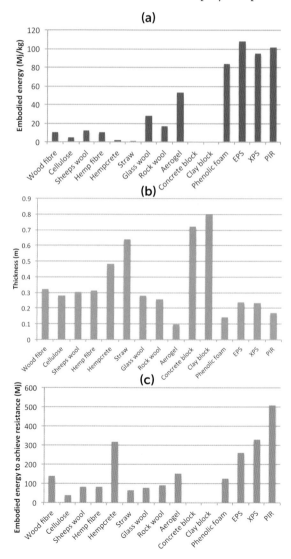

Fig. 6.9 Comparison of the performance of insulation materials: (a) embodied energy values for different materials; (b) relative thickness to achieve a thermal resistance of 8.0m²K/W; and (c) embodied energy to achieve the same resistance.

products, which can be rigid foam, or blown with CFC-free gas. PIR is a technical development of PUR, with superior firmness, strength, thermal resistance and dimensional stability. Prefabricated PIR sandwich panels are manufactured with bonded steel facings and are used extensively on roofs and walls, such as in warehousing, factories and offices. PIR is more fire-resistant than PUR; however, it does burn when exposed to heat and both give off toxic cyanide fumes.

Fig. 6.9 compares the relative performance of different insulation materials. Natural insulation materials have lower embodied energy per unit of weight, but generally require an increased thickness to achieve the required U-value performance. If we compare the relative thickness of different materials to achieve a thermal resistance of 8.0m² K/W, which represents a well-insulated construction, oil-based insulation materials require the least thickness, due to their lower k-values. Oil-based insulation materials have the highest embodied energy to achieve the same thermal resistance when compared to organic and naturally occurring materials, but the differences are not so pronounced.

Glass wool and mineral wool are the most well-established insulation materials, comprising some 58 per cent of the European construction insulation market[6.3]. They have good 'natural' fire protection characteristics compared to EPS, which has about 27 per cent of the European market. However, in some countries the lower priced EPS material often favours its use in construction. PUR/PIR and XPS take up some 8 per cent and 6 per cent of the market respectively, with others totalling 1 per cent. The more environmentally friendly insulation materials have very little penetration in the European markets, although cellulose appears to be popular in North America. There are emerging natural materials, including cornstalk blocks, corncob board, bamboo fibres, palm fibres, kenaf fibres and sunflower stalks, which tend to have k-values from 0.045 to around 0.1W/m².K. There is also the potential for using mycelia, grown on organic waste, for thermal insulation, which can achieve k-values of around 0.08W/m².K[6.4].

Thermal Bridging

The integrity of insulation in a construction may be reduced through thermal bridging. Thermal bridging takes place through the parts of a construction that have a relatively low thermal resistance to heat flow in comparison with the rest of the construction (*see* Fig. 6.10). In colder climates, a cold thermal bridge

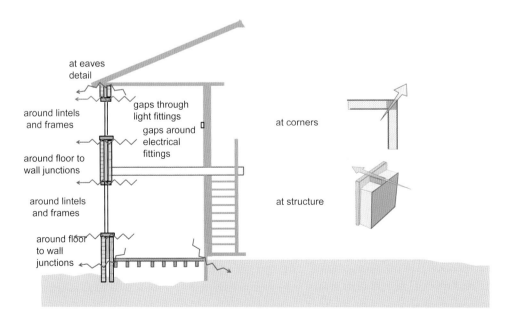

at eaves detail

around lintels and frames

gaps through light fittings

gaps around electrical fittings

around floor to wall junctions

around lintels and frames

around floor to wall junctions

at corners

at structure

Fig. 6.10 Typical sources of cold bridging in housing.

will result in increased heat loss and increased risk of condensation. It may arise due to poor construction details around windows, doors and structural elements, or poor workmanship during construction. In a construction, heat will flow from high- to low-temperature areas by conduction along the path of 'least thermal resistance'. For sills, lintels and door edges, the least resistance path will be through higher conductive materials, such as metal and dense concrete. Insulating components can provide a thermal break to reduce thermal bridging.

Insulation should be continuous around design details, such as at the eaves and floor junctions. Insulation may be compressed during installation, or disturbed when other building work is carried out. As buildings become better insulated, thermal bridging can contribute a greater proportion of the overall heat loss, with thermal bridging accounting for up to 20 to 30 per cent of fabric heat loss in a new home.

Thermal bridging may be classed as repeating or non-repeating. Repeating thermal bridges include structural elements such as wall ties that bridge across cavity insulation, or timber joists in ceilings that regularly interrupt the insulation. They are usually accounted for within a construction's U-value. Non-repeating thermal bridges occur at the intersection of materials with different thermal properties, such as door and window reveals, the intersection of roof slopes, or in corners, where there is a relatively higher proportion of external area for heat loss. Heat loss through solid ground floors is a specific case of non-repeating geometric thermal bridging. Non-repeating thermal bridges are calculated separately based on their type and length. Ψ-values are associated with type (see Table 6.2), measured in W/m K, and are multiplied by the length of the thermal bridge to estimate its heat loss, which is then added to the element's U-value to provide an estimate of overall heat loss.

Missing insulation within a construction, due to poor design or workmanship, may also cause thermal bridging. The integrity of insulation can be measured by a thermographic survey. All objects emit heat energy (infrared radiation), depending on their surface

Table 6.2 Ψ-values[6.5].

Junction details in external walls	Default Ψ-value (W/m.K)
Steel lintel with perforated steel baseplate	0.50
Other lintels	0.3
Sill	0.04
Jamb	0.05
Ground floor	0.16
Intermediate floor within a dwelling	0.07
Eaves (insulation at ceiling level)	0.06
Corner (normal)	0.09
Corner (inverted)	−0.09

temperature and emissivity. Thermography can make this heat energy visible and capable of interpretation. An infrared camera scans the surfaces of a building, producing a 'live' heat picture. The differences in colour or shade correspond to differences in surface temperature. Areas of defective or missing insulation are detected as locally warm (viewed from the outside) or cool (viewed from the inside) areas. Images taken from the inside show greater temperature variations compared to those taken from the outside, due to the relatively higher internal surface thermal resistance, which produces a greater surface temperature difference at any defective areas, and therefore they will be easier to identify (see Fig. 6.11). A thermography survey can be carried out on completion of construction to ensure that the insulation has been installed correctly.

Air leakage through construction details is another form of thermal bridging (top left in Fig. 6.11). Ventilated air cavities should be located on the cool side of the insulation, to avoid heat loss via the ventilated cavity. Cavities may be formed unintentionally, where the thermal insulation is not tightly fixed to the adjacent material (see Fig. 6.12).

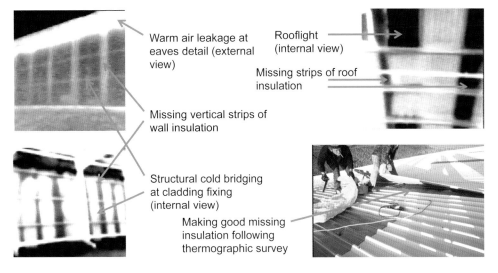

Warm air leakage at eaves detail (external view)

Rooflight (internal view)

Missing strips of roof insulation

Missing vertical strips of wall insulation

Structural cold bridging at cladding fixing (internal view)

Making good missing insulation following thermographic survey

Fig. 6.11 Examples of defective insulation and air leakage detected through a thermographic survey. In the bottom right-hand side photo, a roof structure of a factory is being opened up to make good missing insulation following such a survey.

Thermal Mass

A building's capacity to store heat within its construction is referred to as its thermal mass. Buildings with a high thermal mass can take longer to warm up from cold, but they can retain heat and are relatively slow to cool down. Lightweight buildings warm up quicker and cool down quicker, and are more at risk of overheating in warm weather. The 'thermal lag' for a heavyweight building can delay the external peak temperature effect until later in the day, whereas it is much shorter for lightweight buildings (see Fig. 6.13). Heavyweight buildings provide a more stable indoor temperature over time and are suited for continuous use, whereas a lightweight building may be more suited to intermittent use, benefitting from a quick warm-up period. Hot climates with relatively cooler nights traditionally use buildings of high thermal mass, cooling down at night and retaining a relatively cool mass during the day. Warm humid climates with a lower diurnal temperature variation traditionally use lightweight constructions that shed heat quickly during the night.

Construction materials can be used to store energy, which may reduce overheating in summer, or retain higher indoor temperatures in winter after the heating goes off. The amount of heat stored relates to the thickness of the construction element, its thermal capacity and its exposed surface area. An exposed

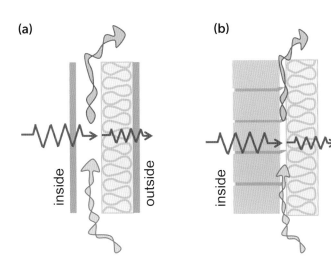

(a)

inside

outside

(b)

inside

outside

Fig. 6.12 Airflow within a construction can provide short-circuiting of heat loss, reducing its overall thermal insulation value: (a) insulation on the cold side of a ventilated cavity; (b) air leakage due to poor butting of the insulation against internal wall, arising from bulging cement joints.

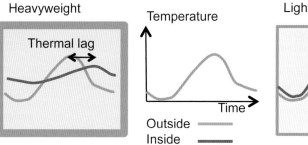

Fig. 6.13
Heavyweight
versus lightweight
building
performance,
illustrating daily
thermal lag and
stability of internal
temperatures.

Heavyweight

Lightweight

Thermal lag

Temperature

Time

Outside ·············

Inside ——

concrete ceiling will absorb excess internal heat gains in the summer, but the heat must later be exhausted, for example, using night-time ventilation cooling. This requires a diurnal external temperature difference with relatively cool nights; so the use of thermal mass cooling depends on the local climate. Reductions in peak internal temperatures using an exposed concrete ceiling can be up to 4°C to 5°C in comparison with a lightweight suspended ceiling (*see* Fig. 6.14).

There are a range of thermal mass strategies (*see* Fig. 6.15), including using the floor slab, exposing concrete ceilings to the space, indirect coupling, active thermal mass and ground ventilation reheat. The ground can be used as a source of heating or cooling, if there is a seasonal temperature variation to 'recharge' the ground

temperature. Direct coupling may just be thermal contact of the floor connected to the ground. Indirect coupling may duct ventilation air through the ground, for cooling in hot weather or to gain heat in cold weather. The ground temperature at depths of two metres or more remains fairly constant throughout the year. The amount of cooling obtained depends on the volume air supply rate and the exposed contact surface area of the pipes. Air may be passed through a basement or labyrinth of tunnels that have a high thermal mass in order to precool it. The heat absorbed by the thermal mass must be extracted through night ventilation or natural seasonal effects. Active mass strategies can cool the thermal mass by installing water pipes or air ducts within the construction to extract the heat.

(a)

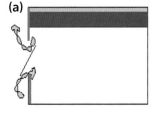

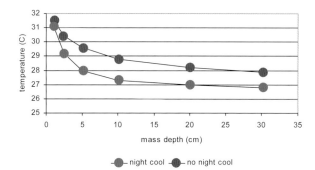

—●— night cool —●— no night cool

Fig. 6.14 Reducing peak indoor temperatures with thermal mass, with and without increased ventilation night cooling: (a) flat exposed ceiling area; (b) exposed ceiling area increased by 50 per cent. Zero thermal mass is equivalent to a lightweight suspended ceiling.

(b)

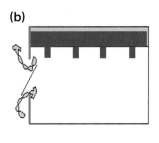

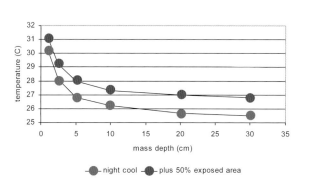

—●— night cool —●— plus 50% exposed area

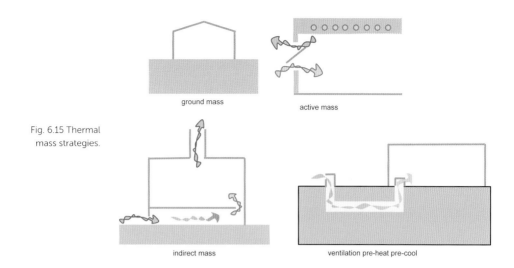

ground mass

active mass

Fig. 6.15 Thermal mass strategies.

indirect mass

ventilation pre-heat pre-cool

Case Study 6.1 Thermal Performance of Solid Ground Floor Slabs

This case study illustrates the thermal performance of large floor slabs such as that found in single storey industrial buildings. A (finite element) computer model was used to investigate the time-dependent heat transfer for a 20m wide slab. Ground temperatures were measured down to 5m, which were compared to the simulated values (see Fig. 6.16). The results show the reduction in ground temperature with depth, and the thermal lag increasing with depth. The building was unoccupied until week 25, at which time the heating was turned on. Two-dimensional contours of the ground temperature over the same time period are presented in Fig. 6.17.

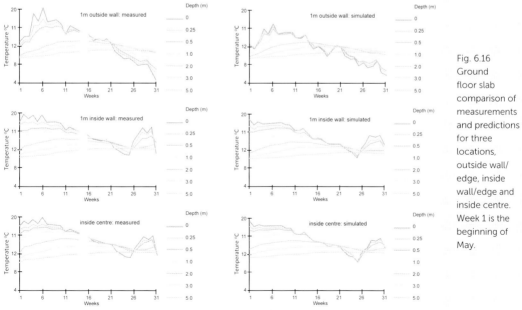

Fig. 6.16 Ground floor slab comparison of measurements and predictions for three locations, outside wall/edge, inside wall/edge and inside centre. Week 1 is the beginning of May.

(continued)

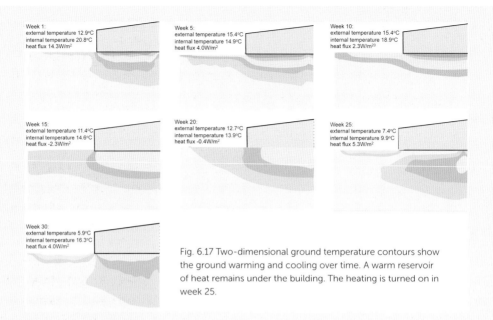

Week 1:
external temperature 12.9°C
internal temperature 20.8°C
heat flux 14.3W/m²

Week 5:
external temperature 15.4°C
internal temperature 14.9°C
heat flux 4.0W/m²

Week 10:
external temperature 15.4°C
internal temperature 18.9°C
heat flux 2.3W/m20

Week 15:
external temperature 11.4°C
internal temperature 14.6°C
heat flux -2.3W/m²

Week 20:
external temperature 12.7°C
internal temperature 13.9°C
heat flux -0.4W/m²

Week 25:
external temperature 7.4°C
internal temperature 9.9°C
heat flux 5.3W/m²

Week 30:
external temperature 5.9°C
internal temperature 16.3°C
heat flux 4.0W/m²

Fig. 6.17 Two-dimensional ground temperature contours show the ground warming and cooling over time. A warm reservoir of heat remains under the building. The heating is turned on in week 25.

Seasonal simulations over a four-year period illustrate how the ground warms up from initial construction of the building (*see* Fig. 6.18(a)). Simulation of a winter day shows that as the building cools down at night, the slab releases heat into the space, and there is a small net heat gain from the ground to the space over a 24-hour period (*see* Fig. 6.18(b)), whereas in the summer there is a relatively large net heat gain to the slab from the space. The edge losses are relatively high for the first metre (*see* Fig. 6.18(c)). Edge insulation can reduce these losses.

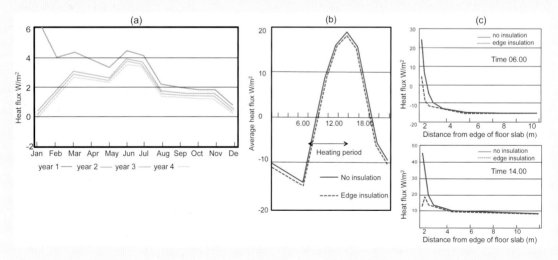

Fig. 6.18 (a) Seasonal heat flux into a slab over a four-year period; (b) daily variation in January; and (c) distance from the edge at two different times.

This is an example of how computer simulation can be tested against measurement data, and then used to explore other detailed aspects of performance.

Phase Change Materials

Thermal mass effects can be increased using the latent heat properties of a phase change material (PCM) to absorb and release energy from and to a space. The most common form of phase change is between the liquid and solid phases. A phase change material is chosen with a melting point appropriate for its application, for example, paraffin wax begins to melt at 26°C. When the indoor temperature approaches this melting point, the chemical bonds of the material will break up, and it will change from solid to liquid, absorbing heat from the space. As the ambient temperature falls, the phase change material will return to the solid state, giving off the absorbed heat. This cycle can stabilize the interior temperature. Fig. 6.19 illustrates how a phase change material can contribute to heating at night and cooling in the day.

Chemical storage materials can potentially provide seasonal heat storage, collecting solar heat in the summer and delivering it throughout the winter. Their moisture content is reduced by heating (in summer), and this heat can be recovered by hydrating them in colder weather. Initial estimates indicate a chemical storage capacity of around one cubic metre could be sufficient to provide a zero energy performance house through the heating season, using solar PV as an energy source, with some topping up during winter sunny periods. Such systems are being explored.

Moisture

The outside and inside air will contain moisture in the form of water vapour. This water vapour will give rise to a vapour pressure, and for a given temperature a high vapour pressure equates to a high relative humidity (RH). In cooler climates, the inside vapour pressure is increased due to moisture generated from occupancy, and the vapour pressure gradient from inside to outside will drive the vapour throughout a construction. Construction materials can both absorb (store) and permeate (transmit) water vapour, depending on their hygroscopic and permeability properties, which is similar to materials having thermal capacity and conductance in relation to heat transfer. If water vapour is stored within the construction, it may be drawn back inside if the inside RH drops, and may then be exhausted through ventilation. Some materials are more hygroscopic than others, and are able

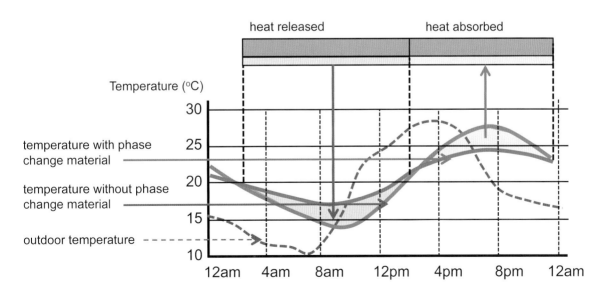

Fig. 6.19 Schematic of a phase change material on a ceiling, absorbing heat in the day and releasing it at night.

to buffer and store moisture without being damaged, while other materials may be adversely affected permanently. Natural materials tend to be more hygroscopic than synthetic ones. Water vapour transfer through a construction can be controlled through the choice of materials and vapour checks. Ideally, the materials towards the inside should be less vapour permeable than those towards the outside.

For a heated building the temperature will change throughout the external construction, getting cooler nearer the outside, with the greatest temperature gradient across the more insulating material layers. If the temperature at any point falls below the dew-point temperature, there will be a risk of condensation. If this occurs on the internal surface, surface condensation may occur; if it is within the construction, interstitial condensation occurs. A vapour barrier, such as polyethylene or foil, placed on the warm side of the insulation will theoretically stop water vapour entering further into the construction. However, in practice it is difficult to achieve a perfect vapour barrier, due to penetrations of the construction. A breathing wall may have a vapour-check layer on the warm side of the insulation, to slow down the passage of moisture to a safe level, combined with permeable materials that allow water vapour to travel through the construction to the outside. It may incorporate a water-resistant breathing membrane towards the outside, with a ventilated gap between this and the weatherproof outer skin, to allow water vapour out, but resist water soaking in from the outside, such as in roofs, where any rain penetration or 'cold night' condensation in the roof's outer layer may be drained. Cold thermal bridges at details should also be designed to avoid condensation risk. Closed cell insulation will have a higher vapour resistance and also reduce condensation risk, although again there may be water vapour leakage around details and any crackage.

The risk of surface condensation can be estimated from the indoor surface temperature (T_s) and the indoor relative humidity (RH), for a given internal air temperature (T_a) and external air temperature (T_e), using the indoor surface resistance (R_{si}) and the U-value of the construction (U):

$$T_a - T_s = UR_{si}(T_a - T_e)$$

For example, if $T_a = 20°C$, $T_e = 0°C$ and $R_{si} = 0.123$ m²K/W

For a single-glazed window, $U = 5.7$ W/m²K

$$T_a - T_s = 5.7 \times 0.123 \times (20) = 14.0$$
$$T_s = 6.0°C$$

For a well-insulated wall, $U = 0.14$

$$T_a - T_s = 0.14 \times 0.123 \times (20) = 0.34$$
$$T_s = 19.64°C$$

If the inside RH is 60 per cent, its dew-point temperature will be 15°C (refer to the psychrometric chart in Fig. 3.19). Surface condensation may occur on the window but not on the wall.

We can assess the risk of interstitial condensation by calculating the temperature drop, $\Delta T = U \times R_{layer} \times (T_a - T_e)$, across layers of a construction. We can similarly calculate the vapour pressure profile through the wall from values of material vapour resistivity (v_r), where the vapour resistance (V_r) of a material of thickness x(m):

$$V_r = xv_r$$

The vapour pressure drop across each layer (ΔV_{layer}) for a total construction vapour pressure drop (ΔV_{total}) will be:

$$\Delta V_{layer} = (V_r / V_{total}) \Delta V_{total}$$

The dew-point temperature is related to vapour pressure (V_p) using a psychrometric chart or the formula:

Dew-point temperature = $(241.88 \times \ln(V_p/610.78))$ $/(17.558 - \ln(V_p/610.78)$

The following calculation (see Table 6.3) provides actual temperature and dew-point temperature profiles through the wall construction shown in Fig. 6.20(a). Adding a vapour barrier (see Fig. 6.20(b)), or adding a lower permeability timber outer layer (Fig. 6.20(c)), or closed cell insulation (Fig. 6.20(d)), can all reduce the theoretical interstitial condensation risk.

Table 6.3 Calculation of temperature and dew-point temperature profiles through a wall construction (see Fig. 6.20(a)).

	Inside	Inside surface	Plaster board	VB	Insulation	Cavity	Brick	Outside surface	Outside
Thickness (m)			0.015		0.1	0.05	0.1		
k-value (W/mK)			0.16		0.04		0.84		
Thermal resistance (m²·K/W)		0.12	0.09		2.5	0.18	0.12	0.055	
Temperature drop (°C)		0.078	0.61		16.3	1.17	0.78	0.36	
Temperature (°C)	20		19.2	18.6		2.3	1.1	0.36	0
V_r (MNs/g)			75		6.0	0	45		
ΔV_r (MNs/g)			1.13		38.6	0	289		
Vapour pressure (kPa)	1000		1000	928		889	889	600	400
Dew-point temperature (°C)	6.99		6.99	5.9	5.3	5.3	5.3	-0.25	-0.25

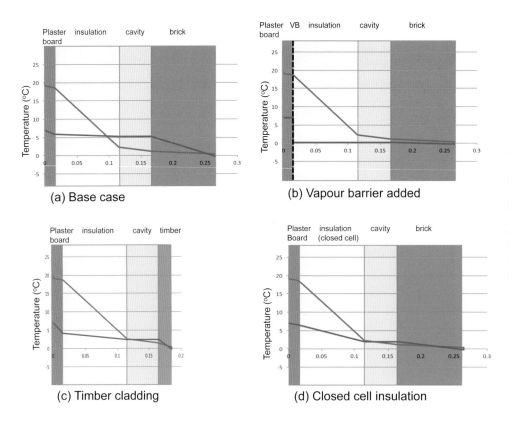

(a) Base case

(b) Vapour barrier added

(c) Timber cladding

(d) Closed cell insulation

Fig. 6.20 Different wall constructions, and actual temperature (red) and dew-point temperature (blue) profiles: (a) base case; (b) vapour barrier added; (c) timber cladding; and (d) closed cell insulation.

Some hygroscopic materials can be used to control inside RH, by a process of absorbing and desorbing moisture at times of high and low RH. Unfired clay brickwork may simultaneously absorb moisture and heat, providing passive thermal and moisture control over the indoor condition[6.6] (see Fig. 6.21). It can be indefinitely wetted and re-wetted, and as little as a 20mm later of clay plaster can substantially moderate the daily cycle of indoor RH, typically maintaining indoor RH levels of 40 to 65 per cent.

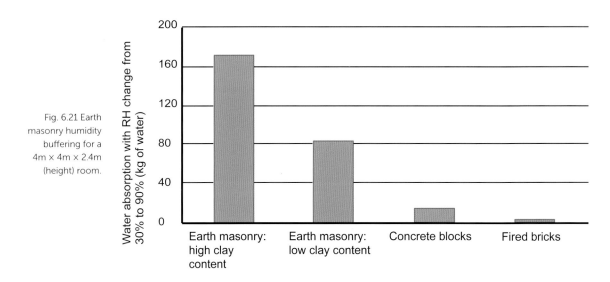

Fig. 6.21 Earth masonry humidity buffering for a 4m × 4m × 2.4m (height) room.

Glazing

Highly glazed buildings have been traditionally associated with high heat loss, cold internal surface temperatures in winter, and overheating and glare in summer. However, modern glazing systems are relatively well insulated, and can provide a range of solar control technologies, through the properties of the glass and through shading devices. Glazing can allow useful solar heat gains, although in modern well-insulated buildings they are generally not needed to supplement space heating. By the time they occur, the building has already warmed up through occupancy, and they may cause overheating, even in winter.

Glass will transmit, reflect and absorb solar radiation, depending on the sun's angle. The total heat gain factor (F), or g-value, is the combined direct transmission plus the absorbed energy that is released inwards to the room (*see* Fig. 6.22). The direct gains themselves will be absorbed by internal surfaces within the space, and the subsequent rise in surface temperature will result in convective and (long-wave) radiant gains to the space. For standard single glazing, most of the radiation will be admitted to the space (*see* Fig. 6.23(a)), varying with solar angle of incidence (*see* Fig. 6.23(b)). Increasing the number of layers of glass will reduce the solar transmittance by about 80 per cent per layer

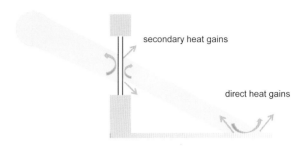

Fig. 6.22 g-value is a measure of the total heat gains through a glazed element: the direct gains absorbed by the interior surfaces and the secondary convected and radiated gains from the heat absorbed by the window.

for standard glass, and blinds may be added to further reduce the g-value (*see* Fig. 6.24(a) and (b)). The outer pane of a glazing system may be used for solar control, by using an absorbing glass, or clear glass may be used to maximize the transmission of solar gains, depending on whether cooling or heating is an issue.

Glass is a good conductor of heat and has practically no thermal resistance. The thermal resistance for single glazing is mainly attributed to its surface resistances. Adding layers of glass will improve a window's insulating properties, through additional surface resistances and the resistance of air cavities, which increases in proportion to their width up to about 20 mm, and remains constant up to 60 mm, after which it decreases slightly due to convection loops in the cavity.

Fig. 6.23 (a) Transmitted, reflected and absorbed solar radiation incident on 4mm single glazing, C and r are the convective heat and (long-wave) radiative transfer from the surfaces to the outside and inside; (b) variation with angle of incidence. F = total heat gain factor $(T + (C_i + r_i))$.[6.7]

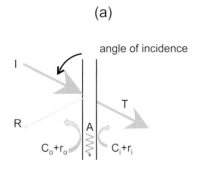

(a)

For a 90° angle of incidence:
Transmitted (T) = 0.84
Reflected (R) = 0.08
Absorbed (A) = 0.08
Convected and radiated outside (C_o+r_o) = 0.06
Convected and radiated inside $(C_i + r_i)$ = 0.02

Total admitted 0.86   Total rejected 0.14

(b)

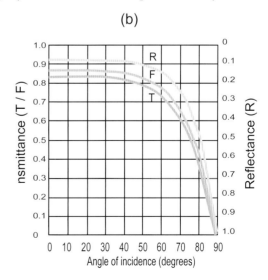

(a)

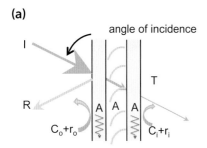

angle of incidence

I

R

$C_o + r_o$ A   A   A $C_i + r_i$

T

For a 90° angle of incidence:
Transmitted (T) = 0.08
Reflected (R) = 0.40
Absorbed (A) = outer 0.18
            blind 0.33
            inner 0.01
Convected and radiated outside $(C_o + r_o)$ = 0.36%
Convected and radiated inside $(C_i + r_i)$ = 0.16%.
Total admitted 0.86   Total rejected 0.14
Convected and radiated outside $(C_o + r_o)$ = 0.36
Convected and radiated inside $(C_i + r_i)$ = 0.16

Total admitted 0.86   Total rejected 0.14

(b)

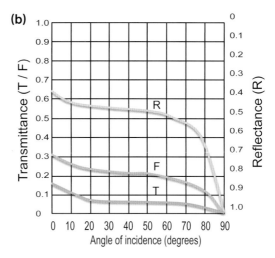

Transmittance (T / F) — Reflectance (R) — Angle of incidence (degrees)

Fig. 6.24 (a) Transmitted, reflected and absorbed solar radiation incident on 6mm double clear glazed with lightweight venetian blind, C and r are the convective heat and long-wave radiative transfer from the surfaces to the outside and inside; (b) variation with angle of incidence. F = total heat gain factor $(T + (C_i + r_i))$.[6.7]

Worked Example

Calculate the U-value of a single 6mm layer of glass (thickness x) with the following properties:
Internal surface resistance (R_{si}) = 0.13m².K/W;
External surface resistance (R_{se}) = 0.04m².K/W;
k-value (k) = 1.05W/m.K.

$$R = R_{si} + x/k + R_{se}$$
$$R = 0.13 + 0.006/1.05 + 0.04$$
$$= 0.176 m^2.K/W$$
$$U\text{-value} = 1/R = 5.7 W/m^2.K$$

Windows radiate and reflect heat depending on their surface properties. Low emissivity glass has a thin coating applied to the glass surface, which reflects solar radiation in the infrared and ultraviolet spectrum. There are two types of low emissivity coating. A soft low-e coating is produced by depositing a silver layer onto the glass through a 'magnetron sputtering' process after the glass has been manufactured. It cannot be exposed to the external environment and needs to be sealed in a double or triple glazing unit, usually on surface 2 (*see* Fig. 6.25); it has good solar control properties. A hard 'pyrolytic' low-e coating has a thin layer of indium tin oxide deposited as the glass is produced. It can be applied to an exposed internal glass surface although it is generally located on surface 3 of a double-glazed unit (*see* Fig. 6.25). It reflects radiant heat back into the space and is therefore particularly useful in cold climates.

A glazing system can be designed to meet a specific requirement for its g-value, U-value, and visible light transmission. The overall g-value is achieved through a combination of changing transmission, reflection, and absorption of the different layers of glass. In general, the lower the g-value, the lower the visible transmission.

Blinds can be incorporated into a layered glazing system to provide additional solar control (*see* Fig. 6.26). Blinds may be venetian or roller, and they will have transmission, reflectance and absorption values, depending on the material and colour, although the transmission value is generally small or zero. Internal blinds heat up and although they shade direct sunshine and reduce glare, much of the solar heat ends up in the space. Blinds located externally or between layers of glass are more effective. It may be necessary to ventilate cavities containing blinds, to release the solar heat gains 'trapped' within the glazing system, which would otherwise heat the internal glass surface. External blinds are the most

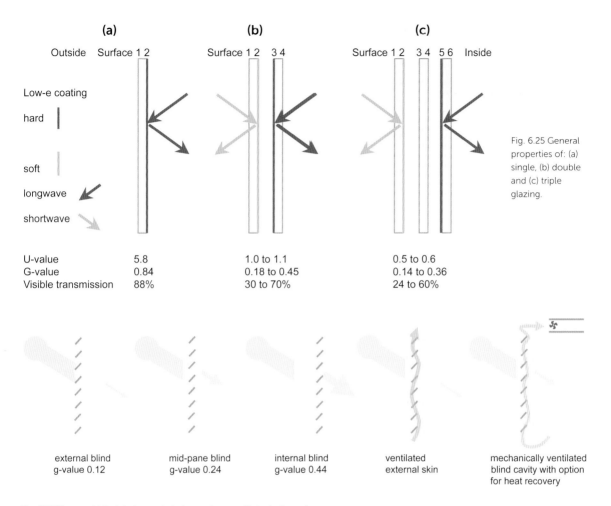

Fig. 6.25 General properties of: (a) single, (b) double and (c) triple glazing.

(a)

Outside Surface 1 2

Low-e coating

hard

soft

longwave

shortwave

U-value	5.8
G-value	0.84
Visible transmission	88%

(b)

Surface 1 2 3 4

| 1.0 to 1.1 |
| 0.18 to 0.45 |
| 30 to 70% |

(c)

Surface 1 2 3 4 5 6 Inside

| 0.5 to 0.6 |
| 0.14 to 0.36 |
| 24 to 60% |

external blind
g-value 0.12

mid-pane blind
g-value 0.24

internal blind
g-value 0.44

ventilated
external skin

mechanically ventilated
blind cavity with option
for heat recovery

Fig. 6.26 Range of blinds in layered glazing systems, with typical g-values.

effective at reducing solar gains, but they are more expensive and difficult to maintain, and they have an effect on the building's aesthetics, although this may be seen as a positive feature. External blinds made of diffuse glass will shade solar heat gains while allowing daylight to enter. Solar control is often achieved by a combination of glazing treatment and blinds.

Electrochromic glass can also be used to control solar radiation and can be adjusted from completely clear to opaque (*see* Fig. 6.27). The g-value can be considerably reduced, although the visible transmission is also reduced. As a rule of thumb when designing a glazing system for summer conditions, internal glass surface temperatures should be less than 5°C above the internal air temperature, to avoid excess secondary heat gains and thermal discomfort.

There is a range of external shading devices (*see* Fig. 6.28). Shading is usually fixed, although it can be moveable, such as venetian blinds, or vertical or horizontal fins. Fixed shading has a limited performance because of the daily and seasonal movement of the sun. In the northern hemisphere, south-facing elevations generally have horizontal shading for peak summer conditions, however, they are exposed to low-angle winter sun. East and west façades experience low sun angles, so vertical shading is often used. External venetian blind shading systems are used extensively in mainland Europe. Computer simulation can be used to optimize blind design for a specific location.

Shade level	Energy transmission g-value	U-value W/m²K	Light transmission %
Bright	0.38	1.1	60
Light	0.12	1.1	18
Medium	0.07	1.1	6
Dark	0.04	1.1	1

Fig. 6.27 Electrochromic glass installation in an office development in Switzerland, showing the difference between an activated and non-activated window. The table compares light transmission for a range of g-values. (Kopitsis Bauphysik AGM)

Green Walls

Green walls and roofs can form an integral part of the external fabric, and in some countries they are required by regulation for flat roofs. They contribute to a building's thermal performance, through reducing fabric heat loss and heat gain, in cold and warm conditions respectively. They absorb pollutants from the air and can convert carbon dioxide into oxygen; 1m² of green wall typically extracts 2.3kg of carbon dioxide per year from the air, while producing 1.7kg of oxygen. Green walls can shade the external façade, reducing solar heat gains, and can reduce external ambient temperatures through evaporative cooling. They can encourage biodiversity in the built environment. There are a range of systems in relation to irrigation and substrate for growth (*see* Fig. 6.29).

(a)

(b)

Fig. 6.28 External blind systems: (a) options mainly for south-facing façades (northern hemisphere); (b) options for east- and west-facing façades and glazed roofs.

A combination of green walls and green roofs can reduce urban temperatures by up to 5°C and reduce wall and roof surface temperatures by up to 15°C and 20°C respectively, depending on the climate of the location (*see* Fig. 6.30)[6.8].

A green wall also acts as a sound barrier, resulting in a much quieter and more natural environment both inside and outside the building. They can provide an aesthetic which people find relaxing. The presence of plants can reduce stress, and improve health and well-being, and greenery can encourage faster recovery for hospital patients. Green roofs can hold rainwater during storms, and delay water entering the drainage system, reducing the risk of flooding; 'sponge city' is a term used to describe natural systems that soak up storm water and release it gradually.

Fig. 6.31 presents two examples of green wall applications. The two 44-storey Bosco Verticale towers were completed in 2014, creating a biological habitat for some 1,000 trees and 10,000 flowering plants. It reduces

Fig. 6.29 Examples of green wall systems.

Climbing facades   Soil substrate pockets   Hydroponic panels   Active walls

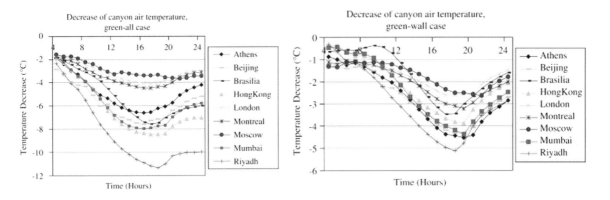

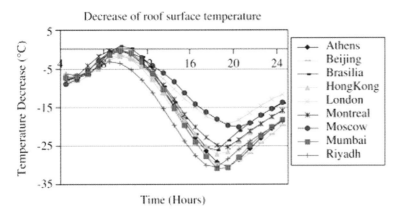

Fig. 6.30 Computer simulation of the temperature reductions from green wall and roofs[6.8].

(a)

(b)

Fig. 6.31 (a) Bosco Verticale towers, Milan; (b) Oasia Hotel Downtown, Singapore. (Photos: Shutterstock)

energy consumption by around 7.5 per cent, and keeps the building 3°C cooler during summer, and warmer during winter. It is irrigated by recycling wastewater.

Singapore's 27-storey Oasia Hotel Downtown was completed in 2016, providing sky terraces and a green façade, which respond to the local climate. The façade creates an outer layer, providing up to 60 per cent shade, absorbing heat, and reducing cooling loads. The open-air sky terraces comprise over 40 per cent of the building's floor area and are naturally cross-ventilated from all directions.

Embodied Energy of Building Materials

Embodied energy is a measure of the total energy required for the extraction, processing, manufacture and delivery of building materials and components to the building site. Embodied energy has associated carbon dioxide emissions, referred to as embodied carbon, which contributes to the overall environmental impact of a construction. Embodied energy is usually measured in mega-joules per kilogram of material used (MJ/kg) for a building element, or GJ/m^2 for a whole building. Embodied carbon is measured in $kgCO_2/kg$ of material used. The relationship between embodied energy and embodied carbon will depend on the primary fuel consumed to deliver the material. Some materials, such as timber and quick growth crops sequester carbon and may be considered to have a negative embodied CO_2.

The embodied energy for insulation materials has been presented in Table 6.1. Data is available for embodied energy and embodied carbon values for a range of construction materials and components (see Table 6.4). These values can then be used to estimate the embodied energy of whole buildings.

Table 6.4 Embodied energy and embodied CO_2[6.9].

Material	Energy MJ/kg	Carbon kgCO_2/kg	Material density kg/m³
Aggregate	0.083	0.0048	2240
Concrete	1.11	0.159	2400
Bricks (common)	3	0.24	1700
Concrete block (medium-density)	0.67	0.073	1450
Aerated block	3.5	0.3	750
Limestone block	0.85		2180
Marble	2	0.116	2500
Cement mortar	1.33	0.208	
Steel	20.1	1.37	7800
Stainless steel	56.7	6.15	7850
Timber	8.5	0.46	480–720
Glued laminated timber	12	0.87	
Cellulose insulation	0.95–3.3		43
Cork insulation	26		160

Material	Energy MJ/kg	Carbon kgCO$_2$/kg	Material density kg/m^3
Glass fibre insulation	28	1.35	12
Flax insulation	39.5	1.7	30
Rockwool (slab)	16.8	1.05	24
Expanded polystyrene insulation	88.6	2.55	15–30
Polyurethane insulation (rigid foam)	101.5	3.48	30
Wool (recycled) insulation	20.9		25
Straw bale	0.91		100–110
Mineral fibre roofing tile	37	2.7	1850
Slate	0.1–1.0	0.006–0.058	1600
Clay tile	6.5	0.45	1900
Aluminium	155	8.24	2700
Bitumen	51	0.38–0.43	
Medium-density fibreboard	11	0.72	680–760
Plywood	15	1.07	540–700
Plasterboard	6.75	0.38	800
Gypsum plaster	1.8	0.12	1120
Glass	15	0.85	2500
PVC	77.2	2.41	1380
Vinyl floor covering	65.64	2.92	1200
Terrazzo tiles	1.4	0.12	1750
Ceramic tiles	12	0.74	2000
Wool carpet	106	5.53	
Wallpaper	36.4	1.93	
Vitrified clay pipe	7.9	0.52	
Iron	25	1.91	7870
Copper	42	2.6	8600
Lead	25.21	1.57	11340
Ceramic sanitary ware	29	1.51	
Paint (waterborne)	59	2.12	
Paint (solvent-borne)	97	3.13	

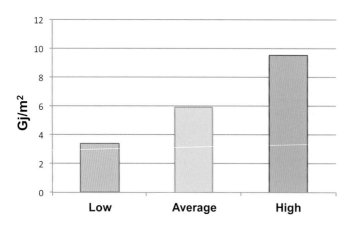

Fig. 6.32 Range of whole building embodied energy values for housing[6.10, 6.11, 6.12].

manufacturing using modular construction methods can significantly reduce this waste. There is data available for whole building embodied energy, with most work centred on housing, which averages around $6GJ/m^2$ (*see* Fig. 6.32).

The split between embodied energy and operating energy varies (*see* Fig. 6.33). For conventional housing, the embodied energy may typically account for 15 per cent of the building's total energy use, with operational energy contributing 85 per cent. For low energy housing the ratio is 33 per cent embodied and 67 per cent operational. The embodied energy increases in proportion as the operational energy is reduced through energy-efficient design, and may increase in absolute terms through the use of more materials, such as thicker layers of thermal insulation. Heavyweight materials generally have a higher embodied energy compared to lightweight materials, but they may offer other advantages that may reduce energy use or improve comfort. They may be more durable or achieve a better performance than less energy-intensive materials. Ideally materials should exhibit both low embodied energy and good operational performance over time.

However, the range of values varies with source and with the boundary selected. The total embodied energy boundary might include the sourcing and processing of the material or component, its transportation to site, the associated energy used on the construction site, the recurrent energy from maintenance and replacement over the building's life, and the energy used for disposal. Different boundary definitions include cradle to gate (the factory), cradle to (construction) site and cradle to grave (including construction, maintenance and demolition). A typical average breakdown of total embodied energy is 6 per cent for transport, 10 per cent for construction, 25 per cent for recurrent costs (over a fifty-year lifetime) and 3 per cent for demolition (although some work suggests < 1 per cent); the remaining 56 per cent will be the embodied energy associated with producing the material (cradle to gate). However, in many cases only cradle to gate or cradle to site is used. Waste on construction sites using traditional construction methods, can contribute around 20 per cent of a building's embodied energy; think of it as one house wasted for every four built! Off-site

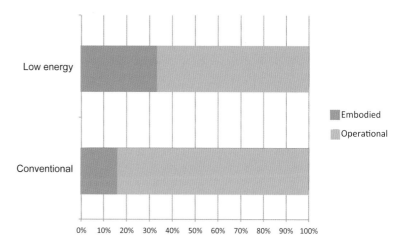

Fig. 6.33 Split between embodied energy and operational energy for low energy and conventional housing[6.13, 6.14, 6.15, 6.16].

Chapter Seven

Ventilation and Infiltration

Introduction

Ventilation and infiltration (or air leakage) account for a major part of a building's thermal load. Ventilation provides fresh air for occupants, dilutes and exhausts pollutants, and may be used for comfort cooling, by exhausting internal heat gains. Too little ventilation and the health and comfort of the occupants is at risk. Too much ventilation during the heating or cooling season will incur an energy penalty. If comfort cooling is used in warmer weather, it will require ventilation rates higher than for fresh air ventilation, typically by a factor of 5 or more. A ventilation system will therefore need to operate at more than one level, generally a background level for normal occupancy, and a boost level for dealing with overheating or pollution episodes. It may also be required to operate at a higher level if there is risk of infectious disease.

Ventilation includes natural ventilation, mechanical ventilation, acting separately or in combination, with air infiltration common to both (*see* Fig. 7.1).

Natural ventilation is the movement of outdoor air into and out of a space through intentionally provided openings, such as windows, doors and ventilator grilles. It is driven by natural forces arising from indoor to outdoor air temperature differences, and external wind pressure.

Air infiltration is the fortuitous leakage of air into and out of a building due to imperfections in the structure, such as cracks around doors and windows; service entries, including pipes, ducts, flues, ventilators; and through porous construction elements, including bricks, blocks and mortar joints. Air infiltration obeys the same rules as natural ventilation, but it is uncontrolled. Both naturally and mechanically ventilated buildings will have some level of air infiltration. Excessive air leakage (similar to thermal bridging) is a major cause of the performance gap between design and as-built energy use.

Mechanical ventilation is the movement of air by active mechanical means, to and from a space. It can be localized using individual wall or roof fans, or centralized with a ducted distribution system. It is controllable and can provide the correct amount of fresh air to spaces, usually based on occupancy levels. It is especially needed in spaces that are deep-plan or highly populated, such as school classrooms, offices and concert halls. It can incorporate heat recovery, filtration and moisture control.

In the past, buildings were often overventilated by virtue of their leaky construction, open fire chimneys, and ill-fitting components. Air infiltration alone generally provided sufficient ventilation for occupancy, and more! Ventilation was uncontrolled and buildings in colder climates were difficult to heat, to maintain comfort. For modern buildings, the balance of reducing ventilation heat loss while maintaining good indoor air quality is a major challenge for energy-efficient design, with the focus on minimizing air leakage and providing controlled fresh air

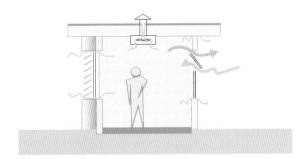

Fig. 7.1 Ventilation may be a combination of natural ventilation, mechanical ventilation and air infiltration.

ventilation. The phrase 'build tight, ventilate right', applies to both natural and mechanical ventilation design.

As the energy efficiency of the fabric improves, ventilation becomes a greater proportion of the thermal load. No matter how energy efficient the building fabric is, we still need ventilation to ensure the comfort and health of occupants. This will incur a heat loss, or heat gain, between inside and outside. In modern buildings, ventilation can become the dominant load for the heating or cooling system. The choice of ventilation strategy has a major impact on a building's form and space planning, so it needs to be decided at an early design stage.

The ventilation rate is measured in air changes per hour (ac/h), or m³/hour/per person (or litres per second per person (l/s/person)). Usually, but not always, ac/h is used in relation to natural ventilation, where 1ac/h would be equivalent to the whole volume of air in a space or building being replaced with outside air every hour. Natural ventilation often relates to whole building requirements, such as for residential buildings, where we might aim for around 0.5ac/h for normal occupancy, which would typically equate to around 35 to 40l/s. For mechanically

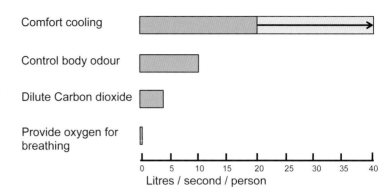

Fig. 7.2 Ventilation levels for occupancy.

ventilated buildings we tend to use l/s/person, which is perhaps related to the more precise nature of mechanical systems and the need to provide for specific occupant numbers, such as for office spaces where each person may require around10l/s.

Reducing odour is generally the most important factor in determining ventilation rates. If enough air is sufficient to get rid of odour, this will generally meet the requirements for carbon dioxide dilution and oxygen supply, although much larger ventilation rates will be needed for comfort cooling, or to deal with pollution episodes (*see* Fig. 7.2). Table 7.1 lists the fresh air rates required to provide ventilation for different buildings alongside typical (maximum) occupation densities, which may vary with specific case.

Table 7.1 Ventilation rates and occupancy density.

Building type	Ventilation rate		Occupancy density
	l/s/person	ac/h	m² per person
Dwellings: living spaces		0.4–1.0	
bathrooms		15	
toilets		5.0	
Educational buildings			
classrooms	10		3
Offices	10		6
Museums and galleries	10		5

Building type	Ventilation rate		Occupancy density
	l/s/person	ac/h	m² per person
Auditoria	10		0.5
Restaurants	10		1.0
Bars (standing)	10		0.3
Retail	10		6–7
Garages		6.0	
Hospital wards		6.0 (rising to 12.0 due to when there is risk of infectious disease)	

Natural Ventilation

Natural ventilation is the controlled ventilation through purpose-made air inlet and outlet devices, such as openable windows. More complex ventilation designs, such as ventilation chimneys and atria, can strongly influence building form (*see* Fig. 7.3). Natural ventilation is often regarded as a major component of passive design. However, it need not be, and other passive design features, such as solar control, the use of daylight and thermal mass, apply equally well to mechanically ventilated buildings.

Spaces with high occupancy levels can be difficult to naturally ventilate, especially in cold weather, when exhausting large amounts of warm stale air incurs an energy penalty, and supplying cold air directly from outside may result in thermal discomfort. Often, recommended ventilation rates are not achieved and air quality is compromised. Given the choice, people will generally choose poor air quality in preference to cold discomfort.

The perception of control is an important feature of natural ventilation, with occupants able to open windows or ventilators, and quickly sense the change in air quality or temperature. Control may be intermittent, such as opening windows in a classroom between lessons to refresh the air, and then closing them before the next session. This rapid ventilation refresh mode may be typical of high-density spaces, where continuous natural ventilation in winter may prove to be too cold. Where lower ventilation rates are required, a continuous low rate of ventilation may be achieved using small controllable 'trickle' ventilators located in window frames.

Natural ventilation is a result of two processes, namely stack effect and wind effect. Stack effect

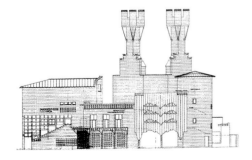
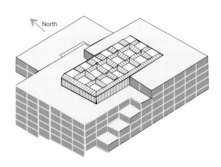

Fig. 7.3 (left)
Contact Theatre
(Alan Short); (right)
Gateway 2.

occurs when there is a difference between the inside and outside air temperatures. If the inside air is warmer than the outside air, it will be relatively less dense and more buoyant. It will rise through the space, escaping at high level through any window openings or air leakage cracks. It will be replaced by cooler, denser air drawn into the space at low level. Stack effect increases with increasing inside-outside temperature difference and increasing height between the higher and lower openings (*see* Fig. 7.4). The so-called neutral plane is established at a height somewhere between the high- and low-level openings, depending on the relative size and distribution of the openings. At this level, the internal air pressure will equal the external pressure (in the absence of wind effects). Above the neutral plane, the internal air pressure will be relatively positive and air will exhaust to outside. Below the neutral plane, the internal air pressure will be relatively negative and external air will be drawn into the space. The further away an opening is from the neutral plane, the greater will be the pressure difference and the greater the airflow through the opening.

The pressure difference between the high and low openings due to stack effect can be estimated from[7.1]:

$$\Delta P = -\rho T g h (1/T_i - 1/T_e)$$

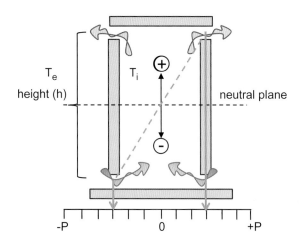

Fig. 7.4 The pressure gradient in a space with reference to the neutral plane.

Where

ΔP is the pressure difference in pascals (Pa)
ρ is the density of air at temperature T (kg/m³)
T is the average temperature $(T_i + T_e)/2$ (K)
g is the acceleration due to gravity = 9.8m/s²
h is the height between openings (m)
T_i is the inside temperature (K)
T_e is the external temperature (K)

Worked Example

Using the above formula and the example in Fig. 7.4, the pressure difference between two openings 8m apart can be calculated, given the following information:

ρ (at 293K) = 1.2kg/m³
T_i = 26°C = 273 + 26 = 299K
T_e = 8°C = 273 + 8 = 281K
h = 8m

ΔP = −1.2 × 293 × 9.8 × 8.0
   × (1/281 − 1/299) = −5.9Pa

The airflow through an orifice type opening such as an open window can be estimated from[7.1]:

$$Q = C_v A (2\Delta P/\rho)^{0.5}$$

Where

Q is the airflow (m³/s)
A is the area of the opening (m²)
C_v is the discharge coefficient (0.61 for a sharp edged opening)
ΔP is the pressure difference (Pa)
ρ is the density of air at temperature T (kg/m³)

Wind flow around buildings is highly turbulent due to its continuous variation in speed and direction. However, a statistical analysis of the wind for a particular location will identify one or more prevailing wind directions, which can then be used in ventilation design. The interaction of the wind across the envelope of a building gives rise to pressures at openings which will drive airflow through the building (*see* Fig. 7.5).

The wind-induced pressure difference between two points on a building envelope is (see also Chapter 5):

$$\Delta P = 0.5\, \rho v_h^2\, (C_{p1} - C_{p2})$$

Where

ΔP is the pressure difference between the two points (Pa)

C_{p1} and C_{p2} are the pressure coefficients across the building

ρ is the air density (kg/m³)

v_h is the wind speed (m/s) at a reference height h(m)

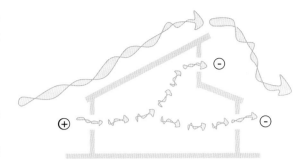

Fig. 7.5 Wind flow around a building in relation to pressure.

Worked Example

What is the pressure difference across a building, at the windows, if the pressure coefficients at the windward and leeward windows are 0.5 and −0.4 respectively, and the wind speed is 5m/s?

wind speed = 5m/s
density of air = 1.2kg/m³
C_{p1} = 0.5, C_{p2} = −0.4

ΔP = 0.5 × 1.2 × 5² (0.5 − (−0.4)) = 13.5Pa

The pressures for wind and stack effects are of a similar magnitude (13.5Pa and 5.9Pa respectively) at typical conditions. When we design for natural ventilation, firstly we usually design for stack effect, with no wind, and then try to ensure that wind effect will not compromise the ventilation design, with reference to the prevailing wind directions.

The flow of air through openings can be calculated using the standard British Standard method [7.2], considering wind effect, stack effect, or a combination of these, for single-sided openings (see Fig. 7.6) and double-sided openings (see Fig. 7.7), where T is temperature (K), H is height (m) and A is area m².

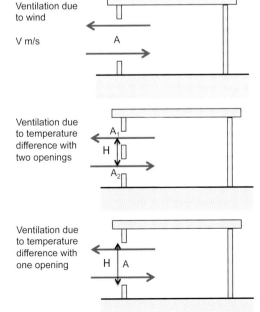

Ventilation due to wind

V m/s

A

$Q = 0.025\, A\, V$

Ventilation due to temperature difference with two openings

A_1

H

A_2

$$Q = C_d A \left[\frac{\varepsilon (2)^{0.5}}{(1+\varepsilon)(1+\varepsilon^2)^{0.5}} \right] \left[\frac{\Delta T g H}{T_{av}} \right]^{0.5}$$

$\varepsilon = \dfrac{A_1}{A_2}$; $A = A_1 + A_2$; $\Delta T = T_i - T_e$; $T_{av} = \dfrac{T_i - T_e}{2}$

Fig. 7.6 Estimating ventilation airflow through single-sided openings [7.2].

Ventilation due to temperature difference with one opening

H   A

$$Q = C_d \frac{A}{3} \left[\frac{\Delta T g H}{T} \right]^{0.5}$$

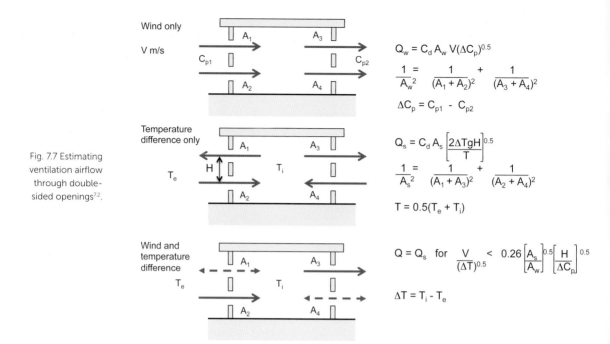

Fig. 7.7 Estimating ventilation airflow through double-sided openings[72].

Wind only

V m/s

$$Q_w = C_d A_w V(\Delta C_p)^{0.5}$$

$$\frac{1}{A_w^2} = \frac{1}{(A_1 + A_2)^2} + \frac{1}{(A_3 + A_4)^2}$$

$$\Delta C_p = C_{p1} - C_{p2}$$

Temperature difference only

$$Q_s = C_d A_s \left[\frac{2\Delta TgH}{T}\right]^{0.5}$$

$$\frac{1}{A_s^2} = \frac{1}{(A_1 + A_3)^2} + \frac{1}{(A_2 + A_4)^2}$$

$$T = 0.5(T_e + T_i)$$

Wind and temperature difference

$$Q = Q_s \text{ for } \frac{V}{(\Delta T)^{0.5}} < 0.26 \left[\frac{A_s}{A_w}\right]^{0.5} \left[\frac{H}{\Delta C_p}\right]^{0.5}$$

$$\Delta T = T_i - T_e$$

Opening windows is the main way of controlling natural ventilation, and there is a range of window types (*see* Fig. 7.8). During winter, background ventilation rates can be achieved by means other than opening windows, such as using fine control small opening 'trickle' ventilators (*see* Fig. 7.9).

There are limits for natural ventilation design relating to depth of space, amount of window opening, and external noise and pollution (*see* Fig. 7.10). Natural ventilation may not be appropriate for high-occupancy spaces during winter in cooler climates, or during summer in hot climates, due to excessive external cold or hot air entering the space. In more temperate climates, there may be limits in achieving sufficiently high ventilation rates for summertime cooling (*see* Fig. 7.11), where we may require natural

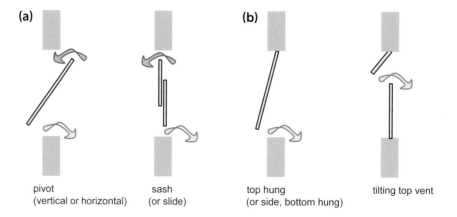

Fig. 7.8 Window opening types: single-sided ventilation requires top and bottom openings, (a) to provide a height difference from the bottom to top openings, allowing warmer air to escape through the top, while drawing cooler outdoor air in at the bottom; (b) top hung windows only work with cross ventilation, or where there are windows at different heights in a space, otherwise they are not effective for stack ventilation, and they do not generally provide a sufficiently large opening for summertime comfort cooling; side-hung windows will provide a continuous vertical height difference, which will allow the stack effect to operate.

Fig. 7.9 Trickle ventilator at the top of a window frame for 'background' ventilation and window opening for higher 'foreground' ventilation.

ventilation rates of the order of 5ac/h or more, to maintain internal air temperatures within a few degrees of external temperatures. In some locations there may also be external noise or pollution, which will inhibit opening windows.

Natural ventilation may be achieved with openable windows, for spaces up to around 6 to 10m deep (roughly two to three times the space height). If the space is cross-ventilated, then depths of up to 15m (roughly five times the height) may be naturally ventilated. Deep-plan spaces can also be cross-ventilated by connecting them to an atrium or chimney to provide an increased stack effect. An atrium should

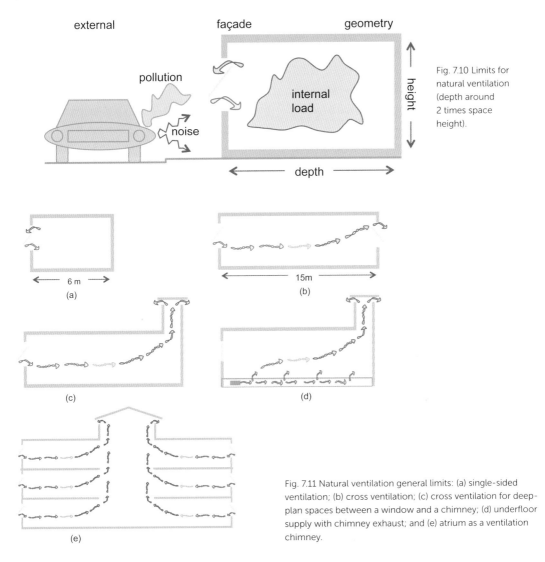

Fig. 7.10 Limits for natural ventilation (depth around 2 times space height).

Fig. 7.11 Natural ventilation general limits: (a) single-sided ventilation; (b) cross ventilation; (c) cross ventilation for deep-plan spaces between a window and a chimney; (d) underfloor supply with chimney exhaust; and (e) atrium as a ventilation chimney.

extend about one floor higher than ceiling of the top floor to create stack effect for the top rooms.

Air Infiltration

Air infiltration, often referred to as air leakage, is a form of uncontrolled natural ventilation. If the infiltration rate is high, a building may prove difficult to heat (or cool) to comfort levels, and this may result in excessive heat loss (or gain). It may also provide a path for external pollutants and moist air to enter the building. It is considered 'best practice' to minimize infiltration, and then use controllable natural or mechanical means to provide the required ventilation rates.

The airtightness of a building is largely determined by its construction, the performance of its components, and the standard of workmanship. For a typical house, around 50 per cent of infiltration arises from leakage through components, such as around windows and doors, and service entries (*see* Fig. 7.12). For new build, doors and windows should have high-quality fixings and furniture, to ensure that they close properly, do not warp, and their frames are well sealed within the construction. Service entries, such as in kitchens and bathrooms, and bath surrounds, need to be sealed. Lobbies, porches and conservatories can reduce infiltration by forming a draught buffer, reducing the impact of wind and outside temperature.

For existing buildings, draught stripping can be applied to existing openable components, such as external doors and windows. A mastic sealant can be applied to joints around window frames. Loft hatches should be draught-stripped to avoid air leakage into the roof space. Infiltration can also take place through porous constructions, such as around mortar joints, which may also reduce U-value performance, especially if air can infiltrate around thermal insulation. As discussed in Chapter 6, this is particularly a problem with rigid board cavity insulation, which often cannot be sealed to the inner skin due to surface irregularities. It is easier to obtain a good seal to the inner skin with mineral wool insulation. Internal dry lining, can also be relatively leaky. Modular construction methods, such as SIPs systems, can produce a relatively airtight construction.

The air leakage of a building can be quantified by its permeability rate, which is the rate of air leakage (m^3/h) per square metre of envelope area when the building is pressurized to 50Pa, using a fan pressurization system (*see* Fig. 7.13), usually carried out on completion of the construction. Generally, new build houses have a target design air permeability rate of $5m^3/h.m^2$ of external envelop. Where mechanical ventilation with heat recovery (MVHR) has been installed, the air permeability rate should be no greater than $3m^3/h.m^2$ for the system to operate effectively. The Passivhaus low energy standard requires $0.6m^3/h.m^2$. The location of air leakage paths can be

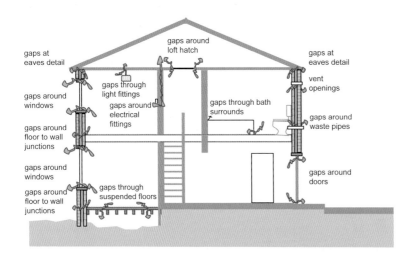

Fig. 7.12 Typical sources of air leakage in housing.

Fig. 7.13 Fan pressurization carried out in a house and small factory. The air leakage of a building can be measured by pressurizing or depressurizing the building using a fan and measuring the volume flow of air needed to maintain a fixed pressure difference between inside and outside. The usual target is a pressure difference of 50Pa, which is above normal pressure differences due to stack and wind effects, and so will provide a relatively reliable comparison with standards, although tests should be carried out during low wind conditions.

determined from smoke tests, with pressurization fans used to depressurize a building and smoke used to visualize incoming air leakage paths. Thermography can also be used, as illustrated in Fig. 6.11.

An approximate estimate of the air leakage, in units of ac/h, can be made by dividing the air leakage measurement value at 50Pa by 20 (called the 1/20th rule). For example, if a house with an envelope area of 250m² has a measured air leakage of 10m³/h at 50Pa, the ventilation rate at normal pressure differences would be equal to: (250 × 10) × 1/20, which is around 125m³/h, which for a house volume of 300m³ equates to around 0.4ac/h of air leakage (125 ÷ 300). Pressurization tests are relatively easily carried out on housing and smaller buildings. For larger buildings, larger fans or multiple fan units are needed. Although a building may be relatively airtight on completion of construction, this may not be the case a year or so later, when the building has 'settled' and grown leakier.

Mechanical Ventilation

Mechanical ventilation can range in complexity, from an individual air supply or exhaust fan unit to a full air conditioning system. Certain spaces may require mechanical ventilation, such as deep-plan spaces that cannot be adequately ventilated from openings in the external perimeter by natural means, or spaces with a high occupancy or high heat gain where natural ventilation alone cannot provide sufficient fresh air or exhaust the internal heat, or where the external environment is hot or polluted. The following are the main types of mechanical ventilation.

Mechanical extract can be used to exhaust pollutants at source, such as mechanical extracts in kitchens, bathrooms and toilets, or local mechanical extracts for processes, such as, photocopying, solder baths and welding booths. The rest of the building may be naturally ventilated or have additional mechanically ventilated.

Mechanical supply systems can be used in situations where a positive flow needs to be established between a space and its surroundings. A positive pressure mechanical supply system in a house or apartment will maintain a minimum ventilation rate and reduce condensation risk (extract may be through trickle ventilators) (*see* Fig. 7.14a). A mechanical supply to an office may have natural extract through an atrium or chimney/tower (*see* Fig. 7.14b).

Balanced supply and extracts, such as in air conditioning systems, provide control of higher

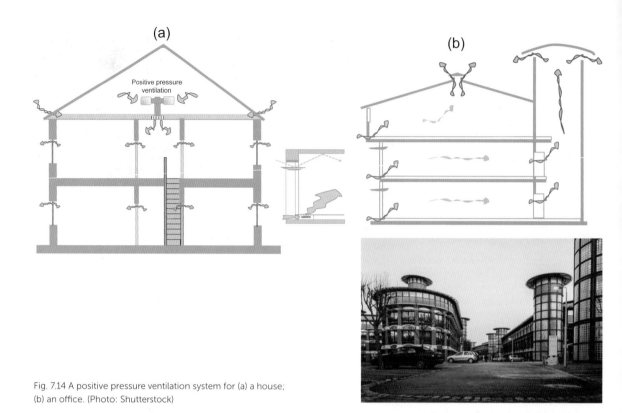

Fig. 7.14 A positive pressure ventilation system for (a) a house; (b) an office. (Photo: Shutterstock)

ventilation rates; heating and cooling of supply air; filtration of supply air; humidity control; and heat recovery by means of the exchange of heat between exhaust air and supply air. Systems might be balanced with a slight excess of air supply to ensure cold, hot, or polluted outside air is not drawn into the building through air leakage paths.

Mechanical ventilation has a number of advantages over natural ventilation. If high ventilation rates are required in winter, mechanical ventilation can incorporate heat recovery, providing energy savings compared to natural ventilation, and without incurring discomfort from cold draughts. Mechanical ventilation will ensure minimum ventilation rates for occupancy, and reduce indoor moisture levels and condensation risk. If external air quality is poor, or if a 'clean' environment is required, then filtration can be used. The air leakage rate in a mechanically ventilated building should be low to avoid the uncontrolled ingress of outside air. Heating or cooling is often combined with mechanical ventilation, which may incorporate ground cooling by passing the supply

air through pipes buried in the ground (*see* Fig. 6.15). During the heating season the supply air may also be preheated through the same system, when the external air temperature is lower than the ground temperature. Zero energy performance generally requires mechanical ventilation with heat recovery.

Mechanical systems are discussed in greater detail in Chapter 8.

Hybrid Systems

A hybrid system combines natural and mechanical ventilation (*see* Fig. 7.15). In temperate climates, a seasonal hybrid approach can be used to naturally ventilate in summer, when the outside air is suitably warm, and mechanically ventilate in winter, when the outside air is cold and mechanical ventilation can be combined with heat recovery. In hotter climates, natural ventilation may be used in winter, and mechanical ventilation in summer with the exhaust cool air being used to precool outside supply air. A spatial hybrid

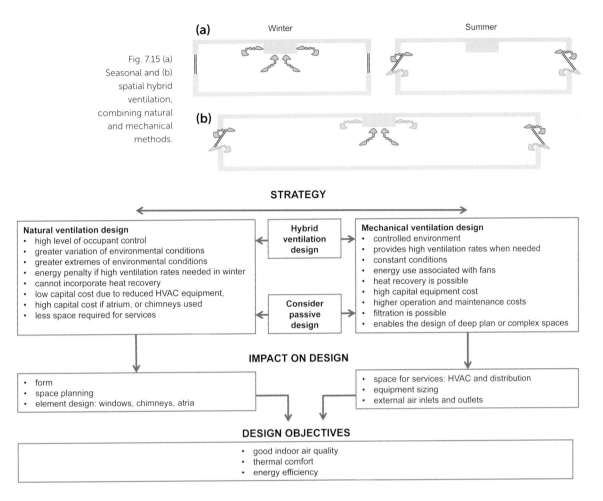

Fig. 7.15 (a) Seasonal and (b) spatial hybrid ventilation, combining natural and mechanical methods.

STRATEGY

Natural ventilation design
- high level of occupant control
- greater variation of environmental conditions
- greater extremes of environmental conditions
- energy penalty if high ventilation rates needed in winter
- cannot incorporate heat recovery
- low capital cost due to reduced HVAC equipment,
- high capital cost if atrium, or chimneys used
- less space required for services

Hybrid ventilation design

Consider passive design

Mechanical ventilation design
- controlled environment
- provides high ventilation rates when needed
- constant conditions
- energy use associated with fans
- heat recovery is possible
- high capital equipment cost
- higher operation and maintenance costs
- filtration is possible
- enables the design of deep plan or complex spaces

IMPACT ON DESIGN

- form
- space planning
- element design: windows, chimneys, atria

- space for services: HVAC and distribution
- equipment sizing
- external air inlets and outlets

DESIGN OBJECTIVES

- good indoor air quality
- thermal comfort
- energy efficiency

Fig. 7.16 Spectrum of ventilation solutions.

approach may be used in deeper plan buildings, with natural ventilation at the perimeter zones, where there is access to openable windows, and mechanical ventilation used for the deeper plan zones.

Ventilation Design

There is a range of solutions for ventilation design, from natural to mechanical with various hybrid combinations (*see* Fig. 7.16).

All can benefit from a passive design approach. Natural ventilation will place constraints on building form and space planning, to allow ventilation air to flow throughout the building, with controllable openings that, in more extreme cases, include atria

and chimneys. For mechanical ventilation the focus is more on providing space for equipment and the vertical and horizontal distribution of ductwork including the access to outside fresh air and to exhaust stale air. Both natural and mechanical systems need to provide good quality indoor air in an energy-efficient way. This may favour mechanical ventilation when heating and cooling is needed, but may favour the option for natural ventilation when active heating or cooling is not needed, or in transitional spaces where comfort needs may be less stringent. Choosing a ventilation strategy must be done at an early design stage, as it impacts on many aspects of building design, and checks needs to be made on the design, during construction and on completion, to make sure the ventilation system has achieved its design performance in practice.

Chapter Eight

Active Systems

Introduction

The active parts of thermal design are those that deliver heating, cooling and ventilation. The term HVAC is used to describe a heating (H), ventilation (V) and air conditioning (AC) system. At its simplest it will involve heating and natural ventilation, extending in complexity to include cooling, mechanical ventilation, moisture control and air filtration. Active HVAC systems are based on engineering solutions, whereas passive design is more associated with architectural solutions. In general, we should maximize a building's potential to provide thermal comfort and ventilation through passive design. However, for most locations, at some time, we will still need to provide heating, cooling and ventilation using some form of active mechanical system, which will consume energy that is traditionally sourced from fossil fuels, but is now increasingly from renewable energy sources.

In our drive towards energy-efficient design, the main emphasis has been on passive design. Although heating, cooling and ventilation systems have become more energy efficient, their basic design has not changed significantly. We now need to be more innovative in how we achieve comfort in zero energy buildings, by providing appropriate and legible ways to generate, distribute and deliver thermal conditions, and, where possible, by reducing the size, complexity, space use and capital cost of HVAC equipment. HVAC systems should be responsive to more efficient design, recognizing the greater significance of internal heat gains from people, lighting, appliances and processes, and the interaction with climate. As the demand on heating and cooling over time becomes more variable, the control of HVAC systems becomes critical. Control can be automated to some extent, and can be smart, but not too smart that people do not understand it, and it must be able to be maintained and adjusted in response to changes in a building's use over time.

The delivery of heating and cooling to a space is central to a successful thermal design, and can be via surface or air systems (*see* Fig. 8.1). Surface systems may use wall or ceiling mounted panels (radiators), or the whole floor or ceiling, with fresh air ventilation

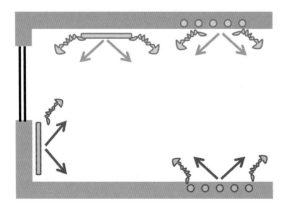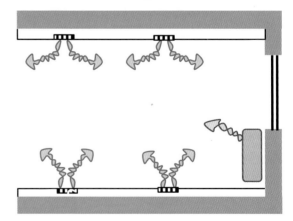

Fig. 8.1 Surface (left) and air (right) heat emitters and their delivery to the space. Surface systems will have a radiant and convective component of heat input, whereas air systems have just a convective heat input.

provided separately. Air systems pass air over heated or chilled coils, which may be located centrally, or locally in the space, with the ventilation often combined.

In the past, the design of HVAC systems has often been 'bolt-on', where the architect designs the building, after which the engineer adds the system. If lucky, sufficient space was provided for HVAC equipment

and the distribution of ducts and pipes. Zero energy design needs to be more integrative, especially as the boundary between architectural and engineering solutions becomes less clear. As energy demand is reduced, building integrated renewable energy systems and energy storage become more viable. Building skins can be used for collecting energy over the external façades, and for delivering heating, cooling and thermal storage on the inside (*see* Fig. 8.2). As HVAC systems and renewable energy generation become more integrated into the building design, a holistic 'whole system' approach is needed (*see* Fig. 8.3). The reduced energy demand and integrative approach should lead to lower cost HVAC equipment, with reduced space needs and better comfort conditions.

We should keep in mind that HVAC systems might be renewed or updated during a building's lifetime, so buildings need to be future-proofed to accommodate these changes. We also need to consider to what extent can the technology developed for new buildings be applied when retrofitting existing buildings.

Fig. 8.4 illustrates the main characteristics and elements of HVAC systems that will be dealt with in this chapter, beginning with the thermal loads on spaces, then moving on to the systems themselves (bounded by the dotted red box), and then a discussion on the overall energy performance and related carbon dioxide emissions.

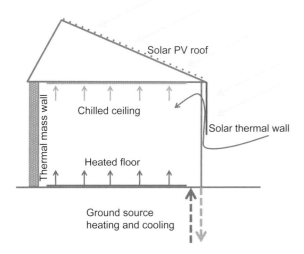

Fig. 8.2 An integrative architectural and engineering approach may involve delivering heat via the internal surfaces: the floor, ceiling, and even the walls. The external façade may collect renewable energy through solar PV and solar thermal. Solar thermal collectors may preheat ventilation air. The ground may be used to precool or preheat supply air, or it may be used as an energy source for heat pumps. Energy storage may be used for thermal (heating and cooling) and electrical power.

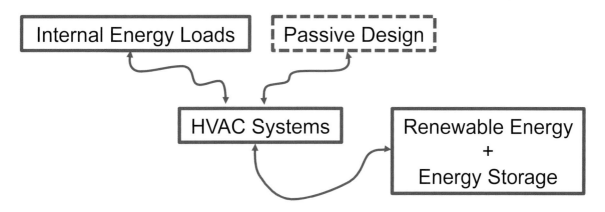

Fig. 8.3 A whole system approach integrates across architectural passive design elements, reducing the internal energy loads from lighting, appliances and control solar heat gains, and reducing HVAC loads that can then be powered from renewable energy generation and energy storage.

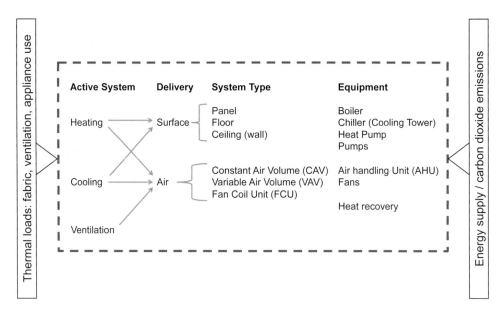

Fig. 8.4 Characteristics of HVAC systems.

Thermal Loads

Before we design an HVAC system, we need to know the thermal loads on the building, taking account of the thermal performance of the fabric (dealt with in Chapter 6), the impact of climate (dealt with in Chapter 5), and the internal incidental heat gains from occupancy.

Incidental Heat Gains

The incidental heat gains from occupancy, people, appliances, lighting and processes may be useful when heating is needed, but increasingly they give rise to overheating and contribute to a cooling load, even in winter for some building types, such as offices and schools. The operation of lighting and appliances also uses electrical energy. If we can reduce these loads, we reduce both cooling energy, and lighting and appliance electricity use. As buildings become more energy efficient, the electrical energy used by lighting and appliances becomes a greater proportion of the overall energy use. Appliances, such as computers and white and brown goods, have become more efficient

with energy rating schemes. In particular, the use of LED lamps has resulted in greater overall lighting system efficiencies. However, there are anomalies in this trend, such as the load from TVs, which seem to have increased as they get smarter, and maybe the same for washing machines[8.1] (*see* Fig. 8.5). So it seems that some appliances are becoming more efficient, but as we get 'smarter', we use more energy. Also, the numbers of some appliances have increased, such as home computers. Many devices are not fully turned off, and left on standby, where they still consume energy. In the UK, electrical appliance loads lie outside the regulated loads dealt with in building regulations, and are set by industry through certification rating schemes, according to their energy efficiency.

Fig. 8.6 illustrates typical daily hour-by-hour domestic profiles of internal heat gains from people (around 80W per person), lighting and appliances[8.2]. The sum of these may peak at around 1kW, which is getting close to the design heat loss of a zero energy house. So, for much of the time the house can be heated by its internal heat gains, not forgetting the solar heat gains. Of course, in relation to occupancy and weather, every building is different, and for each building every day is different.

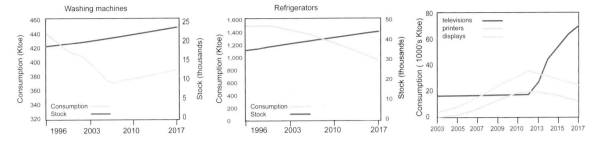

Fig. 8.5 Energy consumption of domestic electrical appliances, showing the recent changes in load for some alongside increases in stock[8.1].

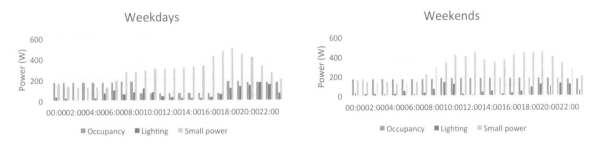

Fig. 8.6 Internal thermal loads from occupancy, lighting and small power for a three-bed house[8.2].

Typical annual electrical appliance loads for housing are around 3,000kWh/year for an efficient house. Using efficient appliances (A++ rating) may potentially reduce the overall appliance loads by around 30 per cent. Table 8.1 presents typical appliance loads based on UK references. However, this varies from country to country, with the UK being around average by global comparison (*see* Fig. 8.7)[8.3].

Table 8.1 Typical UK annual appliance loads (various sources).

	Power rating (W)	**Hours use per day**	**Energy consumed per year (kWh/year)**
Laptop	50	4	73
PC	100	4	146
Broadband router	7–10	24	88
TV	50–170	8	146–496
iPhone charger	6	5	11
iPad charger	12	5	22
Gaming	79–127	4	115–185
Toaster	1200	36.5 hours per year	44
Fan-assisted oven	2500	1	913

(continued)

	Power rating (W)	Hours use per day	Energy consumed per year (kWh/year)
Microwave	800	91 hours per year	73
Kettle	2500	91 hours per year	228
Fridge-freezer	31	24	270
Freezer	22	24	190
Washing machine	600–1000	220 cycles per year	190
Tumble dryer	1300–2300	220 cycles per year	396
Dishwasher	1050–1500		
Iron	2400	2 hours per week	249
Vacuum cleaner	900	1 hour per week	47
Extractor fan	5–36		
Halogen lamp	40	3	44
CFL bulb	11	3	12
LED bulb	5	3	5
Immersion heater	3000		

Fig. 8.7 Global values of domestic appliance loads (kWh/year per house)[8.3].

- below 1000
- 1000 to 2000
- 2000 to 3000
- 3000 to 6000
- above 6000
- no data

Heating and Cooling Demand

Internal heat gains may be enough to heat the space at certain times, and this is especially the case for housing, offices and schools, where even in winter, after an initial warm-up period in the morning, the internal occupancy loads may be greater than the heating demand of the space, and we may need cooling. Fig. 8.8 illustrates the impact of solar gains on the heating and temperature performance of a house fitted with a sunspace. When the sun shines, we observe that the sunspace warms up to over 31°C, when the external air is around 7°C. The heated conservatory and other incidental heat gains raise the indoor temperatures, and during the period of sunshine, the heating system is not operating.

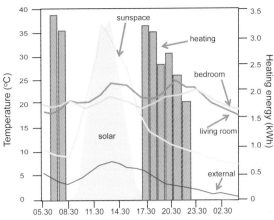

Fig. 8.8 The impact of solar heat gains on heating system operation for a house with a sunspace.

(a)

Internal heat gains (W/m²)		
	Current	Efficient
Internal gain from people (~12m²/person)	6.0	6.0
Small power	10.9	4.9
Lighting	12.0	7.0
Total	**28.9**	**18.0**
For a 6m deep office	173.4W	108W

(b)

Internal heat gains 18 x 6 = 108W   Fabric heat loss = 48W

Fig. 8.9 (a) Typical office internal heat loads for standard and efficient appliances; (b) diagram of heat gains and heat losses.

The peak heat loss in winter of a 6m deep office, with one external wall with glazing, might be typically less than half the internal heat gains, and so cooling would be required even in winter (*see* Fig. 8.9).

Fig. 8.10 illustrates the performance of a school, considering heat gains to the space from occupancy, solar and the heating system. The daily profile illustrates the intermittent operation of the heating system, and the annual energy breakdown shows that only 17

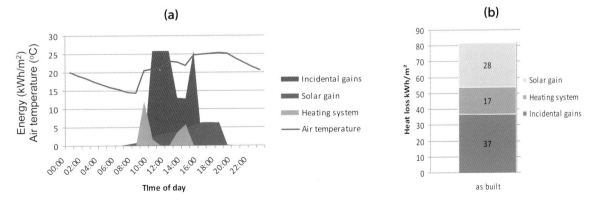

Fig. 8.10 Illustration of solar and internal incidental heat gains: (a) daily profiles in a westerly facing classroom; (b) annual energy inputs that meet the heat loss.

per cent of the annual heating demand is delivered through the heating system. The main heating input is provided by incidental and solar gains, which at times may be excessive and lead to high internal temperatures and overheating. The solar heat gains can be relatively large, depending on area and orientation of windows. As the building becomes more thermally efficient, the intermittent nature of HVAC systems and the risk of overheating becomes more of an issue. North-lit spaces with insulated glazing systems often provide a more appropriate solution for some building types than a bias for south-facing windows.

HVAC Systems

Local Systems

HVAC systems can be referred to as local when the conversion of fuel for heating or cooling is near to the point of use. Coal or wood may be burnt in an open fire or stove, and the products of combustion taken away through purpose-made chimneys. Local gas or electric fires are common, in addition to a central heating system, or to use when whole house heating is not needed. A local heater provides a focal point in the room, and somewhere one can go to warm up quickly. Electric 'storage' heaters can be charged at night when electricity cost is lower. Unit air conditioning 'split' systems are popular in warmer climates, especially in high-rise apartments (*see* Fig. 8.11), although they may be inefficient and an eyesore. They use heat pump technology to move heat from inside to the outside. Local systems are generally only switched on when needed, whereas central systems may operate for the whole building, even though some spaces may be unoccupied. This may provide an energy-efficient solution for some applications.

Central Systems

Central systems use water or air, through pipes or ducts, to distribute heating and cooling around a building,

Fig. 8.11 Local air-conditioning units on a dense urban residential building in Hong Kong. (Photo: Prof. Jianxiang Huang, University of Hong Kong)

from one or more plant rooms. They have common elements of generation, distribution and delivery, whether for a domestic central heating system, or a fully air-conditioned commercial building (*see* Fig. 8.12).

i. Generation: The fluid used for heat transfer, usually air or water, has to be heated or cooled centrally, by a boiler or chiller respectively. For an air system, the provision for fresh supply air and exhaust air will need access to the outside. The chiller will also need to exhaust heat to the outside, using a cooling tower to external air, or to a water or ground heat sink. Flues are needed to exhaust products of combustion from gas, oil, coal or biomass boilers, or electricity may be used to supply heat, using heat pump technology.

ii. Distribution: An air-handling unit (AHU) heats or cools air, using heating or cooling coils, and a fan distributes the air through ducts around the building. The air may also be humidified or dehumidified, and filtered. Another AHU will be needed to extract air. Heated or cooled

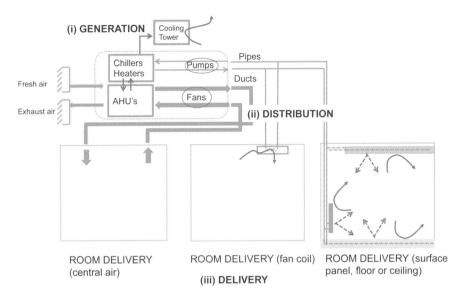

(i) GENERATION

Cooling Tower

Chillers Heaters

Pumps

Pipes

Ducts

Fresh air

AHU's

Fans

Exhaust air

(ii) DISTRIBUTION

ROOM DELIVERY (central air)

ROOM DELIVERY (fan coil)

ROOM DELIVERY (surface panel, floor or ceiling)

(iii) DELIVERY

water is pumped from the chiller or boiler to the AHU, or directly around the building, for a surface heat delivery system. Water can carry some 3,306 times the amount of heat than air per unit volume (*see* page 163), therefore pipes are considerably smaller than ducts for distributing the same amount of heat.

iii. Delivery: For an air system, heated or cooled air is blown into a space through ceiling or floor diffusers. A water system uses heated or cooled surfaces on the wall, ceiling or floor. Heat is then delivered to the point of use in the space by convection, radiation, or a combination of both.

HVAC systems have space requirements, which impacts on the building design. Major equipment, such as boilers, chillers and AHUs, need plant rooms with connection to the outside. Larger developments, such as hospitals, may have a separate 'energy centre' to locate some of this equipment, although there will be thermal losses and increased fan and pump loads if plant rooms are remote from the spaces they service. Distribution ducts and pipes need vertical and horizontal space. Ducts may be very large, where large volumes of air are needed, such as in concert halls. Air and surface delivery devices will take up space in ceilings, floors, or along wall surfaces.

Surface Systems

Surface systems can be used to heat or cool a space. They will have a radiant convective split, depending on surface temperature and whether they are ceiling, floor or wall mounted (*see* Fig. 8.13). For example, a heated floor would have a far greater convective output than a heated ceiling.

Central Heating Radiator System

Wet radiator central heating systems have been a standard method of heating buildings for some time. Although mainly associated with housing, they have been common in other building types, of domestic scale and larger, such as schools, libraries, and offices. In larger building types, they have generally been phased out in preference to air systems, but in housing, up to now, they are still the preferred choice. Even as energy demand has reduced with more efficient design, wet systems have continued to hold favour. They are familiar and acceptable to householders, easy to maintain, and are relatively energy efficient. They have a central boiler, fuelled by gas if available, providing both space heating and domestic hot water. Heat is distributed through pipes to radiators, which deliver heat to the space with water

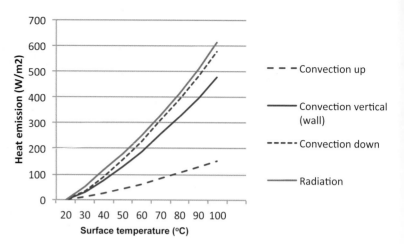

Fig. 8.13 Radiant convective split for surface heat emitters in relation to surface temperature for a space air temperature of 20°C.

temperatures around 70°C. Radiators are usually controlled using TRVs (thermostatically controlled radiator valves), which are often not operated properly, largely because they are not intuitive; people tend to turn them either fully open, with the perception the room will warm up quicker, or fully closed, to turn them off. Radiators take up wall space, which affects furniture layout, and high surface temperatures can be a hazard to the elderly and young. They can be reduced in size to match the lower heating demand of modern buildings, but there is still a relatively large heat loss through distribution pipework, which, although ending up in the building, is uncontrolled.

Modern systems are pressurized, often using a gas combi boiler to heat domestic water on demand (*see* Fig. 8.14). Modern boilers use condensing technology to extract the latent heat from the flue gases, producing efficiencies over 90 per cent. An oil-fired boiler can also be used, although oil needs storage and is more carbon intensive than gas. An electric heat pump is also an option, but the water temperature supply is generally limited to around 40°C, which may be suitable for low to zero energy buildings, but for existing buildings, radiator size would need to be increased to counter the lower water supply temperatures.

Underfloor Heating

Underfloor heating uses the floor surface as the heat source, and can be either a 'wet' system, pumping warm water through pipes in the floor, or a 'dry' system, with electric coils laid under the

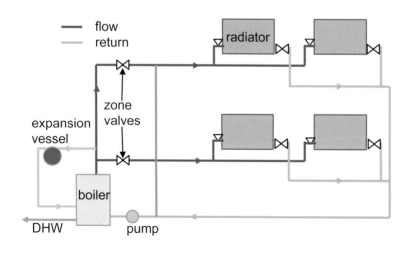

Fig. 8.14 Pressurized wet radiator system also providing domestic hot water.

Fig. 8.15 Wet and electric underfloor heating systems: (a) wet systems circulate warm water through plastic pipes usually embedded in a screed, which helps dissipate the heat; (b) electric systems can be installed directly under the floor finish. (Photos: Shutterstock)

floor surface (*see* Fig. 8.15). An electric underfloor system will be more expensive to run, compared to gas, however, they are about half the installation cost compared to a wet system; they may be more suited to individual smaller spaces, such as bathrooms.

A wet underfloor heating system operates at a lower distribution temperature, up to 55°C, compared to a conventional radiator system, at around 65°C to 70°C. The floor surface temperature should not be higher than 29°C, and preferably be between 23°C and 25°C for comfort. Heat is delivered to the space by radiation and convection (*see* Fig. 8.16), and a proportion of the heat is lost to the slab, so the pipes should have a layer of thermal insulation below them (*see* Fig. 8.15a). The system can also be used for cooling; floor surface temperatures should not be below 19°C, otherwise they may give rise to discomfort and condensation.

For low to zero energy buildings, heated floor temperatures may only be a few degrees above air temperature, at around 23°C. As space temperatures rise, the heat output from the floor will automatically reduce; a temperature difference is needed for heat transfer to take place from the floor surface to the space, so the system self-regulates. The distribution water temperature will typically be 30°C to 40°C, so they are well matched to ground or air source heat pumps, which are more efficient when supplying lower temperatures. Underfloor systems do not take up wall space and therefore allow greater flexibility in room layout. For housing, an underfloor system

Fig. 8.16 Schematic performance of a wet underfloor heating system, delivering typically around 12W/m² by convection and 15W/m² by radiation, for a floor temperature of 24°C.

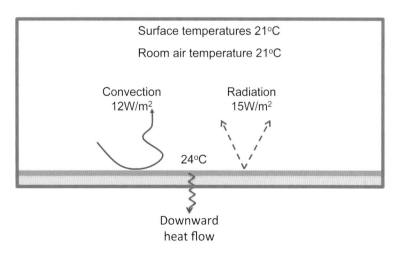

Surface temperatures 21°C

Room air temperature 21°C

Convection
12W/m²

Radiation
15W/m²

24°C

Downward
heat flow

may be combined with a radiator system, typically using underfloor heating on the ground floor and radiators upstairs. The pump energy for water distribution for a house is around 200kWh per year, similar to a wet central heating system.

Ceiling Surface Systems

Ceiling surface systems have become widespread in Europe, especially for offices. They can be used for heating or cooling, although they are probably most suited for cooling, as the ceiling is in direct contact with the warmer layer of air at high level. They can be passive or active. A truly passive system will simply use the thermal mass of an exposed concrete ceiling to absorb heat during peak times in the day. However, it will need to get rid of the heat, generally through night-time ventilation. Active systems extract heat, generally using water. A typical chilled ceiling system has water pipes placed some 10cm into the exposed concrete ceiling, and will extract around 25 to 35W/m² of heat from the space. A chilled panel system is attached to the ceiling and supplied with chilled water by a piped system. It will generally have a cooler surface temperature and typically extract up to 60 to 80W/m² of heat from the space. In cooling mode, systems are supplied with chilled water, typically between 14°C and 18°C, with the return temperature around 2°C to 4°C higher. If used for heating, the supply water temperature is typically 35°C to 40°C. Both chilled ceiling and chilled panel systems use radiant and convective heat transfer (*see* Fig. 8.17).

Fig. 8.18 illustrates the performance of a chilled ceiling over two warm summer days. The ceiling temperature is relatively cool at around 20°C to 21°C compared to the air temperature, which peaks at around 25°C. The heat flux into the ceiling peaks at around 34W/m². Air temperatures are more varied,

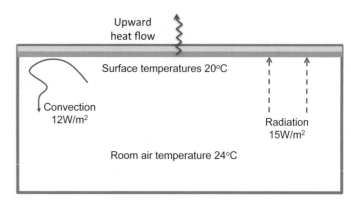

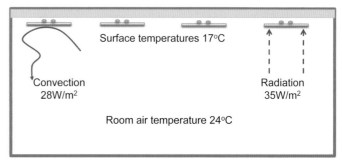

Fig. 8.17 Typical cooling performances for a chilled ceiling and chilled panel system.

but generally produce better comfort compared to a rigidly controlled all-air system.

A chilled ceiling system will generally cover the whole ceiling, whereas chilled panels might cover an appropriate percentage of the ceiling area (*see* Fig. 8.19). Other systems include passive and active chilled beams (*see* Fig. 8.20), which would be located at regular intervals along the ceiling to provide uniform cooling. Passive chilled beams allow warm air at the top of the room to be cooled by direct contact with chilled pipes, and then fall back down to the occupied zone through buoyancy forces; they provide cooling up to 350 to 475W/m² of exposed area. Active chilled beams include a primary air induction supply to enhance and control the air passing across the chilled pipes; they provide cooling up to 700 to 1,250W/m².

Chilled surface cooling decouples the main cooling load from the ventilation, which is provided separately. The ventilation is then primarily designed to provide air for occupants, and not combined with delivering

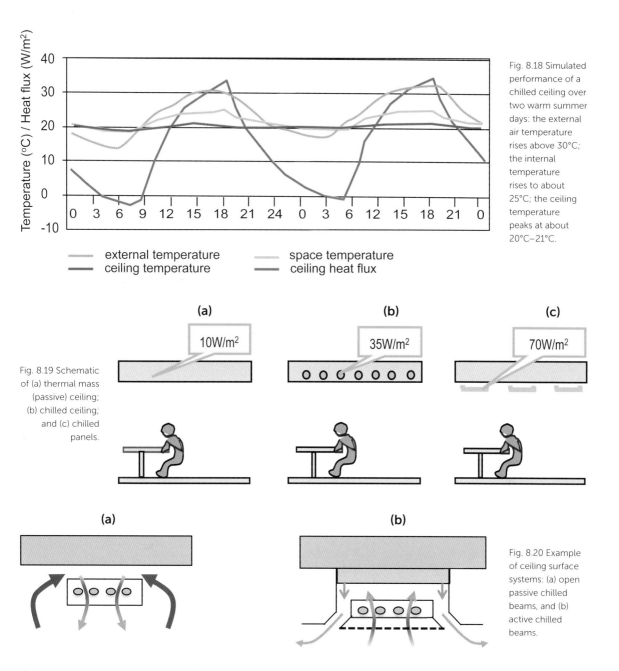

Fig. 8.18 Simulated performance of a chilled ceiling over two warm summer days: the external air temperature rises above 30°C; the internal temperature rises to about 25°C; the ceiling temperature peaks at about 20°C–21°C.

external temperature
ceiling temperature
space temperature
ceiling heat flux

Fig. 8.19 Schematic of (a) thermal mass (passive) ceiling; (b) chilled ceiling; and (c) chilled panels.

(a) 10W/m² (b) 35W/m² (c) 70W/m²

Fig. 8.20 Example of ceiling surface systems: (a) open passive chilled beams, and (b) active chilled beams.

(a) (b)

the main cooling load. The ventilation rate for an office is around 1.5 to 2ac/h, compared to 5 or 6ac/h needed to provide the total space cooling by using an all-air system. Ventilation may still contribute to space cooling by some 10W/m² (with an 18°C supply temperature). Ventilation ducts will be proportionally smaller, which will reduce distribution space and floor-to-floor heights. For high-rise buildings, extra floors may be allowed within planning permission. There is also no need to recirculate air, as all the exhaust air will be regarded as stale, and so the supply air will be 100 per cent fresh air. Chilled surface cooling has a higher radiant component compared to wholly convective all-air systems, and is generally more comfortable. The water supply temperatures are relatively high, typically 14°C to 18°C, compared to the 7°C or

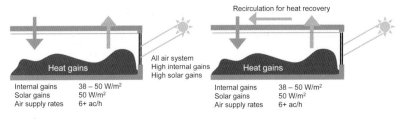

Recirculation for heat recovery

All air system
High internal gains
High solar gains

Internal gains	38 – 50 W/m^2
Solar gains	50 W/m^2
Air supply rates	6+ ac/h

Internal gains	38 – 50 W/m^2
Solar gains	50 W/m^2
Air supply rates	6+ ac/h

From all air to surface cooling

- Air supply only for fresh air ventilation (provides around 10W/m^2 cooling
- Reduced internal gains
- Reduced solar gains

Surface cooling systems with increasing heat gains

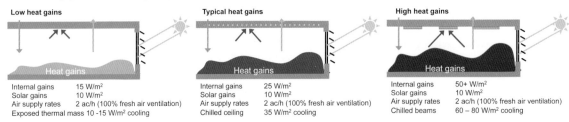

Low heat gains

Internal gains	15 W/m^2
Solar gains	10 W/m^2
Air supply rates	2 ac/h (100% fresh air ventilation)
Exposed thermal mass	10 -15 W/m^2 cooling

Typical heat gains

Internal gains	25 W/m^2
Solar gains	10 W/m^2
Air supply rates	2 ac/h (100% fresh air ventilation)
Chilled ceiling	35 W/m^2 cooling

High heat gains

Internal gains	50+ W/m^2
Solar gains	10 W/m^2
Air supply rates	2 ac/h (100% fresh air ventilation)
Chilled beams	60 – 80 W/m^2 cooling

8°C water supplied to an all-air system's AHU, so the chiller will typically be 20 per cent more efficient.

Chilled surface systems are often combined with 'smart façades', which control solar radiation heat gains and glare, and allow a greater use of space, avoiding no-go areas next to windows caused by excessive solar radiation heat and glare. Fig. 8.21 illustrates the shift from a standard all-air approach to a chilled surface approach for office environments.

Surface systems provide an efficient and effective means of conditioning a space, especially when the cooling is the dominant load. A potential disbenefit of surface cooling is the risk of condensation, especially for the lower surface temperature chilled panels, but probably no different to the localized risk around diffusers in all-air systems. However, the humidity of the supply air can be controlled, and any air leakage from outside air will be minimized by using a high-quality 'smart façade'.

Air Systems

Air systems provide heating and cooling through the supply of conditioned air to a space. In its simplest

form, it can be a fan coil unit to which heated or chilled water is supplied. Or, in a more complex form, it can be a central air system, distributing air through ducts around the building. In cooling mode, different air supply temperatures and flow rates will exhaust different amounts of heat gains from the space (see Fig. 8.22). For a high heat gain space, large amounts of supply air are needed, often at low temperature, so air supply devices cannot deliver air directly to the occupied zone. Air is typically delivered at high level and mixed with air in the space, before arriving in the occupied zone; in which case, air extract grilles need to be located to avoid direct short-circuiting of the supply air.

Fan Coil System

Fan coil units (see Fig. 8.23) are often used in hotels, offices and shops. They are supplied with heated or chilled water from a central plant, and can be ceiling, wall or floor mounted. Air is drawn from the space, often through light fittings for ceiling systems, directly heated or cooled by passing it through a heated or cooled coil, and blown back into the space. A two-pipe fan coil unit is supplied with either cold or hot water depending on the demand for cooling

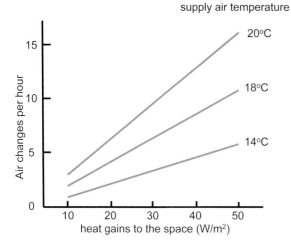

Fig. 8.22 Relationship of air supply rates with internal heat gains (including solar gains) and delivery air temperature.

or heating. Four-pipe fan coil units are supplied with both hot and cold water, allowing heating and cooling of different spaces at the same time, or some systems may have an electric heater. Water supply temperatures may be typically 35°C to 40°C for heating and around 14°C for cooling. In cooling mode, moisture may be condensed out of the air, so a condensate tray and draining is needed.

The ventilation air may be supplied separately to the space or mixed with the conditioned air in the fan coil unit. The stale air will be exhausted separately, via the ceiling void or through the toilet extract. Due to their simplicity, fan coil units are generally low cost. The ventilation system associated with a fan coil system will generally be similar to that of a central air system, and sized to meet the ventilation requirements.

Central Air System

A central air system supplies conditioned air from a central plant room to the spaces it serves. There may be one or more plant rooms, depending on the building size, type and the different spaces served. An AHU conditions the supply air (see Fig. 8.24), and a fan blows air through filters, heating and cooling coils, and humidity control, and delivers air to the building through ductwork. A return fan and its ductwork returns the exhaust air. Often, there will be heat recovery between the exhaust and supply air. The AHU will be connected to heating (boiler) and cooling (chiller) equipment. Central air systems may use a constant or variable volume approach.

Constant Air Volume (CAV) is based on air supplied to spaces at a constant volume, with its temperature varied in response to the space's cooling or heating needs. As the load reduces, the supply air temperature is adjusted, but the fan speed remains

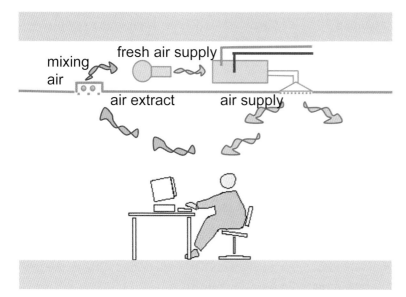

Fig. 8.23 Fan coil unit.

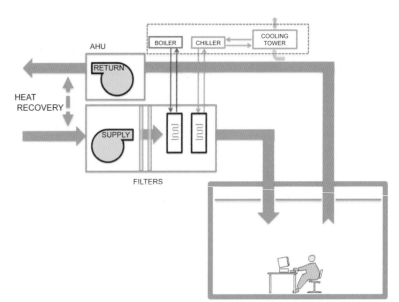

Fig. 8.24 Typical central air system schematic.

constant; this is not energy efficient. If multiple rooms are served, the supply air is cooled to meet the needs of the highest demand zone, and other zones may be overcooled, unless the air is reheated in the room supply units. If the heating and cooling loads are low, as for an energy-efficient building, the ventilation air may provide the majority of the heating and cooling requirement, and the system will be sized on ventilation needs alone. Additional heating and cooling may be provided separately through chilled or heated surfaces. So, CAV combined with a chilled surface system can provide an energy efficient solution.

Variable Air Volume (VAV) is based on the volume of air being controlled in response to the cooling load, while the air supply temperature is kept constant. As the cooling load reduces, the volume of air also reduces, until the minimum air supply for ventilation is reached, after which the supply air temperature may be increased. The variation of fan speed to match the load is where the main energy efficiency gain occurs.

Room Air Delivery

Air can be delivered to a space at high level or low level. The temperature and volume flow rate of the supply air will often determine the type of delivery system used. Many all-air systems are primarily designed for cooling, although they can be also used to heat. The supply air entering the space, which may be as low as 14°C in cooling mode, is mixed with the air in the space to provide satisfactory conditions by the time it reaches the occupied zone. Air is often 'jetted' across the ceiling so that it 'attaches' to the ceiling, termed the Coanda effect, and mixes with air in the space by entrainment and diffusion (*see* Fig. 8.25).

Low-level air delivery is referred to as displacement because it theoretically displaces the air in the space upwards to the extract. Displacement systems require an air delivery temperature greater than 18°C or they may cause cool draughts (*see* Fig. 8.26). Displacement systems may be compromised in practice by thermal convection loops in the space and the movement of people disrupting the displacement flow. They became popular in the early part of this century, often combined with raised floor systems and cable distribution. However, raised floor systems no longer seem to be in fashion, with cable management often replaced with wireless technology, and because ceiling systems are generally less expensive.

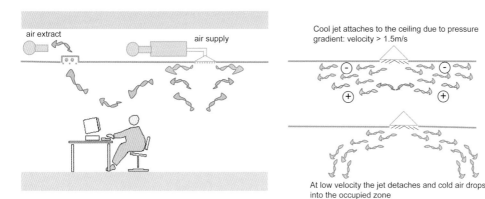

Fig. 8.25 High-level mixing system and the Coanda effect.

Cool jet attaches to the ceiling due to pressure gradient: velocity > 1.5m/s

At low velocity the jet detaches and cold air drops into the occupied zone

air extract

air supply

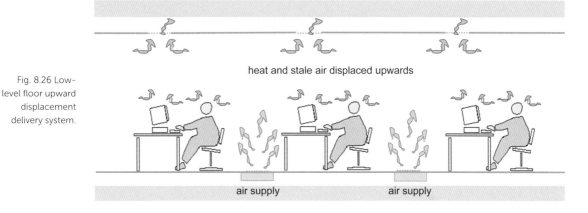

Fig. 8.26 Low-level floor upward displacement delivery system.

heat and stale air displaced upwards

air supply   air supply

Ventilation Effectiveness

The term ventilation effectiveness is used to describe the fraction of fresh air delivered to the space that reaches the occupied zone, which should ideally be 100 per cent. However, if air 'short-circuits' between supply and extract, it could be reduced to as low as 50 per cent.

Ventilation effectiveness depends on the temperature conditions and the location of air supply and extract devices (*see* Fig. 8.27). For ceiling delivery, the warmer the supply air in relation to the room air temperature, the lower the ventilation efficiency, because buoyancy will encourage the air to stay at high level and short-circuit to the extract. For displacement ventilation at low supply air temperatures, the effectiveness can exceed 100 per cent, as the concentration of pollutant will be lower in the occupied zone than at the exhaust, due to the movement of pollutants upwards.

Ventilation effectiveness can be defined for a specific pollutant as its mean concentration throughout the space in relation to its concentration at the extract.

$$\text{Ventilation effectiveness } E = \frac{(C_e - C_s)}{(C_o - C_s)} \times 100$$

Where:

E is the ventilation effectiveness

C_e is the concentration of pollutant in the extract

C_s is the concentration of pollutant in the supply

C_o is the concentration of pollutant in the occupant zone

If there is a significant level of the pollutant in the supply air, then this should be subtracted from the internal and extract concentration levels. If there is complete mixing of air and pollutants, the ventilation effectiveness is 100 per cent. Metabolic carbon

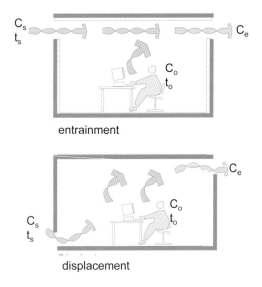

entrainment

displacement

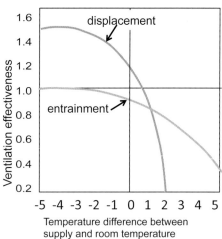

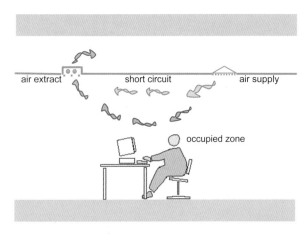

air extract   short circuit   air supply

occupied zone

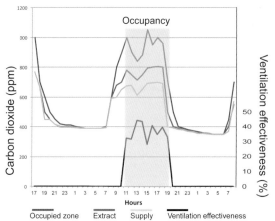

Fig. 8.28 CO_2 measurements used to estimate ventilation effectiveness. The CO_2 levels in the extract are much higher than in the occupied zone, implying short-circuiting of fresh air from supply to extract, with a low ventilation effectiveness of around 40 per cent during occupancy.

dioxide can be used to estimate ventilation effectiveness over time, where concentration is measured in parts per million (ppm). If the occupied zone carbon dioxide level is significantly higher than at the extract (*see* Fig. 8.28), it implies a level of short circuit of the supply air directly to extract.

There may be short-circuiting of air in other parts of the ventilation system, such as poorly controlled dampers in AHUs, giving rise to more recirculation than needed (*see* Fig. 8.29(a)); there could be short-circuiting between the stale air exhaust and fresh air supply at the external louvres (*see* Fig. 8.29(b)).

Heating and Cooling Equipment

Air Distribution Equipment

An AHU is central to an air distribution system (*see* Fig. 8.30). It supplies and returns air around the

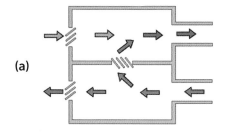

(a)

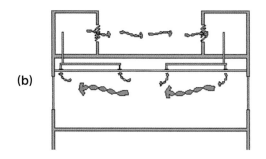

(b)

Fig. 8.29 (a) Poor damper control resulting in excessive recirculation; (b) Short-circuiting of exhaust air into the supply air stream, as shown within a rooftop courtyard. Initially the kitchen air was also exhausted into this courtyard but has since been ducted out (blue circle), possibly due to kitchen smells being spread throughout the building.

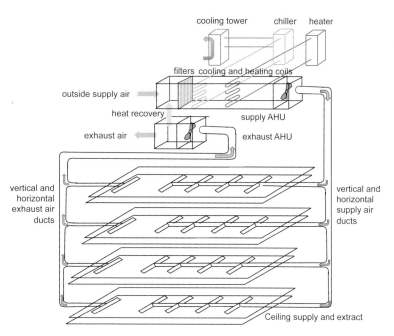

Fig. 8.30 Schematic of a typical central air distribution system for a four-floor building, showing main plant items and duct distribution.

building through vertical and horizontal ductwork, the dimensions of which will depend on the amount of air transported and its velocity. The AHU will connect to boilers and chillers, which need to dissipate heat to outside air, cooling towers, or to a ground or water source.

A typical AHU (*see* Fig. 8.31) draws in supply air from outside, passing it through coarse and fine filters, and then through cooling and heating coils, which are activated depending on what supply temperature is needed. A fan draws the air through the AHU and supplies it to the internal spaces; air is then extracted from the internal spaces using a return AHU. Dampers are located in supply and return AHUs to control the flow. In colder climates, frost protection is needed at the outside air inlet, which

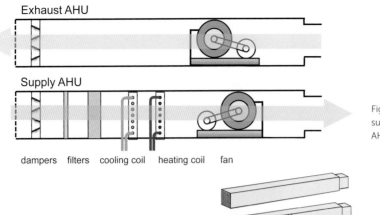

Exhaust AHU

Supply AHU

dampers   filters   cooling coil   heating coil   fan

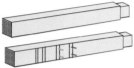

Fig. 8.31 Typical supply and return AHUs.

generally uses electric heating, or waste heat if it is available.

AHUs generally have two sets of filters. Primary filters will remove dust down to 4 to 5 microns, which protects people and the AHU fan, coils and ductwork. The more expensive secondary filters catch pollen, bacteria and fine dust. As filters get blocked their resistance to airflow increases, as does the fan power, so they need regular replacement. Filters are rated in terms of their performance with highly efficient MERV 13 filters able to remove a wide range of particulates, as well as larger amounts of bacteria and even some viruses.

The AHU cooling coil can also be used to dehumidify the air, with moisture condensing on the coils and then drained. This is a latent heat load that can be typically 20 per cent or more of the total thermal load. The air leaving the cooling coil may then need to be reheated using the heating coil; this is energy-intensive and so reheat is often not done. Buildings in hot humid climates may therefore have overcooled internal environments, with people wearing warmer clothes inside a building than outside! There is a limit to how much dehumidification can be done with cooling coils alone, so other means, such as desiccants may be used. Steam humidifiers can be used to increase supply air RH in dry climates, although this tends to be in buildings where specific moisture criteria apply, such as museums, hospitals and libraries.

Heat recovery may be used for energy efficiency, for both cooling and heating modes of operation:

- In its most basic form, a proportion of the exhaust air is mixed with the outside supply air (*see* Fig. 8.32(a)). The supply air will usually be much more than what is needed for fresh air ventilation, and up to 80 per cent of the return air may recycled. This may incur air quality problems, as mixing stale exhaust air with fresh air, although filtered, still results in a level of stale supply air, which is unsuitable for many applications, such as hospitals or other clean environments.

- Run-around coils provide heat recovery with complete separation of the supply air and the return air (*see* Fig. 8.32(b)). A fluid is heated or cooled in the return air stream and this thermal energy is transferred to the supply air stream. There is the added benefit that the return and supply AHUs do not have to be adjacent to each other.

- A thermal wheel heat recovery system has elements that are heated or cooled in the return air stream, transferring heating or cooling to the supply air stream as the wheel revolves (*see* Fig. 8.32(c)). There may be a small amount of leakage between the return and supply air streams, which makes it unsuitable for clean environments.

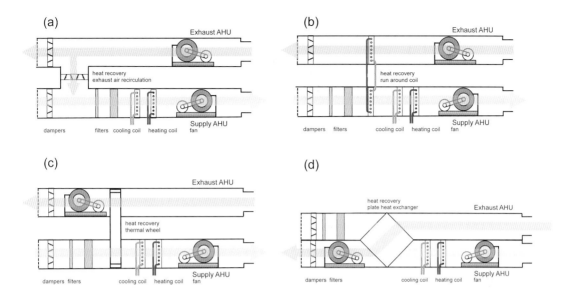

Fig. 8.32 AHU with heat recovery: (a) direct recirculation of exhaust air; (b) run-around coil; (c) thermal wheel; and (d) plate heat exchanger.

- A plate heat exchanger retains separation between supply and return air streams (*see* Fig. 8.32 (d)).

All methods of heat exchange incur an energy penalty, through motors and pumps, and a pressure drop across the device, increasing the AHU fan power. Heat recovery systems have a range of efficiencies (*see* Table 8.2), and only become cost-effective when the cost savings associated with the use of the recovered heat outweigh the [initial] cost

Table 8.2 Heat recovery system efficiencies.

System type	Efficiency (%)
Run-around coil	50–70
Thermal wheel	65–80 (up to 85% with enthalpy wheels that recovery sensible and latent heat)
Plate	60–75

Note: Heat recovery systems produce a pressure increase of 200–500Pa, which could increase fan power by up to 50%.

of the heat recovery equipment and any increase in its running costs.

Many building applications use rooftop AHUs that combine the exhaust and supply air, and the heating and cooling equipment, as a self-contained single unit, often incorporating a reverse cycle heat pump, which can be used to heat or cool (*see* Fig. 8.33).

To improve energy efficiency, an air system may be run in 100 per cent recirculation mode, normally outside of occupancy when no fresh air is required. This needs a connection between exhaust and supply air ducts. Free cooling may operate with 100 per cent fresh air, when outside air conditions are relatively cool and the maximum flow of outside air is used without any cooling added by the AHU.

Heat Pumps

Heat pumps are used for heating and cooling, by transferring the heat between inside spaces to outside air, or to a ground or water source, and vice versa. The amount of heat transferred is greater than the energy needed to power the heat pump. A heat pump's operation is based on the properties of refrigerants, which

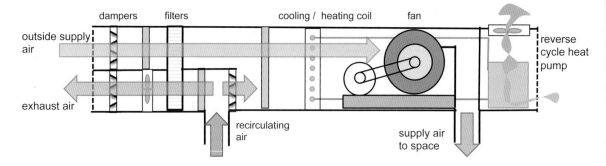

Fig. 8.33 Schematic showing a typical rooftop AHU.

boil at relatively low temperatures. Commonly used refrigerants R134a and R410A boil at −26.3°C and −48.5°C respectively, at atmospheric pressure. As the refrigerant boils (in the evaporator) it changes from liquid to gas, absorbing heat from the surrounding air or liquid, and then cooling it. When a refrigerant is compressed (in the compressor), its pressure increases and it changes from a gas to a liquid, heating the surrounding air or liquid. Think of the surface of

an aerosol can cooled through evaporation, and the hot surface of a bicycle pump when operating under compression. The cycle of compression and expansion transfers heat, from one medium to another. Fig. 8.34 illustrates the operation cycle of an air-to-air heat pump used for cooling. A heat pump can also transfer heat between different sources: air and water, air and ground, and ground and water. A heat pump can be simply reversed to provide heating.

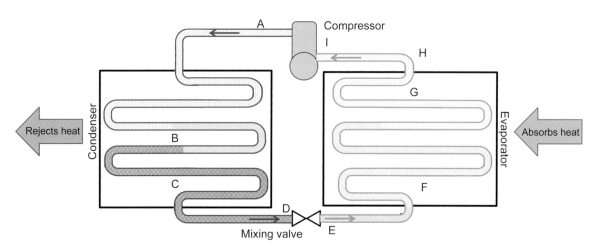

A. Refrigerant vapour compressed and becomes high pressure super heated* vapour. Begins to reject sensible heat, the temperature reduces and the vapour enters condenser.
B. Midway through the condenser the vapour begins to condense into a liquid, rejecting latent heat due to change of state. The refrigerant temperature remains constant.
C. Around 90% of the way through the condenser all the vapour is changed to liquid and the refrigerant begins to reject sensible heat, and subcools.
D. The refrigerant then enters the mixing valve as a 100% super cooled** liquid.

*Super-heated occurs when the refrigerant is above its boiling point
**Super-cooling is when the refrigerant is below its bolling point

E. As the refrigerant passes through the mixing valve its pressure is reduced and it flashes to a mix of 75% liquid 25% vapour.
F. It starts to boil and enters the evaporator where it continues to boil, absorbing latent heat.
G. Around 90% of the way through the evaporator all the liquid has boiled to a vapour.
H. The refrigerant leaves the evaporator as a 100% vapour, and travels under suction to the compressor. It absorbs sensible heat and becomes super-heated. This insures that the refrigerant is 100% vapour before it enters the compressor, otherwise it could cause damage.
I. The refrigerant absorbs heat from the compressor and is drawn into the piston chamber and compressed adding the heat of compression; and the cycle continues.

Fig. 8.34 Operation of a heat pump in cooling mode.

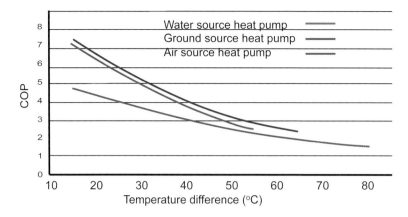

Fig. 8.35 Variation of COP with temperature difference between source and use.[8.6]

A heat pump's efficiency is measured by its coefficient of performance (COP), which is the heat delivered divided by its electricity consumption for the compressor, plus any fan and pump loads. Values of COP are typically in the range 3 to 6; so for every 1kWh of electricity consumed, 3 to 6kWh is delivered as heating or cooling. The heat pump is only a means of transferring heat energy from one location to another. Even if the outside air is cold, it will still contain heat. A simplistic analogy might be a truck load of coal being transferred from the coal mine to the user. The energy content of the coal is far greater than the fuel used to drive the truck. Likewise, the energy used to operate the heat pump (to drive the compressor) is less than the heat transferred. A heat pump is therefore a very efficient means of heating and cooling buildings, especially when it can be operated with energy from renewable energy generation.

The heat pump COP varies with the temperature of the heat source, and the characteristics of the heat pump (see Fig. 8.35)[8.6]. In heating mode, the COP will be higher if the heat gained from compressor heat loss is captured. The Seasonal COP (SCOP) is the average value over time under variable operating conditions, which will generally be lower than the COP, depending on source temperature (see Fig. 8.36).

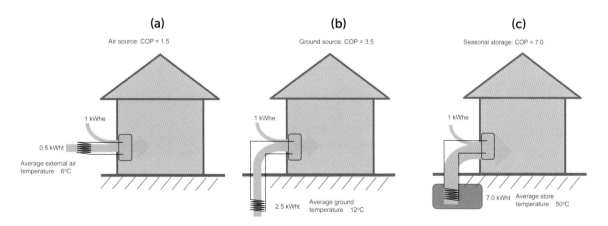

Fig. 8.36 Heat pumps with air, ground and heat storage connections: (a) for an air source heat pump, where the average heating season external air temperature is around 5°C (UK), the SCOP is around 1.5; (b) for ground source heat pumps, where the seasonal average ground temperature is around 11°C–12°C (UK), the COP is around 3.5; and (c) for a water storage medium of, say, 50°C, the COP would be around 8.0.

Fig. 8.37 Schematic operation of a vapour compression chiller.

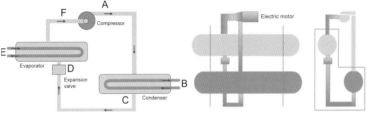

An electric motor operates the compressor, which transforms the refrigerant into a high pressure vapour (A). As this travels through the condenser it changes state to a high pressure liquid giving off heat which is extracted to outside the system (B). The refrigerant loses enthalpy (C). It passes through an expansion valve, which reduces its pressure (D), and as the refrigerant passes through the evaporator it boils absorbing heat from the chilled water return from the AHU (E), which is cooled and supplied back to the AHU. Chilled water leaves the evaporator at 6°C which is supplied to the AHU and returns to the chiller at 12°C. The refrigerant boils and changes state to a low pressure liquid, which is drawn into the compressor (F), and the cycle repeats.

Compression Chillers

In large buildings, chillers are used to produce chilled water for cooling. They are based on heat pump technology, using either vapour compression or vapour absorption. Vapour compression is the most common type (*see* Fig. 8.37), comprising a compressor, a condenser, an expansion valve and an evaporator.

A chiller can be air-cooled or water-cooled (*see* Fig. 8.38). A water-cooled chiller is more efficient and can deal with larger loads. They are open systems and exchange sensible and latent heat. They have a longer life, but they need a supply of clean water. Water-cooled chillers are typically connected to rooftop cooling towers for rejecting heat into the environment. Air-cooled chillers are generally simpler, cost less, use less space, and require less maintenance, but they are less efficient, and because they are a closed system they only exchange sensible heat. Air-cooled condensers tend to be used more on smaller packaged systems.

There is a range of these chiller types and their COPs vary from around 2.5 to 7, which relates to the type of compressor used. The main types of compressor are listed in Table 8.3.

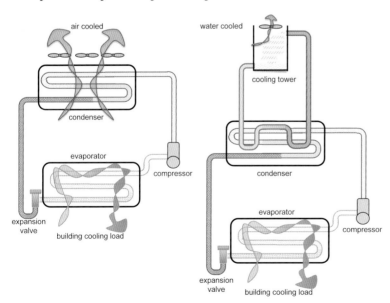

Fig. 8.38 Air and water-cooled chillers.

Table 8.3 *Types of chiller compressor.*

Type of compressor	Size	COP	Cooling	Application
Reciprocating	50–500kW 170–1700kW	4.2–5.5	Air or Water-cooled	• Older technology. • Less efficient and noisy, but reliable.
Scroll compressor	140–1400kW	3.2–4.86 4.45–6.2	Air-cooled Water-cooled	• Small to medium cooling loads. • Often in banks.
Rotary screw	70–600kW 250–2100kW	2.9–4.15 4.7–6.07	Air-cooled Water-cooled	• Small to medium cooling loads.
Centrifugal compressor	530–21000kW	5.8–7.1	Water-cooled	• Medium to large cooling loads. Most efficient of the large-capacity chillers.
Turbocor	210–5200kW	4.6–10.0	Air or water-cooled	• Latest technology. • Similar to centrifugal, but 2-stage. Very efficient. Variable speed, low maintenance.

Source: *Chiller Types and Application, Engineering Mindset.com*

Absorption Chillers

An absorption chiller uses heat as an energy source instead of an electric motor driving a compressor. A thermochemical process increases the pressure of the refrigerant from evaporation level to condensation level. Water is used as the refrigerant and combined with an absorbent, usually lithium bromide or ammonia, as outlined in Fig. 8.39. Absorption chillers can be direct-fired, using natural gas or fuel oil, or indirect-fired, using hot water or steam from a boiler, steam from a district heating system, or waste heat. Their COP is between 0.9 and 1.6, which is relatively low compared to vapour compression chillers, and they are most suitable when free waste heat is available.

Split Systems

Split systems are commonly used for cooling in residential buildings in warmer climates; often, but not exclusively, associated with high-rise apartment blocks in cities (*see* Fig. 8.40). There is an outdoor unit that houses the compressor, condenser coil and the expansion valve; and an indoor unit that contains the cooling coil, air filter and blower fan. The COP is typically 3.6, with a 1kW supply delivering 3.6kW of cooling. There is a multi-split system option, where more than one indoor unit is connected to a single outdoor unit. This can cool multiple rooms or have more than one fan unit for larger rooms. They can be noisy, generally with on and off cycling, running at full capacity when on.

Variable refrigerant flow (VRF) systems are similar to split systems, but have a variable motor speed, which varies the refrigerant flow. They are relatively quiet and energy efficient, and can be operated at the turndown ratio required to meet the capacity needed. For a two-pipe system, the zones within a building must be either all in cooling mode or all in heating mode. A three-pipe version can simultaneously heat and cool different zones.

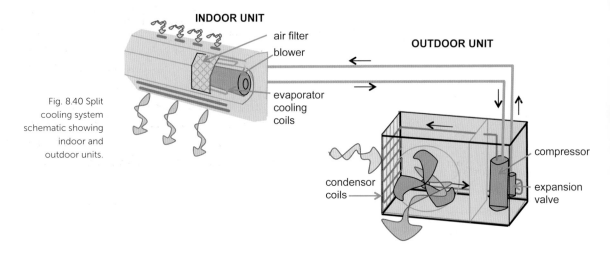

A. The generator provides heat to the mix of LB and water which is sprayed into the high pressure chamber.

B. The water boils leaving the heavier LB liquid at the bottom.

C. The water vapour is condensed by contact with the cooling coils of the condenses and is captured beneath.

D. The water then passes through an expansion valve and is sprayed onto the evaporator coil

E. The water vaporises at a temperature of 4.5°C. Any water that is not vaporised is collected and pumped back to the spray.

F. Chilled water enters at 12°C and is cooled to 6°C, as the water absorbs heat and boils (at 4.5°C).

G. The water vapour is attracted to the LB, which is sprayed into the absorber, and it is absorbed by the hydroscopic effect of LB. This produces an almost vacuum of 0.84Pa within the low pressure chamber.

H. The mixture of LB and water is collected at the bottom of the low pressure vessels and pumped via a heat exchanger to the high pressure cylinder.

I. The heat exchanger cools the LB. If it is too warm the reaction with water does not take place.

.... and the cycle repeats.

80°C

Hot water heat source

90°C

High pressure

A generator

B

water vapour

condenser

C

D

expansion valve

Low pressure

6°C

Chilled water

12°C

E

F evaporator

G

water vapour

absorber

H

I

chilled water from a cooling tower

Fig. 8.39 The operation of an absorption chiller. A mixture of 60 per cent lithium bromide (LB) and 40 per cent water is used. The system uses hot water as the generator; waste heat or solar heat is ideal.

INDOOR UNIT

air filter

blower

OUTDOOR UNIT

Fig. 8.40 Split cooling system schematic showing indoor and outdoor units.

evaporator cooling coils

compressor

condensor coils

expansion valve

Exhaust Air Heat Pumps

Mechanical ventilation heat recovery using a plate heat exchanger to transfer heat from exhaust air to the supply air can be combined with an exhaust air heat pump. This takes the remaining heat out of the exhaust air, after the heat exchanger, to heat the supply air to the space (*see* Fig. 8.41). Exhaust air heat pumps can also be used with underfloor heating systems, or to supply heat for domestic hot water systems. They are becoming a preferred option in the design of Passivhaus and zero energy buildings (*see* page 216), where the heating demand can be met with the ventilation supply air.

Boilers and Furnaces

Boilers produce hot water or steam, at low or high pressure. In the UK and Europe, boilers and wet

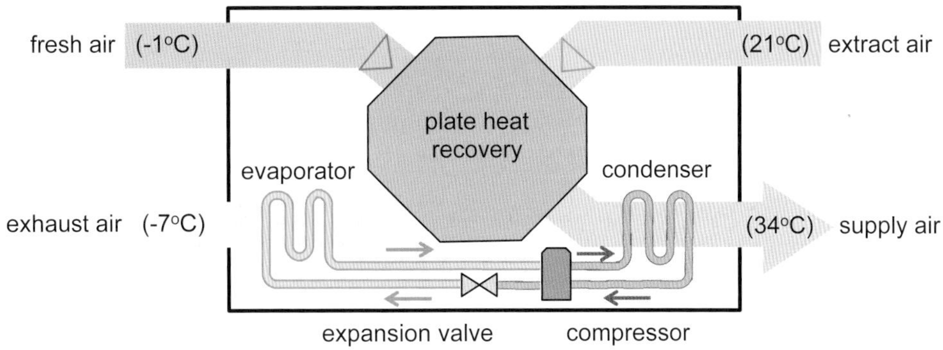

Fig. 8.41 Exhaust air heat pump showing typical temperatures for heating.

plate heat recovery

evaporator   condenser

exhaust air (-7°C)   (34°C) supply air

expansion valve   compressor

systems are favoured for domestic and non-domestic applications. Furnaces are more common in the United States for domestic installations. Both boilers and furnaces convert fuel to heat. In the past, the fuel was coal, oil, gas or electricity, with gas more recently being regarded as the less carbon intensive fuel. Biomass, from a sustainable timber source, may be regarded as low or zero carbon. Any exhaust products of combustion contain heat, which is an energy loss to the system. Condensing boilers are able to recover latent heat from the flue gases and therefore have a higher efficiency. At full-load operation, gas boilers are around 95 per cent efficient, but this may be reduced at part-load operation. In larger buildings, modular boilers maximize efficiency by sequencing a number of smaller boilers, so that the majority operate at full load. Boilers are also used to heat domestic hot water. Domestic combination (or combi) boilers heat hot water directly on demand, avoiding the need for water storage and reducing any storage cylinder standing heat losses. The efficiency of a gas combination boiler reduces (to around 84 per cent) when they are only used for heating domestic hot water, where no space heating is required.

Electric heat pumps are becoming more popular for heating, for domestic and non-domestic use, especially in low to zero energy buildings. Hybrid systems, which are a combination of an electric heat pump, coupled with oil or gas boilers, are now being tested. The heat pump operates in milder weather, when its COP is relatively high, but when heat pump's COP drops in colder weather, the system switches to oil

or gas. Such systems may be more appropriate for existing houses, which already have a gas or oil boiler. In new housing, with a low heat demand, a heat pump system alone should suffice.

Fans and Pumps

Fans and pumps are an integral part of air and water HVAC systems, driven by electric motors, which account for a major part of HVAC energy use. Many fans and pumps run continuously at full speed, with their output varied using throttling devices, such as vanes or valves, which is not energy efficient. For a given pressure in the system, fan and pump energy is related to the speed value cubed (see Fig. 8.42). A 20 per cent reduction in speed results in a 50 per cent

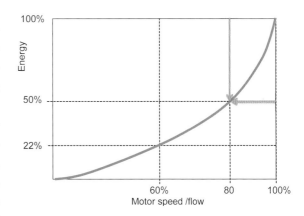

Fig. 8.42 Cube law for fan and pump energy in relation to motor speed as a percentage of full load, showing a 50 per cent reduction in energy for a 20 per cent reduction in speed.

reduction in energy. A variable speed drive fan therefore produces considerable energy savings. Modern efficient EC (electronically commutated) motors are efficient and can vary their speed, producing 30 to 60 per cent energy savings overall compared with traditional AC motors.

Energy savings can also be achieved by reducing the total pressure drop in the system, using low-pressure equipment and relatively larger ducts or pipes. Fan power is related to the total pressure drop in the system, including the AHU, the ductwork and room terminals. Table 8.4 presents performance values for poor, typical and good systems.

For a piped water system, the pressure drop is related to items of equipment, such as boilers, chillers and heat exchangers; the distribution system, such as pipes and valves; and the end devices, such as radiators, fan coils, and floor/ceiling, heating/cooling coils. Typical pressure drops in piped water systems are in the order of 300Pa/m, and water velocities range from less than 1m/s, for small domestic systems, to 3m/s for pipework of 50mm diameter or greater.

For HVAC systems, we refer to specific fan and pump powers, SFP and SPP respectively, which is the electrical power input related to the volume flow rate:

Table 8.4 Typical pressure loss, fan efficiency and SFP in an air system for poor, typical and good design[8.6].

Equipment	Poor	Typical	Good	Units
AHU				
Face velocity	2.5	2.0	1.5	m/s
Filter EU3 bag	80	70	50	Pa
Filter EU5 bag	140	115	75	Pa
Filter EU9 bag	190–250	160	110	Pa
Rotary heat exchanger	200–250	150	90–100	Pa
Heater battery	120	80	40	Pa
Cooling battery	140	100	60	Pa
Humidifier	60	40	20	Pa
Fan silencer	80–235	50	30	Pa
Total AHU	670	420	175	Pa
Air distribution				
Ductwork	340–490	200–230	100–115	Pa
Ductwork silencers	15	10	0	Pa
Plenum box	100	50	30	Pa
ATD (supply or exhaust)	70	50	20	Pa
Exhaust stack/jet	175	175	175	Pa
Total air distribution		285		Pa
Fan system efficiency	40%	50%	63%	
SFP	6	3	1.3	kW/m³/s

$$SFP = P_{ef}/V$$
$$SPP = P_{ep}/V$$

Where

V is the volume flow rate (m³/s)

P_{ef} and P_{ep} are the electrical power input (kW) to the fan and pump respectively

Typically, SFP may vary from 0.6kW/m³/s for an exhaust fan system, to 1kW/m³/s including heat recovery, to 1.5kW/m³/s for supply and exhaust fan systems without heat recovery, to 2.0kW/m³/s including heat recovery. Fan energy use may be some 17 per cent of total energy use for an office, rising to some 34 per cent for hospitals, and greater than 50 per cent for swimming pools and restaurants.

SPP may vary from 301kW/m³/s for a heating system, to 349kW/m³/s for a cooling system. This will be around 3.5 to 5 per cent of the total electricity use for most building types, but may rise to 6 per cent for specific buildings such as swimming pools. The SFP is considerably less than the SPP for equal amounts of energy. However, water can carry more energy per unit volume (3,306 times) than air. Therefore, fans tend to use more energy than pumps to deliver the same amount of heat.

The data below compares the heat carrying capacities of water and air.

Specific heat capacity of water = 4,186J/kg.K
Specific heat capacity of air = 993J/kg.K
Density of water = 1,000kg/m³
Density of air = 1.275kg/m³
Volumetric heat capacities of water = 4,186,000J/m³.K

Volumetric heat capacities of air = 1,266J/m³.K
Therefore: 4,186,000 ÷ 1,266 = 3,306

Space for Services

Allowing sufficient space for services and their maintenance is an early design decision. Clearly there needs to be good communication between the architect and the engineer to optimize the architecture and engineering and provide an integrated solution. If not, there will be clashes, which will then need to be resolved, often during the latter design stages, or even in the construction phase. Table 8.5 shows typical plant areas for natural, mechanical and air-conditioned buildings.

The size of AHUs and their associated ductwork can be estimated if the volume air flow rate is known. The volume flow rate is related to the ventilation rate and the building volume, and any increase in volume of air due to cooling and heating demand. The velocity of the air passing through the AHU should not exceed 2m/s, and the velocity in other parts of the system should be kept as low as possible to reduce noise and fan power (*see* Table 8.6). The cross-sectional area of ducts (m²) can be calculated from their volume flow rate (m³/s) and air velocity (m/s) (*see* Fig. 8.43). Where air enters or leaves a system through louvres, its velocity should be less than 1.5m/s to avoid excessive noise. The air velocity will also need to be reduced as it nears the air diffusers, and to do this the diameter of the duct will need to be increased. Attenuation may be required to reduce the noise to acceptable levels, the main source being fan noise. Round steel ducts

Table 8.5 *Space for services for offices or non-specialist buildings: approximate space needs as a percentage of total floor area.*

Type of system	Heating	AHUs	Chillers	Total
Natural ventilation	1.5%	–	–	1.5%
Mechanical ventilation and heating	1.5%	2%	–	3.5%
Air conditioning	1.5%	4%	2%	7.5%

Table 8.6 Recommended maximum duct velocities for low-pressure systems (m/s).

Building type	Controlling factor				
	Noise reduction	Duct friction			
	Main ducts	Main ducts		Branch ducts	
		Supply	Return	Supply	Return
Housing	3.0	4.0	5.0	3.0	3.0
Apartments Hotel bedrooms Hospital wards	5.0	7.5	6.5	6.0	5.0
Offices	6.0	10.0	7.5	8.0	6.0
Theatres and auditoria	4.0	6.5	5.5	5.0	4.0
Restaurants Banks	7.5	10.0	7.5	8.0	6.0
Retail Cafeterias	9.0	10.0	7.5	8.0	6.0
Industrial	12.5	15.0	9.0	11.0	7.5

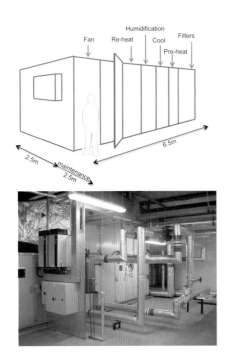

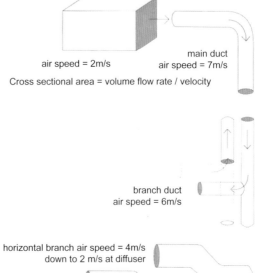

Humidification
Fan   Re-heat   Cool   Filters
Pre-heat

6.5m
2.5m
maintenance 2.5m

air speed = 2m/s

main duct
air speed = 7m/s

Cross sectional area = volume flow rate / velocity

branch duct
air speed = 6m/s

horizontal branch air speed = 4m/s
down to 2 m/s at diffuser

Fig. 8.43 Typical AHU and ductwork sizing, with velocities based on general office design.

Table 8.7 Typical values for volume flow, air speed and duct diameter for a 1,000m² office.

Operation mode	Volume flow		Speed	Main duct diameter*
	ac/h	m³/s	m/s	m
Ventilation	1.2	1.0	7	0.43
Cooling	5.9	4.9	7	0.94 (or 2 × 0.61)
Heating	0.3	0.25	7	0.11

Assumes a single main duct off the AHU. In practice this would typically be divided between two main ducts.

are more efficient than rectangular ducts, because the relative surface area to cross-sectional area is less, reducing friction losses.

The volume flow rates will be different for ventilation, heating and cooling, say, for a typical office design (*see* Table 8.7). Heating can, in general, be delivered within the fresh air ventilation supply (0.3ac/h for heating, compared to 1.2ac/h for ventilation); however, if cooling is delivered through the air system, much larger volume flow rates are needed (5.9ac/h), which requires larger ducts and/ or higher air speeds.

Other Building Types

So far we have considered HVAC systems targeted mainly at housing and offices. The type of HVAC system will vary with building type, its spatial form, and its occupancy density and hours of use. The spatial form will vary with the floor area, the space volume and its height, the number of floors and the amount of glazing. Many buildings will have a mix of spaces, such as retail malls, public buildings (galleries, libraries) and schools. Some buildings may include external and transitional spaces as part of their function.

School Classrooms

School classrooms have a high-density occupation over distinct time intervals. They have a high people heat gain and relatively high fresh air ventilation rates. Historically, school classrooms had high ceilings, which provided a large volume of air to dilute pollutants over the occupied period, while modern classrooms generally have lower ceilings. Natural ventilation in winter, drawing cold air directly from outside, may cause discomfort. A classroom of thirty pupils would require some 240l/s (30 × 8l/s) of fresh air, typically 3ac/h. Classrooms are therefore generally best served by mechanical ventilation with heat recovery in winter (*see* Fig. 8.44). In summer, windows may be opened if the outside air is clean and there are no noise issues; this would be a seasonal hybrid solution.

Carbon dioxide levels can be used to provide a measure of classroom air quality[8.7]. This should be less than 1,000ppm for mechanically ventilated classrooms, corresponding to a fresh air ventilation rate of 8l/s/person, and not exceed 1,500ppm for more than twenty consecutive minutes each day, corresponding to a ventilation rate of around 5l/s/person. For natural ventilation, the daily average concentration of carbon dioxide should be less than 1,200ppm, and not exceed 2,000ppm.

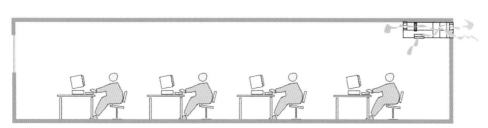

Fig. 8.44 A typical ventilation, heating and heat recovery system for a classroom.

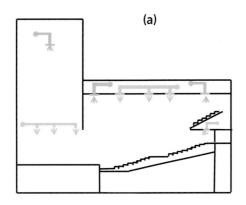
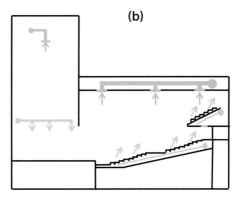

(a) **(b)**

Fig. 8.45 Air delivery to auditoria: (a) from above; (b) from below.

Auditoria

Auditoria typically have a high occupancy density for relatively short periods. Air can be delivered mechanically either from above or below (*see* Fig. 8.45). They are usually in cooling mode during a performance, exhausting heat gains from the audience and performance lighting. If cool air is delivered from above, swirl diffusers can be used to mix the air, otherwise it may fall directly on the audience due to negative buoyancy, and cause discomfort. Air may be introduced at low level, such as under the seat, and then extracted at high level. If there is a curtain, then the back of stage must also be conditioned such that when the curtain is opened there are similar conditions either side to avoid bulk buoyancy-induced air movement. Duct dimensions may be relatively large to deliver the large volume of air and to minimize noise.

Galleries

Galleries need to provide specific environmental conditions for works of art as well as for people. In particular they need good control of relative humidity, which is difficult to maintain due to the constant influx of people, causing both temperature and humidity to fluctuate. Even minor fluctuations in humidity can cause damage over time. The most frequent design condition is a relative humidity of between 45 and 55 per cent, although this may be relaxed at times to between 40 and 65 per cent, with air temperatures

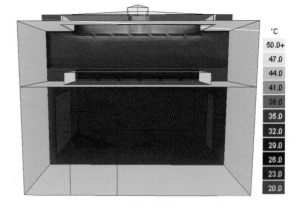

Fig. 8.46 Gallery air delivery and lighting: CFD simulation of spatial variation in temperatures. (Jones Kopistis)

maintained in the range 18°C to 26°C. Generally the speed of change in environmental conditions over a 24-hour period should be within 10 per cent for relative humidity, and within 4°C for air temperature. The air delivery system for new galleries typically introduces conditioned air at floor level and extracts at high level. The ceiling may include a mix of artificial and natural lighting designs, which may be integrated with the ventilation extract system, with solar gains being exhausted with ventilation air (*see* Fig. 8.46).

Factories

Factories often have large volume spaces, where thermal conditions relate to the tasks carried out. Comfort temperatures can range from 13°C to

16°C, for heavy work and light work respectively. There are two main types of industrial heating system, namely warm air and radiant heaters (*see* Case Study 9.2).

Warm air systems use a fan to blow air across a heat exchanger, distributing the heat evenly throughout the space, and are generally used where a constant temperature is needed across a large area. The heat exchanger may have heat provided by hot water, piped from a central boiler, otherwise it may use direct electric or be gas-fired, the latter requiring a flue. They are usually ceiling or wall mounted so as not to intrude on the workspace.

Radiant heaters may use radiant plaques, which are usually gas-fired and flued directly into the space (assuming the volume of the space is large enough to dilute pollutants to a safe level); or they can use radiant tubes, which can be gas-fired or supplied with medium-pressure hot water. Both produce infrared heat that is directed downwards by a reflector. Radiant heat is immediate, taking only minutes to reach comfortable temperatures. Radiant plaques operate at temperatures of around 500°C, whereas radiant tubes are at around 150°C to 450°C (hotter nearer the burner) for gas-fired tubes, and around 110°C for medium-pressure hot water tubes. The higher temperature systems, with their fast warm-up times, are particularly useful when the heating requirement is 'occasional' rather than 'full time'. Lower temperature tubes or panels may be more effective for whole space use, and for less labour-intensive clean manufacturing activities. Comfort is achieved when people are in a 'direct line of sight'

of the radiant heat source so that they heat people rather than the whole space, thus saving energy. They are also suited for areas with high ventilation rates, such as in loading bays. The air temperature in a radiant heated space is typically lower than in a warm air heated space.

For both radiant and convective systems there may be high vertical temperature gradients; radiant systems also have a large convective heat output. Destratification fans located at high level can blow the warm air downwards, reducing vertical air temperature gradients from 10°C to less than 2°C (*see* Fig. 8.47), potentially saving 20 to 50 per cent heating energy. Air curtains are often used with large loading doors to block the cold air from coming into the building when the doors are open. Air curtains are usually heated and in some cases more energy is used to heat the air curtain than the rest of the space. Smaller air curtains are also used in other building types, such as malls and large retail stores.

High-Rise

High-rise buildings need to distribute HVAC equipment over a large numbers of floors. Therefore, they generally have a primary air delivery, from one or more central AHUs, which takes fresh outside air and delivers it to a number of secondary AHUs, which condition the air, typically for each floor or maybe for pairs of adjacent floors. The secondary AHU is supplied with chilled or heated water, delivered from one or more boiler/chiller plant rooms

(a)

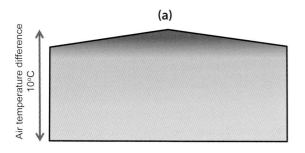

(b)

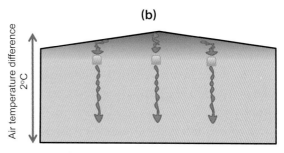

Fig. 8.47 Vertical temperature gradients in a factory: (a) without and (b) with destratification fans.

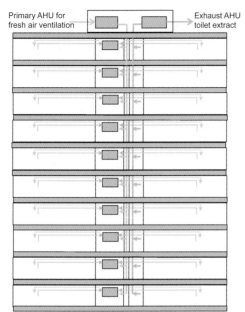

Primary AHU for fresh air ventilation

Exhaust AHU toilet extract

HVAC floor

HVAC floor

HVAC floor

HVAC floor

Typical arrangement with each floor having a dedicated AHU which mixes recirculated air with primary fresh air supply from a roof plant room. The extract, which balances the fresh air supply will be via the toilet.

For super high-rise buildings, HVAC rooms which supply fresh air will be located throughout the height of the building.

Fig. 8.48 Typical HVAC layout for a high-rise building.

Fig. 8.49 Shanghai Tower, with its HVAC floors and outer skin buffer spaces. (Shutterstock)

(*see* Fig. 8.48). Some buildings will have a single primary AHU on the roof, while others may have a primary AHU located, say, around every ten floors. For each secondary AHU zone, air will be recirculated from the spaces and mixed with the fresh primary air. The extract will typically be through toilets, which will be balanced with the primary fresh air supply.

The Shanghai Tower has a series of dedicated service floors, each serving fourteen floors (*see* Fig. 8.49). It also has an atrium space that creates a double-skin façade, which acts as a climate buffer zone.

Renewable Energy

As buildings reduce their energy demand and are more efficient to heat, cool, ventilate and light, renewable energy can contribute more, or even wholly, to the energy supply. The energy scene is rapidly changing, and over time the energy supply grids themselves, both electricity and gas, are being decarbonized, with an increasing proportion of renewable energy supplied to them. However, renewable energy at building scale can be applied immediately to many projects, both new build and retrofit, which will reduce the pressure on the grid to expand, reduce energy distribution losses, and future-proof building occupiers against uncertainties over energy supply and costs. The main options for building integrated renewable energy are solar thermal for heat and solar photovoltaic (PV) for electricity generation. For larger buildings or groups of buildings, it may also be effective to use wind power.

Solar Thermal

Solar thermal includes hot water and air systems. Solar hot water systems are used mainly for heating domestic hot water (DHW), and are relatively efficient, typically 50 to 60 per cent, in converting solar radiation into heat. The payback period for a DHW system is between five and fifteen years, depending on the cost of the fuel being saved and the level of solar

Fig. 8.50 Solar thermal water pipes used as a balcony rail in Tianjin Eco-city.

radiation for the location. Solar thermal is around three to five times as efficient in capturing the sun's energy compared to solar PV. However, solar PV has the advantage of producing electricity, which has a greater range of uses, displacing grid electricity, which is a more expensive fuel, compared to solar thermal, which would generally displace gas or oil.

A solar thermal water heating system could simply comprise pipes integrated into a building façade (*see* Fig. 8.50). However, most systems tend to be flat plate collectors or evacuated glass tubes, which can be fixed on top of roof tiles or integrated into the roof structure (*see* Fig. 8.51). Flat plate collectors contain water pipes within a narrow metal box, usually with a glass outside layer. The evacuated tube system comprises a series of

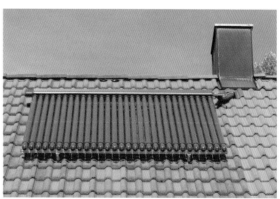

Fig. 8.51 Flat plate collectors and evacuated tubes. (Photos: Shutterstock)

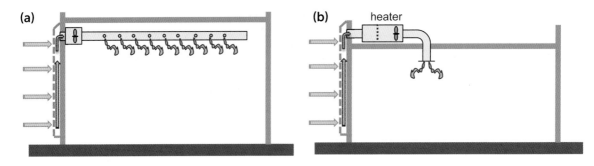

Fig. 8.52 Transpired solar collector (TSC): (a) direct supply and (b) ventilation preheat.

evacuated tubes that collect the solar heat and pass it to a manifold, where a fluid (usually water) collects the heat. They are more efficient than flat plate collectors. An electric pump, which may be powered by solar PV, is needed to circulate the water through the system to a storage tank. In cloudy weather, domestic hot water will need to be heated by an auxiliary system, such as an electric immersion heater.

Air collectors may be in the form of a transpired solar collector (TSC), which is integrated into a southerly facing wall or roof (*see* Fig. 8.52). The (TSC) has an outer metal sheet, which is heated by the sun. Small holes allow outside air to be drawn through and heated by contact with the external and internal metal surface, although the amount of heat absorbed on the external surface will depend on wind conditions. A TSC can be used to preheat air in a balanced mechanical ventilation system, or to feed warm air directly into a space; typically a large volume space, such as a warehouse, where exhaust is by natural air leakage. Fig. 8.53 shows a TSC applied to a public convenience in Lhasa, Tibet.

Solar PV

Building integrated solar PV systems can range from relatively small arrays of a few kilowatts to larger arrays of several tens of kilowatts, attached to the roof or wall of a building. They may be fully integrated as part of a roof or wall construction (*see* Fig. 8.54), or they may act as a shading device, rather than just installed as an independent element on the roof or wall. They can therefore contribute to the function of the outer skin of the building, as well as generating electricity, potentially saving on overall material costs.

The main types of PV cell include monocrystalline and polycrystalline silicon, and thin-film (*see* Fig. 8.55). The most well-established 'first-generation' technology is crystalline silicon (c-Si) solar cells. They have a high power output, and relatively long lifetime. The cost of crystalline silicon solar PV has fallen dramatically by some 90 per cent over the last twenty years, and further cost reductions of around 50 per cent are possible by 2050. The purest form of c-Si cells are monocrystalline silicon cells, which have the highest efficiency rates, reaching above 20 per cent. Polycrystalline silicon (Poly-Si) solar panels use a faster and cheaper process, which leads to a

Fig. 8.53 TSC applied to a community public convenience in Tibet (red cladding), as part of an energy retrofit carried out by Cardiff University and Xi'an University researchers.

Fig. 8.54 Zero Energy Office, Malaysia. A zero energy building may be typified by a large contribution from building integrated renewable energy generation systems, such as the large PV integrated roof. The PV also acts as shading for the atrium roof, allowing a relatively small amount of daylight to enter, but sufficient to light the space.

Fig. 8.55 Solar PV cells.

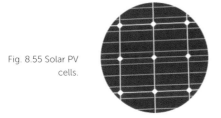
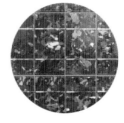
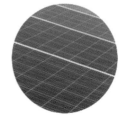

Monocrystalline silicon   Polycrystalline   Thin-Film Solar Cells

lower price, but also lower efficiencies of around 15 per cent, and are affected by high temperatures, and have a shorter lifespan.

'Second-generation' cells are based on thin-film technologies, such as copper indium gallium selenide (CIGS), cadmium telluride (CdTe), gallium arsenide (GaAs) and amorphous silicon (a-Si:H), have efficiencies of around 18 per cent. CIGS cells have achieved efficiencies of 22.6 per cent, although they are relatively expensive. Thin film PV is lighter in weight, more flexible and available in semi-transparent form, so more suitable for integrating into building design. They are less affected by high temperatures, operate at relatively higher efficiencies at lower sun angles and with diffuse solar radiation, and are less energy intensive to produce.

'Third-generation' cells include a variety of 'emerging' thin-film technologies that are less commercially advanced, including organic PV materials (OPVs), copper zinc tin sulphide (CZTS), perovskite solar cells, dye-sensitized solar cells (DSSCs), and quantum dot solar cells. Of particular interest are perovskite solar cells, which promise low cost, low environmental harm, good performance and easy manufacture. They are based on a solution-processed hybrid organic-inorganic tin or lead halide-based material. Efficiencies have increased from below 5 per cent in 2009 to over 20 per cent. However, most types of perovskite solar cells have not reached sufficient operational stability to be commercialized, although recent developments have indicated that coating traditional silicon based cells with a thin layer of perovskite can achieve overall efficiencies of some 27 per cent.

Solar panels are specified in relation to their kilowatt peak power (kWp), which is obtained from testing panels under standard test conditions (STC). The STC is the power output (kW) of a panel irradiated by 1,000W/m², with a panel temperature of 25°C and AM 1.5. (AM is the distance solar radiation travels through the atmosphere relative to the vertical distance at sea level.) If 1,000W/m² of sunlight falling on a 1.6m² panel generates 320W, this would correspond to a panel kWp value of 0.32kWp. The solar panel efficiency is the energy generated (W/m²) in relation to the solar energy falling on it. A 0.32kWp panel would have an efficiency of 20 per cent: $((320 \div (1.6 \times 1000) \times 100))$. The total energy generated includes a time period of operation, so a PV panel of 1.6m² with a peak power of 0.32kWp, working at its maximum capacity for one hour, will produce 0.320kWh. A typical installation (40m²) will produce around 8kWh of energy in an hour at peak conditions. However, real world conditions will be different from the STC, so panels rarely produce their kWp performance in practice.

Solar panels generally operate at higher temperatures than 25°C when irradiated by the sun. For an outside air temperature of 20°C, a panel's temperature may rise to around 40°C. Temperature affects a panel's efficiency, which can be estimated from its temperature coefficient Pmax, which is the percentage decrease in panel output per °C above 25°C. For example, if a 0.15kWp module has a Pmax of −0.40 per cent per °C, and a panel temperature of 40°C, the reduction of panel output would be −6 per cent, or −9W. Ventilating the back of the panel can cool it. For temperatures below 25°C, the panel output is increased. Temperature effects vary with cell type, for example, crystalline silicon cells have a Pmax of around −0.5 per cent per °C, compared to that of amorphous silicon cells of around −0.25 per cent per °C. The electricity generated by solar PV is direct current (d.c.) and an inverter will be needed to change the electric current from d.c. to a.c.

Solar PV thermal (PVT) systems combine solar PV and solar thermal, collecting heat from the panel, which improves the overall efficiency.

The overall annual energy generated from a solar PV panel can be estimated from the following formula:

$$E = A \times \mathit{eff} \times H \times PR$$

Where

E is the energy (kWh)

A is the panel area (m²)

eff is the solar panel yield given by the ratio: kWp divided by the area of the panel (kWp/m²)

H is the annual average solar radiation on the panel, allowing for inclination (slope, tilt) and orientation (azimuth); for example, 200kWh/m²/year (Norway) and 2,600kWh/m²/year (Saudi Arabia)

PR is the performance ratio coefficient for all losses, which includes inverter losses (4 to 10 per cent), temperature losses (5 to 20 per cent), cable losses (6 per cent), dirt on panels (2 per cent), resulting in a typical overall default value of 75 per cent of STC performance

The cost of a panel is usually quoted in cost per kWp. Presently, the typical cost of solar PV panels ranges between £1,000 to £1,500 per kWp. For a typical domestic system of 1.5 to 3kWp, each kWp should generate around 800 to 850kWh per year if unshaded and south-facing, with a tilt of 30 to 50 degrees. A solar roof array would typically generate 1,200 to 2,400kWh per year depending on size; if the whole south facing roof of a UK house had PV panels, it would generate around 5,000kWh/year. An average home uses around 3,000kWh of electricity per year for lights and appliances. However, an energy-efficient home using A++ rated appliances and efficient lighting may only use half this value.

Panels will degrade over time, by an average of about 0.8 per cent annually. So after a lifetime of thirty years, it will produce 76 per cent of its as-new performance. It may therefore prove cost-effective to replace panels before their end-of-life date. More expensive panels may have lower degradation rates, closer to 0.3 per cent. A warranty given by panel manufacturers is typically twenty-five to thirty years, retaining at least 85 per cent of the rated capacity, which is around a 0.5 per cent drop in efficiency per year. However, it is likely that panel efficiencies will improve over time, so replacement may still occur earlier. In fact, there is an

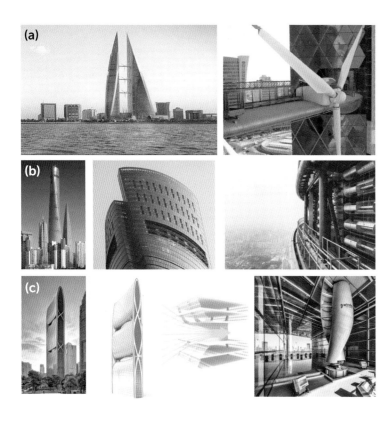

Fig. 8.56 Examples of building integrated wind generation: (a) Twin Towers, Bahrain; (b) Shanghai Tower; and (c) Guangzhou Pearl River Tower. (Photo: Tom Griffiths and Minggang Yin)

indication that some future panels may adopt a short lifetime, low-cost approach, and use less harmful materials. It may therefore be more cost-effective and sustainable to replace panels within a shorter period. So we should design for easy replacement. A PV panel will have an embodied energy associated with its manufacture. A rooftop system will typically recover its embodied energy within 0.7 to 2 years, producing some 95 per cent of net clean renewable energy over a thirty-year service lifetime.

Wind

There are examples of building integrated horizontal and vertical axis wind turbines, usually best suited for larger buildings, typically providing around 10 per cent of a building's energy needs. The Bahrain Towers generate nearly 1MW of power from its three wind turbines located on bridges spanning from tower to tower (*see* Fig. 8.56(a)). The Shanghai Tower has some forty-five horizontal axis wind turbines located at the top of the tower, generating 54,000kWh per year (*see* Fig. 8.56(b)). The Pearl River Tower has 270 vertical axis turbines capable of generating up to 350,000kWh, located within voids that channel the wind (*see* Fig. 8.56(c)). For smaller buildings, wind energy generated is generally low and is not cost-effective; and there will also be structural and aesthetic issues to deal with.

Building Energy Use

The successful thermal design of a building will integrate across the fabric, ventilation and heating and cooling systems, to provide comfort and low to zero energy performance. We sometimes refer to this as a whole building approach. The actual solution for a specific building will depend on the building type, its location and whether it is a new building or a retrofit of an existing building. Fig. 8.57 presents an example of how thermal and electrical systems can be integrated, with the following points of focus:

- Grid electricity: The grid is used to provide electricity when there is insufficient renewables or stored energy to power the building. Energy can be exported to the grid when there is excess renewable energy produced, or stored energy may be exported if needed by the grid.
- Building integrated renewables: These should be maximized to provide as much energy autonomy as possible, in order to be resilient against future energy price rises, with security of supply, and to reduce the pressure on the supply grid to expand. Renewable energy is most likely to be solar PV and solar thermal.
- Energy Storage: This can be used to store renewable energy when there is excess generated to what is immediately needed. Alternatively, grid energy may be imported and stored when its cost is low, and exported to the grid when the grid is under pressure and exported energy can return a cost benefit. Hot water may be used to store energy from the grid when costs are low.
- Electricity use: Electricity used for lights, appliances, specialist equipment and lifts should be mimimized by using efficient devices. This reduces electricity use and unwanted heat gains from the operation of electrical equipment.
- Fabric losses: These should be minimized to provide an optimum level of energy demand and material (thermal insulation) use. For some buildings, cooling may be required throughout the year, even in colder climates, so increasing insulation may not be worthwhile beyond a certain point.
- Infiltration losses: These should be minimized to reduce conditioned air leaving the building and to avoid unwanted polluted air from entering the building.
- Heat pumps: This technology can provide efficient means of heating and cooling, providing suitable temperatures for surface and air heat delivery in low energy buildings. It can be incorporated into heat recovery systems. Absorption heat pumps are appropriate for capturing waste heat, for example, from any processes within or attached to the building.
- Air supply: This should be minimized for occupancy, and for low to zero energy buildings, the amount of air delivered to the space should also be sufficient for heating and cooling. Any additional heating or cooling may be provided by surface systems, which are particularly appropriate for office-type spaces. If high levels of air supply are needed for occupancy or related to any process, the heating and cooling can be delivered through the air supply. Perimeter heat may be needed in certain locations, for example, to counter downdraughts where there are large areas of glazing.

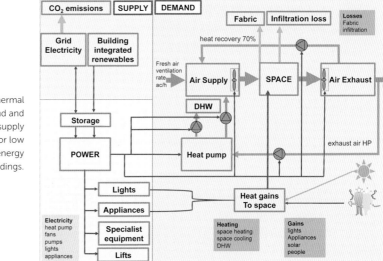

Fig. 8.57 Thermal demand and energy supply strategy for low to zero energy buildings.

- Air exhaust: This can provide heat recovery through heat exchangers and can also be a thermal source (heating and cooling) for exhaust air heat pumps.
- Fans and pumps: These should use efficient direct-drive electronically commutated (EC) variable speed motors. To minimize fan power, duct lengths should be kept short and air speeds low. AHU's should be located close to the spaces they serve.
- DHW: This can be the highest heat demand, especially in new houses. It can be delivered using heat pump technology, perhaps integrated with water- or air-based solar thermal heating.

The above may be regarded as an example checklist. Computer simulation is usually needed to evaluate the optimum level of reduced demand, in relation to HVAC efficiency, heat gains, and renewable energy supply and energy storage. Table 8.8 summarizes potential heating and cooling solutions for a range of space types.

Table 8.8 Heating (H) and cooling (C) solutions for a range of space types, for low to zero energy buildings.

Space type	Occupancy	Ventilation rates	Comments*
Housing	Low	Low	The heating load can be met through the mechanical ventilation system. If cooling is required this can also be met with the same system. Windows can be opened for natural ventilation at appropriate times of the year.
Offices	Medium	Medium	The office heating load can be met through the mechanical ventilation system. Cooling may require additional ceiling surface cooling.
Classrooms	High	Medium	The heating load can be met through the mechanical ventilation. Windows may be opened in summer (or winter in hot climates) if conditions allow.
Hospital wards	Medium	High	The heating and cooling loads can be met through the mechanical ventilation. Windows may be opened in summer (or winter in hot climates) if conditions allow.
Retail	High	High	The heating and cooling loads can be met through the mechanical ventilation. CO_2 occupancy sensing can reduce ventilation for low occupancy.
Auditoria	High	High	The heating and cooling loads can be met through the mechanical ventilation. CO_2 occupancy sensing can reduce ventilation for low occupancy.
Factories	Low	Low	Ventilation preheat using TSCs may be appropriate. Radiant heating will provide direct delivery of heat to the occupied zone in high ceiling areas. The ventilation may be met through air leakage in large volume spaces, even though rates should be low.
Transition spaces	Low	Low	Natural ventilation should be the preferred option without any whole-space heating or cooling. Spot heating and cooling may be used in extreme cold and hot conditions.

* In all cases of mechanical ventilation, heat recovery and heat pump technology should be considered.

Chapter Nine

Low Energy to Zero Carbon

Introduction

From a thermal design perspective the start of the twentieth century saw the growing influence of new materials, technologies and design thinking, and, as the century progressed, the increasing availability of energy. The cost and environmental impact of a high energy dependence was not a major issue, nor was energy efficiency high on the agenda. It was not until the 1970s that we became more aware of global energy and environmental issues, and also the impact that the indoor environment has on people's comfort, health and productivity. Since then, there has been a gradual improvement in energy efficiency, but not enough to satisfy international targets for greenhouse gas reductions. We must now achieve a zero carbon built environment by the middle of this century. Since the 1970s oil crisis, a range of more efficient thermal design approaches have been considered. Some have been successful, while others have perhaps been more wishful thinking. If we are to develop a zero carbon, and maybe even energy positive, built environment, we need to understand and learn from our previous successes and failures. We can then develop our design thinking based on real examples, as well as from our more theoretical insights. This chapter traces developments over the last four to five decades, identifying a range of innovative approaches to thermal design, and preparing the way for a transition to a zero carbon built environment.

The 1970s

The 1970s saw a 'new beginning' in the thermal design of buildings, and in particular the efficient use of energy to maintain a good standard of thermal comfort. This was triggered by the oil crises, which caused a dramatic increase in the cost of energy, first in 1973 with the Arab oil embargo, and then in 1980 with the Iran–Iraq war. There was a quadruple increase in oil price in 1973 (*see* Fig. 9.1), and then almost doubling again in 1980, demonstrating the sensitivity of oil price to global events, and the need to use less energy and use energy more efficiently[9.1]. Since World War II there had been an increase in construction in the West, with little thought about energy use. At the start of the 1970s, energy was plentiful and relatively cheap, so the oil crises were a shock to the system, and although we languished through a period of relatively cheap oil in the 1990s, it was not to last long, with prices continually rising from the start of the millennium. It began to sink in that fossil fuel reserves had a finite lifetime, and we would eventually loose our supply of cheap fossil fuel energy, although there seemed no great urgency to address the problem.

It had already been a decade since Rachel Carson's *Silent Spring* (1962) drew attention to the adverse environmental effects caused by the indiscriminate use of pesticides, focussing attention on the environmental damage of modern living. *The Limits to Growth*, a 1972 report from the Club of Rome, stated that 'if growth trends continued unchanged, the limits of growth on this planet would be reached sometime within the next 100 years'. Towards the late 1970s, the use of chlorofluorocarbons (CFCs) as refrigerants in air conditioning systems, and other products, was identified as damaging the ozone layer. Concern over the environment continued over the proceeding decades. The Brundtland Report in 1987 on sustainable development focussed on the relationship between energy use, economic development and environmental

Fig. 9.1 Global oil prices in relation to global events[9.1].

harm. The 1990s saw the first IPCC report, and the Earth Summit of 1992 was the first to address urgent problems of environmental protection, adopting the Agenda 21 plan for achieving sustainable development in the 21st century. In 2004, Bioregional launched its One Planet Living vision, recognizing the planet's limits to providing future resources, and that if we continued our use of resources and discharge of pollution, we would need three planets to support the one planet we live on. In fact, it appeared that we had ceased to be self-sustaining as a planet since the mid-1970s. Stern's report *The Economics of Climate Change* in 2006[9.2] identified climate change as the greatest and widest-ranging market failure ever seen, with the potential impacts of climate change on water resources, food production, health, and the environment, being equivalent to losing some 5 to 20 per cent of global gross domestic product (GDP) each year.

The 1970s also saw a growing concern that many buildings were suffering from poor indoor

environmental conditions. In the UK, housing was difficult to heat in winter, with little or no thermal insulation, and with many still using coal as the main fuel, often supplemented by direct electric heaters, or unvented paraffin heaters. When the installation of central heating became more widespread, boilers were relatively inefficient, with early gas boilers being around 60 per cent. Other building types also suffered. Offices were becoming increasingly highly glazed, and usually single-glazed, suffering glare and overheating in summer, and cold discomfort in winter. There had been some recent glorious failures. Stirling's History Library at Cambridge University, completed in 1968, was celebrated architecturally with the Royal Institute of British Architects Gold Medal in 1970, but was a disaster from the point of its internal environment. A rotation of the plan due to site constraints left the highly glazed façades facing south, with the internal space suffering from intense solar heat gains and visual

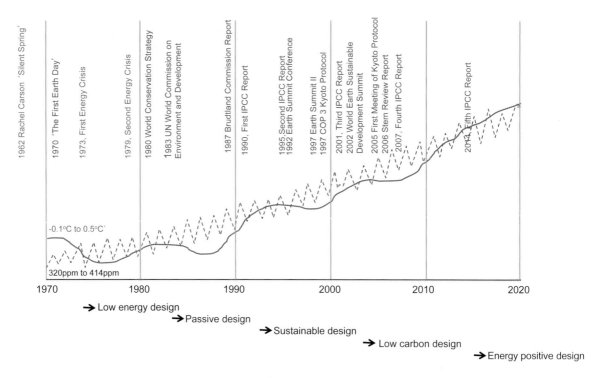

Fig. 9.2 Four decades of environmental design and environmental events, alongside increasing global carbon dioxide level and temperature.

glare. Environmental design appeared to be largely ignored by the architectural profession in favour of more aesthetic drivers. In general, thermal design was not considered and energy was used in a profligate way. The architecture and building services engineering were generally dealt with as separate items; the architect designed the building and then the services engineer added the heating, ventilation and air conditioning.

There was a brief glimmer of hope, when, in 1972, the Welsh architect and president of the Royal Institute of British Architects (RIBA), Sir Alex Gordon, described good architecture as buildings that exhibit long life, loose fit and low energy[9.3]. This very much fits with our current ideas relating to sustainable building design. However, his ideas fell on deaf ears within the architectural profession. And over much of the period since then, many buildings have tended to be shorter life, more inflexible, and with a relatively high energy consumption.

However, a new era of 'building environmental design' was beginning to happen, starting with 'low energy design' of the late 1970s, followed by 'passive design', 'sustainable design', and 'low and zero carbon design', being renamed every decade or so. Now we have 'energy-positive design'. Each has built on the previous, changing the focus, but all aiming to produce a more sustainable energy-efficient design, with low environmental impact, and comfortable and healthy indoor conditions. Although, throughout this period of growing environmental awareness, atmospheric carbon dioxide levels and global warming has continued to rise at an alarming rate (*see* Fig. 9.2).

Building Regulations and Environmental Assessment Schemes

In many countries, building regulations have changed significantly since the 1970s, specifying minimum energy performance standards. In 1965, the UK set maximum U-values for the first time, mainly to reduce condensation risk. This applied to roofs, walls and floors. Walls could achieve the required U-value of $1.7W/m^2K$ without added thermal insulation, while roofs required some 28mm thermal insulation to achieve a U-value of $1.4W/m^2K$, which was then lowered to $0.6W/m^2K$ in 1973. New regulations in 1976 required wall U-values of less than $1W/m^2K$ for domestic buildings. In 1984, the UK building regulations were revised 'for the purposes of securing the health, safety, welfare and convenience of persons in or about buildings, [and] furthering the conservation of fuel and power'. At the time, single glazing was sufficient to comply with building regulations, with double glazing not required until 1990. Energy-related building regulations were updated in 1990 and 1995, and then again in 2002, 2006, 2011 and 2014. Fig. 9.3 summarizes housing U-values since 1965, alongside corresponding annual heating consumption, assuming whole house heating, which would have been uncommon in 1965. Building regulations dictate minimum standards, and although energy performance has improved through successive releases of the regulations, the construction industry has generally adopted a minimum standards approach; it has rarely shown an appetite to exceed minimum standards. It was also relatively easy to make significant improvements

early on, when standards were so poor to begin with. It should be noted that UK building regulations only apply to the regulated loads of heating, cooling, ventilation and lighting. Appliance load is not covered and is left to industry certification and rating systems, for example, an A+ rated refrigerator. And of course, many UK houses were built before 1965.

A more aspirational approach that exceeds minimum building regulations led to the development of voluntary environmental assessment schemes, which address energy, as well as a range of other environmental categories, including water use, health and wellbeing, pollution, transport, materials, waste, ecology and management processes. The first major scheme was the UK BREEAM, which has been continually developed since its initial introduction in 1990. Other schemes followed. In 1996, HKBEAM, now called BEAM Plus, was launched, loosely based on UK BREEAM, but written specifically for Hong Kong. One of the most widely used schemes is US LEED, launched in 1998, and now used in many countries outside of the US. Most schemes are based on the original UK BREEAM structure, covering a range of environmental performance attributes, although some, such as the Swiss Minergie scheme and Passivhaus standard, only focus on energy. The Passivhaus standard sets a total energy use target of less than $120kWh/m^2/an$ of primary energy and less than $15kWh/m^2/an$ for

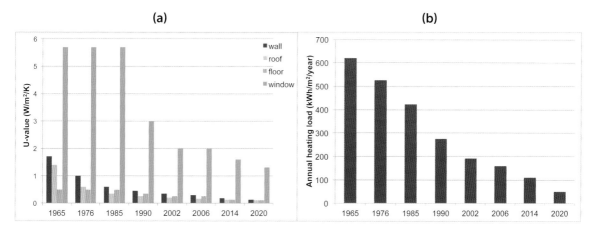

Fig. 9.3 (a) Changes in housing U-values over time, as prescribed by UK building regulations, (b) corresponding annual heating load, although whole house heating was not common in the earlier period, and most houses built then would have subsequently had some energy efficiency measures added.

heating. Although generally a success, these schemes have attracted criticism. The construction industry often takes the easiest low-cost route to achieve a high assessment score, and in some cases not following this through into design. The predicted energy savings are often not realized in practice, and it seems that the actual rating is more important to developers than the environmental and energy benefits. Some Environmental Assessment Schemes have versions that can be applied to the retrofit of existing buildings, such as BREEAM Refurbishment and Fit-Out (RFO) and LEED-EB (Leadership in Energy and Environmental Design – Existing Buildings), and some for urban scale developments, such as BREEAM Communities and LEED for Cities and Communities. LEED now has a complementary scheme called SITES, which assesses sustainable landscaping.

In 2003, the European Energy Performance of Buildings Directive (EPBD) was launched, which required EU member states to adopt a whole building calculation method for assessing the carbon emissions of new buildings. The latest version of the EPBD requires all new buildings to be nearly zero energy, by the end of 2020, through reducing energy demand, with a significant proportion of this energy demand to come from renewable generation, either on the building or nearby.

In 2006 the UK introduced the non-mandatory national standard, the Code for Sustainable Homes, for rating and certifying the environmental performance of new homes, covering energy, carbon dioxide emissions, water, materials, surface water run-off, waste, pollution, health and wellbeing, management and ecology. However, in 2015 the government withdrew the code, albeit consolidating some of its features into building regulations.

Since the 1970s there has been an increasing environmental awareness in relation to the environmental design and energy use of buildings. On the positive side, much has been achieved, albeit at a painfully slow rate of progress, but things would be far worse without this. However, there is still much to do, both for new build and for retrofitting the existing building stock. There has been a lot of innovation, some of which has been more successful than others. In this chapter, we will review progress through a range of case studies, which are presented in approximate chronological order.

Low Energy Design

From the mid-1970s through to the mid-1980s, the interest in 'low energy' buildings grew. In the UK, the immediate attention was focussed on a combination of reducing energy demand and providing more efficient heating, through:

i. Thermal insulation: Building regulations began to require better insulation levels, firstly focussing on housing, followed by other building types, although at a slower pace. Increased levels of thermal insulation significantly reduced building heat loss and improved energy efficiency. After all, relatively large improvements could be made with relatively little effort, when standards were so low to begin with.

ii. Reduced air leakage: Improved airtightness became a major feature of low energy buildings, using better sealing and draught stripping around construction elements. However, as a consequence of improved sealing, sometimes buildings became too airtight. In housing, some spaces were becoming practically unventilated. Trickle vents were introduced to provide a more controlled and balanced background ventilation distribution, becoming an option for meeting building regulations for natural ventilation.

iii. Efficient heating systems: Whole house central heating was becoming standard, and heating system boilers were becoming more efficient, with thermostatic valves on radiators to control space temperatures. Gas was the preferred solution, if available, with oil and electric storage used in areas without a natural gas supply.

The UK government funded research into low energy building design, to inform of the requirements for the design of low energy housing, and the development of future building regulations. Two case studies illustrate research developments of the time. The Abertridwr Better Insulated Housing project and the Low Energy Factory project both evolved into extended research programmes, providing evidence on how energy monitoring and measurement experiments can provide a greater understanding of thermal design and low energy performance.

Case Study 9.1 Abertridwr Better Insulated Housing Research Programme, from 1978 to 1984

In response to the energy crises of the 1970s, a series of research projects were set up under the UK Department of Environment: Housing Development Directive (HDD), to investigate the energy performance benefits resulting from higher levels of thermal insulation, combined with more efficient heating systems. The Abertridwr Better Insulated Housing project was carried out between 1978 and 1984 by researchers at the Welsh School of Architecture, Cardiff University, in collaboration with the Rutherford Appleton Laboratory. It involved the detailed energy and environmental monitoring of thirty-nine houses, of which twenty 'test' houses had higher levels of thermal insulation and reduced heating system size, compared to nineteen 'control' houses, built to the then current building regulations (see Fig. 9.4).

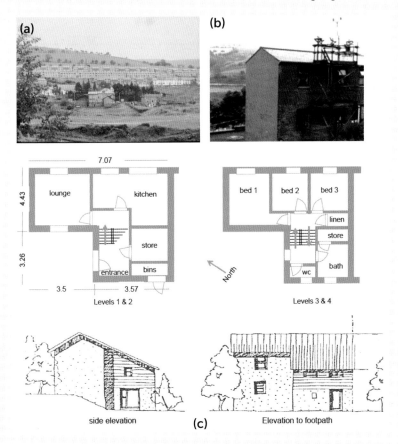

Fig. 9.4 (a) Photograph of the Abertridwr houses; (b) test house with attached weather station; and (c) drawings of plans and elevations.

The houses were built as a series of terraces on a steep sloping site, with a north-east, south-west aspect. The U-values for the control house were 1.0, 0.5 and 0.6W/m².K, for the walls, roof and floor respectively, reduced to 0.5, 0.3 and 0.45 W/m².K for the test houses. The wall insulation in the test houses used an internal dry lining board, considered appropriate for the exposed, hilly South Wales valley location. The roof insulation was 60mm and 120mm for the control and test houses respectively. The test houses also had a 1m slab of perimeter edge floor insulation. Both house types had single glazing at the start of the project, with double glazing not being standard at that time. The boiler capacities in the control and test houses were 14.7kW and 8.3kW respectively, and the respective estimated design heat losses were 10kW and 6.5kW. All thirty-nine houses were intensively monitored, and an on-site weather station was installed (as shown in Fig. 9.4(b)). Data was collected every five minutes, and a social scientist lived on site to observe occupant behaviour in relation to energy use, and their perception of comfort.

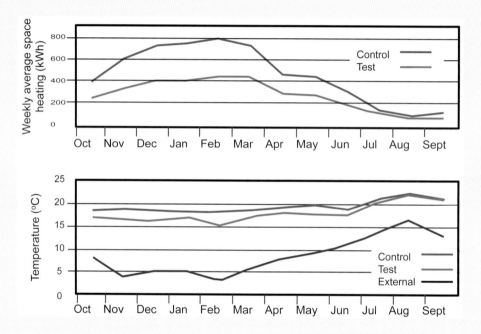

Fig. 9.5 Annual space heating and average internal air temperatures.

Average energy use over the heating season was measured to be 37 per cent less in the test houses compared to the control houses (see Fig. 9.5). The measured whole house average internal temperatures were lower in the test houses during the heating season, which was partly attributed to only one radiator being installed on the first floor landing, to match the reduced whole house heat loss. The combined heat gains from occupancy and solar radiation contributed an estimated 20 to 30 per cent of the overall heat input to the houses, although a proportion of this was considered to have resulted in higher internal temperatures rather than a reduced heating demand. Measured boiler efficiencies for the test houses were on average 80 per cent at high loads (above 6kW) and 50 to 60 per cent at lower loads (typically 2kW), while for the control houses, they were 75 per cent at high loads (above 8kW) and 50 to 60 per cent at lower loads (typically 3kW).

A number of 'calibration' tests were carried out, considered to be pioneering at the time, to assess the thermal integrity of the construction. Thermographic surveys, which assessed the installation of thermal insulation, showed up a number of problems due to deficiencies in both design and construction, now referred to as the performance gap (*see* Fig. 9.6).

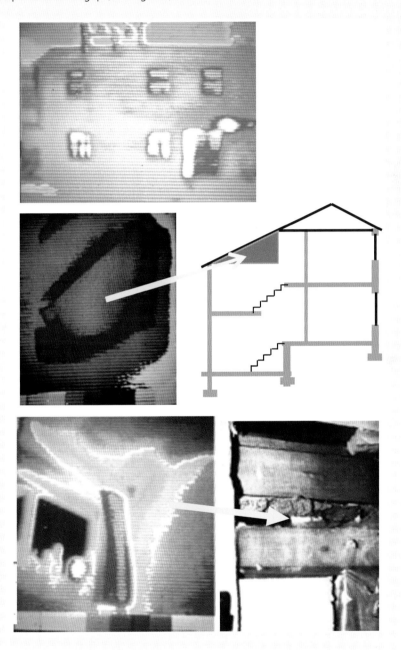

Fig. 9.6 Thermographic survey of the Abertridwr housing, indicating missing insulation and poor detailing: insulation was missing in the wall between the top of the stairway and adjacent roof space, and there was a discontinuity of insulation at the eaves detail.

Tracer-gas air infiltration rate and fan pressurization leakage measurements indicated that the houses were constructed to be relatively airtight. Measured air leakage rates were between 5.6m³/h.m² and 8.5m³/h.m² (at a 50Pa internal external pressure difference) on completion of construction, which is not far from current (2020) UK maximum air leakage rates of 5m³/h.m² at 50Pa (some forty years on). However, further tests performed two years later showed that air leakage rates had risen to between 8.6m³/h.m² and 14m³/h.m², through houses losing their airtightness shortly after construction.

The Abertridwr project hosted two other highly significant trials. Titon trickle ventilators (*see* Fig. 9.7(a)) were installed in both half of the test and half of the control houses to investigate the potential energy savings due to reduced window opening. Although no significant energy savings were identified, and the window opening was only marginally reduced, there was a significant reduction in condensation noted in the houses with trickle ventilators. Air leakage measurements indicated an increase of 10 per cent with trickle ventilators open, which although not a large increase in overall ventilation rate, provided a better distribution of background ventilation throughout the house, without incurring a significant energy penalty. In particular, the very low background ventilation in bedrooms was improved with trickle ventilators.

The second trial tested the performance of Pilkington's low emissivity 'Kappafloat' double glazing units, which were installed in half of the houses. Some 14 per cent energy savings were achieved, and thermal comfort improved. Condensation at window reveals (*see* Fig. 9.7(b)) was eliminated, which was attributed to the reveal surface not radiating so much heat to the relatively warmer double-glazed surface.

(a)   **(b)**

Fig. 9.7 (a) Trickle vents and (b) condensation on the window reveal.

The results of the Abertridwr research programme played a major role in defining UK housing energy performance and component design, and informing the development of future building regulations. The project demonstrated that heating energy could be significantly reduced through low energy design. It demonstrated the additional benefits of trickle ventilation and low emissivity double glazing, not only to reduce energy demand but also to reduce the risk of condensation and improve comfort. The project pioneered what are now more commonplace measurements, such as thermography surveys and air leakage tests, to help understand and check the performance of low energy design on completion of construction, and to help reduce the performance gap. It is a great pity that, some forty years later, we are still challenged by similarly poor quality construction and performance gap issues.

Case Study 9.2 Low Energy Factories

Fig. 9.8 Examples of the WDA advanced factories programme.

In 1981 the Welsh Development Agency (WDA) set up a programme to deliver 'advanced' speculative factory units across industrial South Wales, in order to provide employment opportunities in areas hit hard by the recent closure of coal mines. They included a range of sizes, from smaller units of around 200m^2, mid-range units of around 1,000m^2, to larger units of around 2,000m^2 (see Fig. 9.8). Thermal insulation in the walls and roofs achieved U-values of 0.35 and 0.45W/m^2.K respectiviely (depending on construction type), which were lower than the then current building regulations of 0.7W/m^2.K. The smaller units had wall-mounted warm air heaters or direct gas-fired radiant plaques; the mid-range units had gas-fired radiant tubes; the larger units had medium-pressure hot water radiant panels (see Fig. 9.9). Attention was given to reducing air leakage, especially around loading doors and roof ventilators. Researchers at the Welsh School of Architecture, Cardiff University, investigated their performance compared to standard factory units, including measuring air leakage rates, the thermal performance of the fabric, the performance of heating systems, and the overall annual energy use. The research programme took place over an extended period of time from 1984 to 1990.

Fig. 9.9 Heating systems: (a) radiant plaque; (b) radiant tube with destratification fans at high level; and (c) hot water radiant panels.

Thermography was used to assess the integrity of the thermal insulation. A major source of heat loss for the smaller standard factory was the poorly insulated loading door, which, combined with a high air leakage, accounted for an estimated 25 per cent of the overall building heat loss. This compared to 3 per cent for an insulated door in the new factory (*see* Fig. 9.10). The measured air leakage rates of the new low energy factories were 60 per cent less than the existing standard factory (*see* Fig. 9.11(a)). U-value measurements indicated that the as-built U-value performance for the better insulated new factories exceeded their design value (*see* Fig. 9.11(b)), but were still lower than the building regulations values. The negative performance gap resulting from the reduced U-value performance was exceeded by the positive performance gap from improving airtightness, so the overall energy use of the low energy factories was reduced by up to 40 per cent compared to factories designed to the then current building regulations.

Measurements of indoor temperatures showed a range of vertical air temperature gradients (*see* Fig. 9.12). The warm air system initially had the highest temperature gradients, attributed to its on-off control, which reduced when replaced with a modular control. Overall energy savings were greatest for the smaller units, where components, such as loading doors and roof ventilators, accounted for a greater proportion of the total losses (*see* Fig. 9.13).

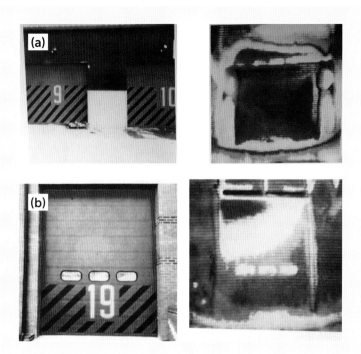

Fig. 9.10 Thermography images: (a) for the leaky poorly insulated door in a standard factory; and (b) the insulated airtight door in a low energy factory. Thermography pictures were taken from the inside: blue to red is relative cold to hot.

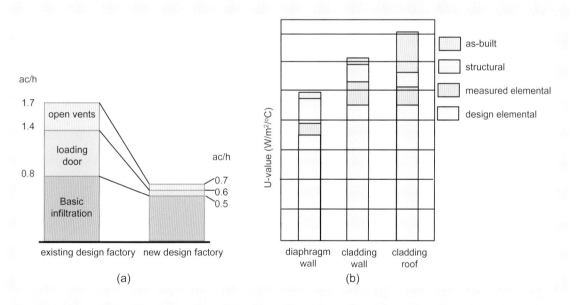

Fig. 9.11 (a) A comparison of measured air leakage for a standard and low energy small unit; and (b) U-value measurements for the range of wall constructions carried out over a four-week period, with increases from the design value due to poor as-built elemental performance, alongside structural and workmanship deficiencies.

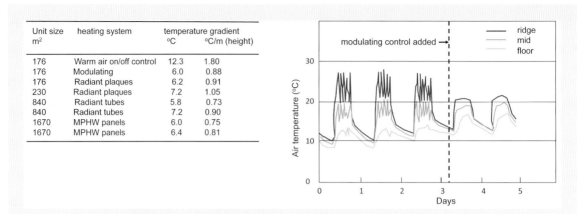

Unit size m²	heating system	temperature gradient °C	°C/m (height)
176	Warm air on/off control	12.3	1.80
176	Modulating	6.0	0.88
176	Radiant plaques	6.2	0.91
230	Radiant plaques	7.2	1.05
840	Radiant tubes	5.8	0.73
840	Radiant tubes	7.2	0.90
1670	MPHW panels	6.0	0.75
1670	MPHW panels	6.4	0.81

Fig. 9.12 Temperature gradients for a range of heating systems (left). Adding modulating control to an air heater (right).

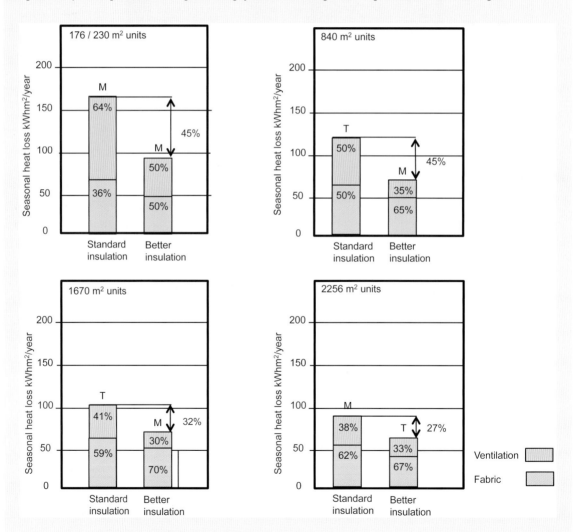

Fig. 9.13 Overall annual energy performance of four factory unit sizes.

The WDA factories research programme showed the potential for energy savings from increasing thermal insulation and reducing air leakage, and the importance of selecting energy-efficient components, such as loading doors and roof vents. It identified a performance gap between as-built and design. The elemental U-values were higher than the design, and there was structural cold thermal bridging and missing insulation due to poor workmanship. As a consequence of these findings, the WDA specified thermographic surveys for all future projects, and where insulation was defective, the contractor was required to make good and pay for a second survey to check the work (*see* Fig. 6.11). This quickly led to improvements in the standard of construction.

Passive design

Low energy designs of the 1970s focussed on reducing energy demand. Many buildings became 'climate rejecting', excluding the positive passive design attributes of the climate that utilize 'free energy' from solar radiation, daylight, and thermal mass, which potentially can further reduce energy demand. In contrast to this, many commercial buildings of the time were in 'climate overload'. Large areas of single glazing resulted in excessive solar heat gains in summer, and excessive heat loss in winter, leading to high cooling and heating energy loads, together with environmental discomfort from direct solar radiation and visual glare. The high radiant gains could not be countered by simply increasing air conditioning cooling. In cold weather, the cold internal surfaces of the glazing resulted in a cold radiant environment and downdraughts.

Around the mid-1980s, greater attention was given to a 'passive design' approach, with greater controlled contact with the external natural environment, and creating more pleasurable internal environments. It added to the principles of low energy design, but widened the approach by adding environmentally selective design features, including:

i. Solar design: Solar heat can be used to contribute to space heating in winter, especially for housing. However, solar design needs to be controlled to avoid overheating, especially in offices and schools, where for a modern well-insulated building, the internal heat gains from people and equipment can often meet, and may exceed, the heat demand of the space. Glazing systems became more insulated. Passive designs were used to buffer solar gains, collecting them in non-occupied or transitional spaces, and then transferring them to occupied spaces when needed, or using them to drive natural ventilation. Atria and sunspaces were often used in this role.

ii. Daylight: This can be used to reduce the need for electric lighting, providing energy-efficient solutions. With the change to more thermally insulated glazing systems, larger windows became a 'low energy' option, providing good levels of daylighting. Innovative blinds and shading systems were used to allow daylight into a building, but control solar heat gains. North-facing glazing became more appropriate to achieve good daylight levels and to avoid excessive solar heat gains.

iii. Ventilation: As buildings became more airtight, purpose-designed ventilation needed to be better controlled. Natural ventilation was generally limited to a narrow plan design, so for a deeper plan, window opening could be combined with ventilation 'stack effect', using chimneys and atria. Wind effect might be used at times to enhance natural ventilation performance. Hybrid mixed-mode systems could use natural ventilation in summer and mechanical ventilation in winter, when a more controlled air supply is needed, possibly combined with heat recovery.

iv. Thermal mass: This can be used to stabilize internal temperatures over periods of high heat gains, to avoid overheating. This requires exposing relatively large surface areas of wall or ceiling that are constructed from high thermal mass materials, such as concrete, to soak up the heat gains when they occur, which are then exhausted, either through active systems or passively through night-time ventilation. The thermal mass of the ground may be used as a source of cooling or heating.

v.   Responsive systems: A low energy performance needs mechanical systems that can respond to the reduced thermal demand, and the fluctuation in conditions, for example, reducing their output when solar gains occur. However, controls need to be responsive and legible for the user; the simpler they are, the less likely they will fail, or fail to be used properly. A simple responsive control system should be able to ensure a good thermal and energy performance throughput the year.

The period from the 1980s to the 2000s saw a range of building environmental design ideas be developed. Whereas previously the attention had mainly been on housing, other building types also became the focus. Commercial buildings began to use atria as part of their environmental solution, or multi-layered glazed façades, providing daylight, thermal insulation and solar control. A more modern version of passive design was emerging, which rediscovered design with climate, but within a modern context, using innovative built forms and design elements to select the benefits of the external climate. Architects, including Thomas Herzog in Germany, Ken Yeang in Malaysia, and Short Ford in the UK, led the way. Building physics emerged as a discipline, with pioneering practices such as Kopitsis Bauphysik in Switzerland. The following case studies illustrate this period of innovative design.

Case Study 9.3 Passive Solar Housing: Energy Performance Assessment (EPA), from 1988 to 1994

From 1988 to 1994 the Energy Performance Assessment (EPA) research programme, funded through the UK Energy Technology Support Unit (ETSU), investigated passive solar design for a range of buildings. The project was carried out at the Welsh School of Architecture in collaboration with DataBuild Ltd. A number of houses (see Fig. 9.14), featuring sunspaces integrated to a greater or lesser extent into the living spaces of the houses, were investigated to assess their energy and environmental performance, together with computer simulation[9.4, 9.5, 9.6, 9.7].

The wall and roof U-values of these houses were as good as, or better than, the test houses of Abertridwr described in Case Study 9.1, typically 0.3 to 0.5W/m². K and 0.2 to 0.35W/m².K respectively. The measured annual heating loads varied from 45 to 132kWh/m², with an estimated useful solar contribution to the heating load of between 10 and 30 per cent. Not all solar heat gains were useful, with a proportion resulting in higher indoor air temperatures, sometimes causing overheating. As houses became more 'passive', they needed more responsive heating system controls, sometimes using thermal mass to reduce extremes of internal temperature. Solar gains displaced heating energy, with the heating system not operating for much of the day (see Fig. 8.8).

The estimated additional cost associated with the passive solar design measures ranged from 2 to 46 per cent, with the higher costs resulting from considerable design additions in the form of advanced

Fig. 9.14 A range of sunspaces were considered.

glazing systems and sunspaces, and the lower costs mainly associated with redistribution of glazing and improved thermal insulation. The EPA programme drew attention to the costing procedures associated with passive design. If the cost analysis was based on an additive approach, starting with a standard design and then adding passive design features, the cost of the passive building would be more expensive than a standard design. However, when whole building costs for passive buildings were compared to standard buildings, cost differences were not that obvious. Cost analysis tends to ignore cost savings associated with passive design, such as reducing heating system capacity, and the benefits of a holistic approach to design.

The EPA houses could be considered to have an improved low energy performance relative to the Abertridwr test houses, showing that a significant amount of energy savings could be achieved through solar heat gains, although responsive control is required to avoid overheating. However, the occupants need to understand and become more active in controlling their environmental conditions.

Conflicting design strategies were encountered, such as the passive use of a sunspace versus the increased heating loads when occupants choose to heat them. A successful passive design needs a holistic approach and a clear statement of design aims, with continuity throughout the design and construction process.

It is interesting to note that the interest in sunspaces for housing was relatively short-lived, with today's low to zero energy house designs rarely including a sunspace feature. This perhaps implies that when houses are super-insulated, solar heat gains may not be useful, and the allocation of space only for seasonal use may be profligate for many house types.

Case Study 9.4 Naturally Ventilated Atrium: Gateway II Office

The Gateway II office building (*see* Fig. 9.15) combines a solar-assisted, naturally ventilated atrium connected to deep-plan naturally ventilated offices that have an exposed thermal mass ceiling. This combination is used to ventilate and reduce peak summer internal air temperatures.

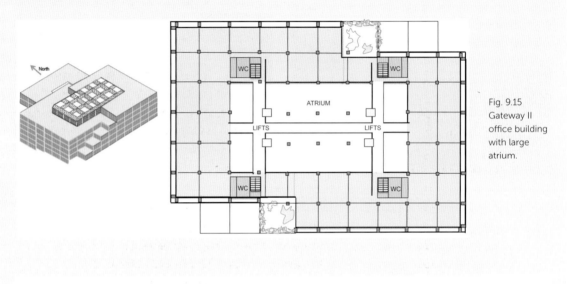

Fig. 9.15 Gateway II office building with large atrium.

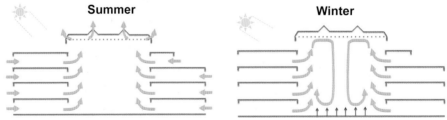

Fig. 9.16 Schematic of the summer and winter operating modes.

Gateway II was designed by Arup Associates and was completed in 1984. It represented an innovative passive approach to office design, based on natural ventilation and thermal mass cooling. The main feature of the environmental design was the use of a central atrium as part of the natural ventilation system (*see* Fig. 9.16). The roof of the atrium is partially glazed, and in summer, openings allow the warm air at the top of the atrium to escape, drawing outside 'fresh' air in through window openings at the office perimeter. The high-level metal walkways that are used to service the roof glazing, trap the solar heat gains above the walkways, therefore avoiding overheating in the atrium. During sunny conditions, the air temperature above the walkway is some 6°C higher than below, enhancing the stack-induced ventilation. In winter, the atrium's underfloor heating system used waste heat from the computer suite. The atrium provides an attractive naturally lit space, although the roof is only partially glazed (*see* Fig. 9.17). The exposed thermal mass of the office ceiling reduced peak summer internal air temperatures. In winter, the roof openings were closed, and the deep-plan offices ventilate to outside and to the atrium.

Fig. 9.17 Gateway II internal design features and roof glazing system, showing the service walkways and the roof glazing system.

Measurements of air movement in the atrium in colder weather indicated a distinct pattern of air circulation, with relatively warm air rising from the side of the atrium with five floors of offices, and falling on the opposite side where there are only four floors. This circular pattern of air movement was visualized on site using neutral buoyancy balloons and simulated using airflow modelling (*see* Fig. 9.18). The resulting downdraught fell on the café area (on the right side of the atrium, above the restaurant) open to the atrium, which could be felt as a cool downdraught[9.8].

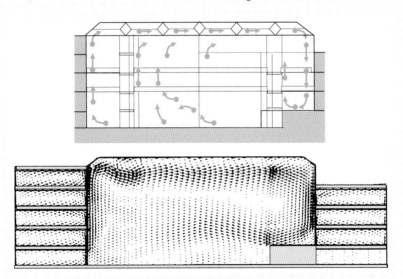

Fig. 9.18 Visualized and simulated airflow in the atrium.

This case study demonstrated using an atrium as part of an integrated environmental solution using natural ventilation. It also demonstrated how CFD airflow simulation might be used to help understand a building's internal environmental performance.

The Gateway II building was successful when first used. However, over time a number of changes resulted in performance issues. Some of the open-plan office space became partitioned, interrupting the ventilation cooling strategy; internal office ventilation airflow paths need to be maintained between the perimeter window inlets, and outlets through window openings into the atrium. The computer suite was moved, and the floor heating system lost its waste heat source. These changes over time illustrate that a fully integrated design strategy may not be continued throughout the building's lifetime, and passive design may be inflexible to change in use.

Case Study 9.5 Innovative Glazing and Hybrid Ventilation: Linz Exhibition Hall

Fig. 9.19 Linz Exhibition Hall external and internal views. (Thomas Herzog and Partner)

The Linz Exhibition Hall was designed by Thomas Herzog and Partner, and was completed in 1993 (see Fig. 9.19)[9.9]. The main environmental design feature is its daylit exhibition space with a double-skin-glazed curved roof incorporating a mid-pane matrix solar shading device (see Fig. 9.20). The building's curved roof design meant that the angle of the small matrix shading fins had to vary with location on the roof, to let daylight through but restrict solar heat gains. The overall solar transmission was 42 per cent with a 33 per cent daylight transmission[9.10].

A spatial hybrid ventilation system incorporates natural ventilation openings along the side and top of the building to allow air to enter and leave the main exhibition space (see Fig. 9.21). A wing-shaped feature above the top opening channels the wind under the wing creating a relative negative pressure, enhancing the extract of air from the space. There is also a floor level mechanical supply ventilation system with cooling if needed during exhibitions, with warm air mechanically extracted at high level for heat recovery. The building can be operated as a spatial hybrid, with the upper space being naturally ventilated and the lower space (if additional cooling is required) being air-conditioned.

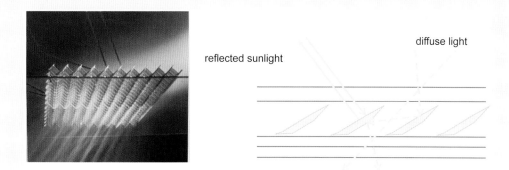

reflected sunlight

diffuse light

Fig. 9.20 Matrix glazing system. (Thomas Herzog and Partner)

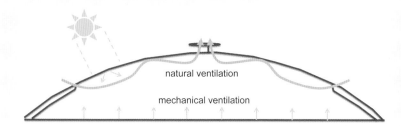

natural ventilation

mechanical ventilation

Fig. 9.21 Schematic of environmental design, indicating the hybrid ventilation system, with natural ventilation at the upper level and mechanical ventilation through the floor, and the solar shading daylight strategy.

Airflow analysis was carried out as part of the natural ventilation design. It showed that as the internal air temperature increased above the external air temperature, due to space heat gains, some of the air entering at the perimeter would fall and maintain the inside temperature close to the outside temperature, with the remainder of the air exhausting the heat gains next to the inside of the glazed roof (see Fig. 9.22). If the internal air temperature in the occupied zone was controlled by air conditioning, the natural ventilation of the upper space would just exhaust the heat gains next to the glazed roof.

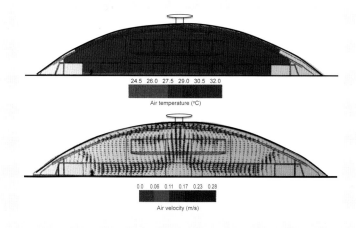

24.5 26.0 27.5 29.0 30.5 32.0

Air temperature (ºC)

0.0 0.06 0.11 0.17 0.23 0.28

Air velocity (m/s)

Fig. 9.22 CFD airflow analysis of natural ventilation showing air entering from side vents and leaving through the top vent. The heat from the glazing is ventilated out.

The building demonstrated a spatial hybrid ventilation system, and a double-skin-glazed roof that shaded solar gains while allowing a daylit space. It has provided a successful daylit exhibition space, whereas most exhibition spaces would be artificially lit.

Case Study 9.6 Ventilation Design: Hall 26, Hannover

Hall 26, designed by Thomas Herzog and Partner, was built for the EXPO 2000 trade fair in Hannover (*see* Fig. 9.23)[9.11]. Its naturally lit exhibition hall uses north-facing steeply pitched roof glazing, whereas the south-facing part of the roof uses a timber construction with triple-glazed roof lights that reflect solar radiation. It has a hybrid natural and mechanical ventilation system, which cost around 50 per cent less than full air conditioning. Fresh air is delivered mechanically through large triangular transparent ducts beneath the lower part of the roof at a height of 4.70m, and directed downwards and distributed evenly over the floor. As the air is heated in the space by internal gains, it moves

Fig. 9.23 A daylit exhibition hall with the option for natural ventilation. (Photo: Thomas Herzog and Partner)

slowly upwards through buoyancy forces and leaves the building via ridge vents located beneath the external 'wings'. These can be opened or closed by a system of individually controlled adjustable flaps, depending on the direction of wind currents, so that only suction forces are active, and air does not enter at ridge level due to positive wind pressure (*see* Fig. 9.24). CFD airflow simulation indicates the temperature distribution due to stack effect, with cool air entering at low level and being extracted at high level (*see* Fig. 9.25). Wind tunnel studies carried out at the Welsh School of Architecture were used to estimate the wind pressure at vent openings for different wind directions, to determine the vent control strategy (*see* Fig. 9.26).

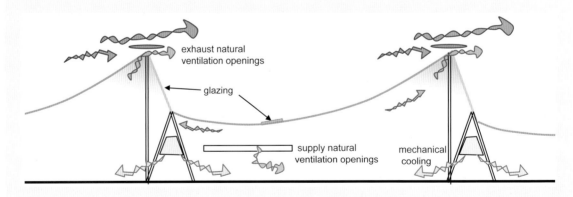

exhaust natural ventilation openings

glazing

supply natural ventilation openings

mechanical cooling

Fig. 9.24 Schematic of environmental design.

Fig. 9.25 Internal temperature distribution by CFD simulation.

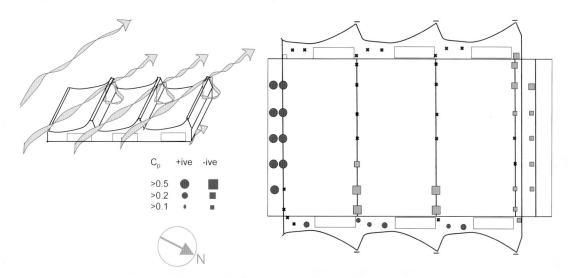

Fig. 9.26 Wind tunnel testing of Hall 26: pressure coefficients for south-easterly wind, indicating positive and negative pressure distribution at inlet and outlet locations.

Case Study 9.7 Saga Office Atrium, Folkestone

The Saga office in Folkestone designed by Hopkins & Partners (see Fig. 9.27) includes a naturally ventilated atrium (see Fig. 9.28). The atrium provides daylight to the rear of the lower single level ground floor, and a double skin for the southerly facing offices behind. Wind tunnel tests were carried out at the Welsh School of Architecture to test the performance of the atrium. An area of relatively high pressure was identified at the opening at the top of the atrium from the southerly onshore wind (see Fig. 9.29), which would interfere with the natural air extract. It was proposed to fit a wing spoiler in front of the extract to create a relative negative pressure, to draw the air out. A CFD airflow simulation indicated that this would prove effective. As with the two previous case studies, a wing device has been used to assist natural air extract from high spaces.

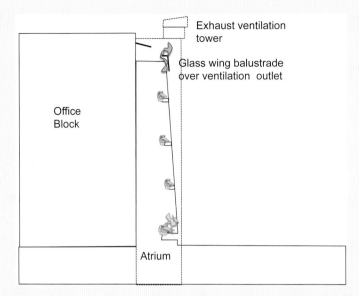

Exhaust ventilation tower

Glass wing balustrade over ventilation outlet

Office Block

Atrium

Fig. 9.27 Saga Office schematic, Folkestone; Architects, Hopkins & Partners.

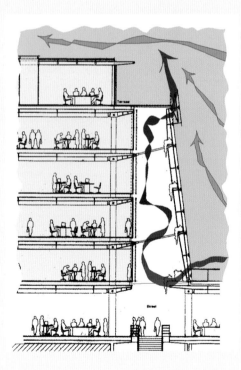

Fig. 9.28 Atrium ventilation with wing spoiler.

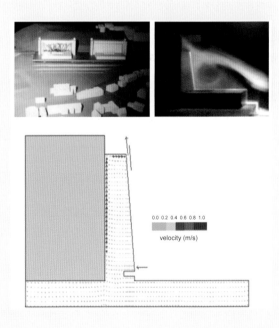

0.0 0.2 0.4 0.6 0.8 1.0
velocity (m/s)

Fig. 9.29 Wind tunnel test model, smoke visualization and CFD simulation.

Case Study 9.8 Contact Theatre, Manchester

The Contact Theatre in Manchester, designed by Short Ford Associates, has two naturally ventilated auditoria. The ventilation design is based on a stack-induced system using 'H-Pot' chimneys for both the studio theatre and the main auditorium. The chimney design was developed with the aid of wind tunnel and CFD modelling in order to ensure that the flow of air up the chimney was relatively insensitive to wind direction, but still providing sufficient ventilation to satisfy occupancy needs and to exhaust the heat gains from the audience and stage lighting. Wind pressure measurements were conducted on a 1:150 scale physical model of the theatre building in the context of the surrounding buildings using the Welsh School of Architecture's boundary layer wind tunnel (see Fig. 9.31). Pressure taps were located at inlet and exhaust positions inside the H-pot terminations of the chimneys. The results showed the H-pots provided a relative negative pressure for a range of wind directions, with positive pressure gradients between the low-level inlet and chimney outlet. Natural buoyancy-driven stack ventilation, with no wind, could be considered the worst-case condition and any wind would assist ventilation.

Fig. 9.30 Contact Theatre, Manchester. (Photo: Shutterstock)

Main auditoria   Studio auditoria

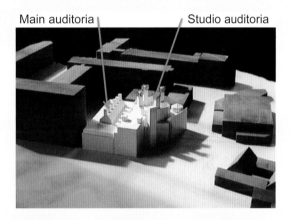

Fig. 9.31 Wind tunnel model showing the main elements of the building.

In summer, the ventilation air is precooled by passing it through a basement where it is cooled by contact with the construction's thermal mass. A CFD airflow analysis was carried out on the main theatre auditorium and studio theatre (see Fig. 9.32) to assess the buoyancy-driven stack ventilation performance due to the heat gains in the space and the precooling in the thermal mass basement.

This case study demonstrates the combination of wind tunnel testing and CFD airflow modelling to provide a means for developing and testing design solutions, and in particular the development of innovative ventilation chimneys.

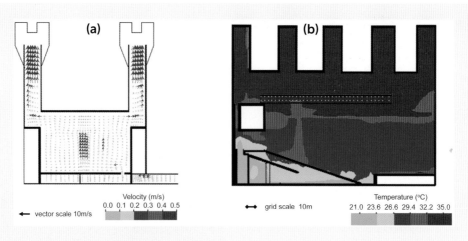

Velocity (m/s)
0.0 0.1 0.2 0.3 0.4 0.5
← vector scale 10m/s

Temperature (°C)
21.0 23.6 26.6 29.4 32.2 35.0
↔ grid scale 10m

Fig. 9.32 CFD analysis: (a) air speed in studio theatre; (b) temperature distribution in main auditorium.

Case Study 9.9 Double-Skin Façade Hybrid Ventilation: Hannover Office HQ

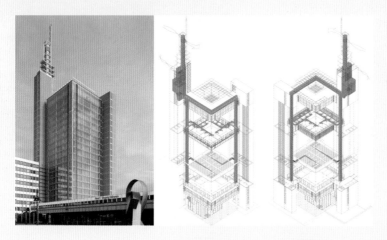

Fig. 9.33 Hannover EXPO Office HQ and overview schematic of the ventilation design. (Thomas Herzog and Partner)

This twenty-storey office building designed by Thomas Herzog and Partner was the headquarters for the Hannover EXPO 2000 (see Fig. 9.33)[9.12]. It incorporated a horizontal double-skin façade that is sealed at every floor by a cantilevered floor slab, so each floor was a self-contained fire zone. Both glazing layers are double-glazed. Outside air enters the double skin through openings, which are automatically controlled depending on wind speed and direction (see Fig. 9.34). The double skin incorporates solar blinds to control solar heat gains, which can be easily maintained by access to the walkway between the glazing layers. Occupants can open windows into the double skin for natural ventilation. Air is exhausted through a vertical shaft rising above the top floor to outside. The offices can also be mechanically ventilated, but if this option is chosen, windows cannot be opened in that zone at the same time. Each floor has a number of controllable louvres that allow external air to be drawn into the double skin and exhausted depending on wind direction. The Welsh School of Architecture's wind tunnel was used to provide information on which to base the control of the louvre openings (see Fig. 9.35).

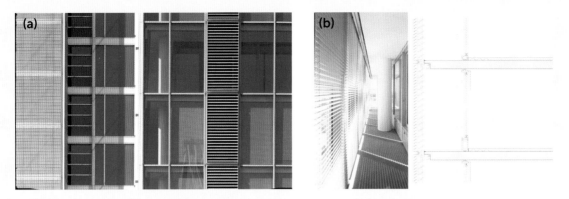

Fig. 9.34 Hannover EXPO Office HQ: (a) controllable louvre vents in façade to allow air to enter; (b) double-skin façade. (Thomas Herzog and Partner)

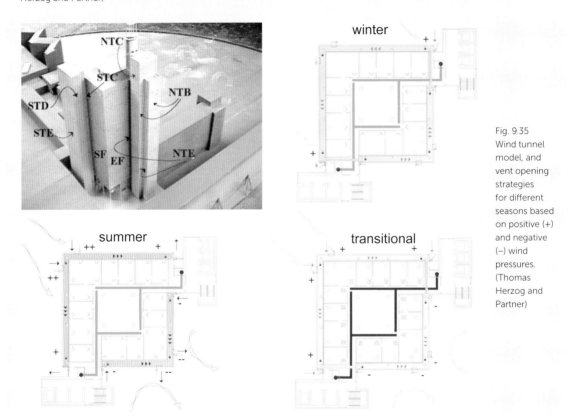

Fig. 9.35 Wind tunnel model, and vent opening strategies for different seasons based on positive (+) and negative (–) wind pressures. (Thomas Herzog and Partner)

The exposed concrete of the office ceiling provides thermal mass for temperature stability. There are also embedded pipes in the floor slab for heating and cooling, with a design floor temperature of 23°C for heating and 21°C for cooling. The central mechanical ventilation system uses a thermal wheel for heat recovery.

The Hannover office demonstrates a hybrid ventilation approach, using a double-skin façade, together with active thermal mass heating and cooling.

Case Study 9.10 Double-Skin Façade: Alpine Finanz, Zurich

Fig. 9.36 Alpine Finanz office in Zurich.

The Alpine Finanz office building in Zurich, designed by Burckhardt and Partner, with building physics by Kopitsis Bauphysik AG, and HVAC by Polke, Ziege, von Moos AG, features a 100 per cent double-skin-glazed façade (*see* Fig. 9.36). Blinds are contained within the continuous vertical double-skin walls to control solar heat gains. Air is allowed to enter the double skin at ground level and leave above the top floor level, to exhaust solar heat gains (*see* Fig. 9.37). The central T-shaped atrium has a double-skin-glazed roof, which also contains blinds for solar shading. The south-facing elevation has an external green wall for additional solar shading, which takes some time to grow to the whole building height.

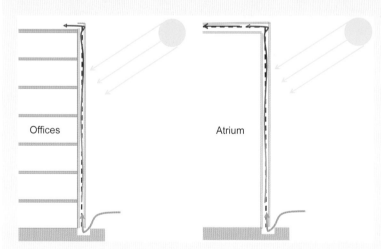

Fig. 9.37 Schematic of double-skin wall.

A CFD airflow analysis (*see* Fig. 9.38) shows the solar heat being captured within the double-skin roof (top) which in summer is ventilated to outside. In winter (bottom), the double skin is not ventilated and it acts as a thermal buffer, adding an insulating layer. The main office cooling uses chilled ceiling panels (*see* Fig. 9.39), with chilled water at 16°C supply and 19°C return. Heating is by perimeter convectors.

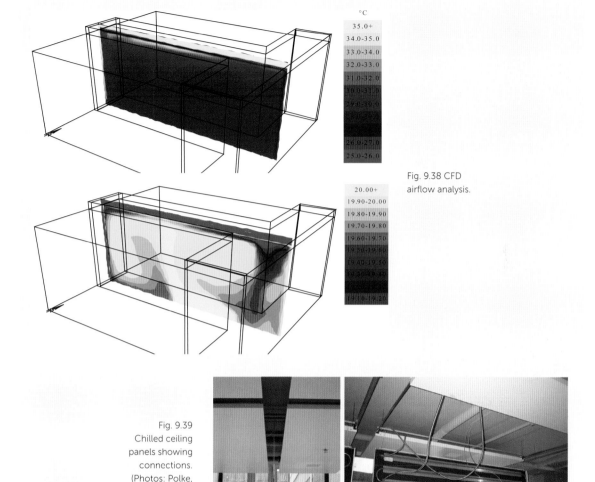

°C

35.0+
34.0-35.0
33.0-34.0
32.0-33.0
31.0-32.0
30.0-31.0
29.0-30.0
28.0-29.0
26.0-27.0
25.0-26.0

Fig. 9.38 CFD
airflow analysis.

20.00+
19.90-20.00
19.80-19.90
19.70-19.80
19.60-19.70
19.50-19.60
19.40-19.50
19.30-19.40
19.10-19.20

Fig. 9.39
Chilled ceiling
panels showing
connections.
(Photos: Polke,
Ziege, von
Moos AG)

This case study shows how a totally glazed building, using a high-quality double-skin design, can provide a controlled environment, maximizing daylight and views.

Case Study 9.11 TX Group AG Office

The TX Group AG office building in Zurich was designed by Atelier WW with building physics by Kopitsis Bauphysik AG. It has totally glazed façades with adjustable external blinds. The diffuse glass blinds let the daylight through while shading solar heat gains, and can be completely raised when not needed (*see* Fig. 9.40). A chilled ceiling cooling system has water pipes cast into the floor slab that forms the ceiling for each floor, which has an acoustic panel fixed to provide a good acoustic environment. Because the majority of cooling is achieved through the chilled ceiling, ventilation is based on the occupant's fresh air needs, and so the air supply ducts are relatively small.

Fig. 9.40 TX Group AG office with external blinds: (a) and (c) down; and (b) withdrawn. (Photos: TX Group)

Computer modelling was used to predict the internal summer temperatures (*see* Fig. 9.41), taking account of the façade system, the chilled ceiling and the ventilation design. The internal air temperature peaked at around 24°C, for an external air temperature of 36°C, which is close to measured values during the first year of occupancy. CFD modelling was used to evaluate the performance of the façade and chilled surface cooling in relation to internal comfort (*see* Fig. 9.42).

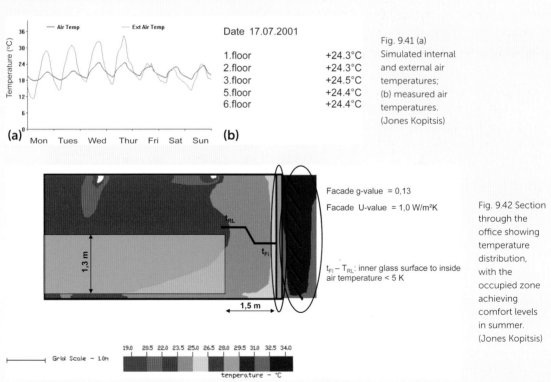

Date 17.07.2001

1.floor	+24.3°C
2.floor	+24.3°C
3.floor	+24.5°C
5.floor	+24.4°C
6.floor	+24.4°C

Fig. 9.41 (a) Simulated internal and external air temperatures; (b) measured air temperatures. (Jones Kopitsis)

Facade g-value = 0,13

Facade U-value = 1,0 W/m²K

$t_{FI} - T_{RL}$: inner glass surface to inside air temperature < 5 K

Fig. 9.42 Section through the office showing temperature distribution, with the occupied zone achieving comfort levels in summer. (Jones Kopitsis)

This case study illustrates the combination of a smart façade, with external controllable blinds, combined with chilled ceiling cooling.

Case Study 9.12 EMPA EWAG Zero Energy Office

Fig. 9.43 EWAG main office building: Forum Chriesbach, external view and atrium. (Photos: EAWAG)

The EWAG office building designed by Bob Gysin and Partner, with building physics by Kopitsis Bauphysik AG, was completed in 2005, and was Switzerland's first zero energy office design (see Fig. 9.43). The external walls are highly insulated with external translucent glass blinds, which track the sun, allowing daylight to enter the internal spaces while protecting from solar overheating. It has a layered façade system with an exposed concrete thermal mass ceiling (see Fig. 9.44).

Fig. 9.44 EWAG façade system and a typical office space. (EAWAG)

The building does not have a conventional heating or cooling system. During the day in summer, mechanical ventilation incorporates ground cooling and heating through a series of some eighty 15m length pipes buried in the ground, delivering ventilation air to the occupied space (see Fig. 9.45). The ground ventilation system can produce around 8°C of cooling when the external air temperature peaks at around 35°C.

The exposed thermal mass ceiling in the offices absorb peak daytime temperatures and the heat is then exhausted at night by natural ventilation using the central atrium, which has a double-skin roof and blind system, to avoid overheating in the day. Renewable energy is generated by solar PV and solar thermal systems located on the roof. The ventilation system provides enough fresh air for occupants, and not the larger quantities that would be associated with more traditional air conditioning systems. So fan power, and space for ducts and air conditioning systems, is reduced.

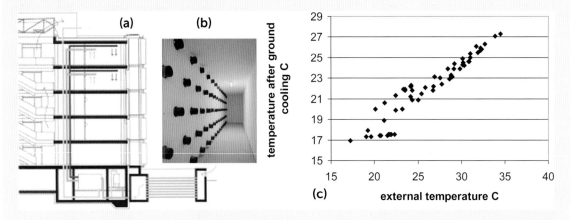

Fig. 9.45 (a) and (b) Ground cooling system; (c) simulated cooling performance with varying external air temperature. (EAWAG; Jones Koptisis)

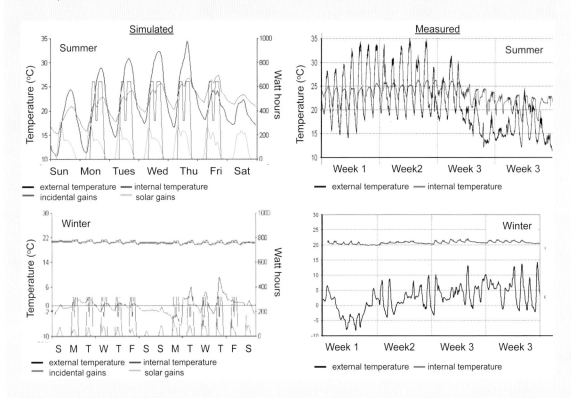

Fig. 9.46 Comparison of simulated and measured conditions for summer and winter. (Jones Kopitsis)

The building was extensively modelled using the Welsh School of Architecture's building energy model, HTB2[9.13]. Simulations were performed for summer and winter conditions at an early design stage. They were compared against measured data during the first year of occupancy (*see* Fig. 9.46). Summertime air temperatures were predicted to peak at around 26°C, which was acceptable as the relatively cool concrete ceiling maintained lower radiant temperatures. Winter temperatures were predicted to be very stable at around 21°C. Measurements were carried out during the first period of occupancy, and they compared well against predictions. An analysis of overall energy performance indicates a relatively low energy use, and the operating energy over a thirty-year period equivalent to the building's embodied energy (*see* Fig. 9.47).

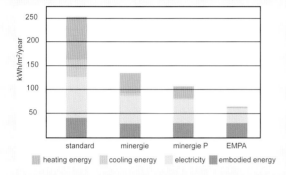

Fig. 9.47 Energy comparison of the EWAG office with a Swiss standard office and Minergie standards. (EAWAG)

This case study demonstrates the success of integrating a range of energy efficiency and environmental measures, including external controllable shading, exposed thermal mass, solar PV and solar thermal renewable energy generation, the use of waste heat, and a diurnal hybrid ventilation system, with natural ventilation night-time cooling and mechanical ground precooling (or preheating) during the day. Thermal modelling was shown to be capable of integrating a number of energy-saving features within the thermal design.

This twenty-year period from the 1980s to the 2000s saw the development of a range of innovative solutions that might be termed a modern passive design approach. A number continue to be used, while some have become less popular. Integrated natural ventilation solutions, using atria and chimneys, have not borne the test of time. They tend to have a major impact on the architecture, and can be relatively expensive, compared to mechanical ventilation. They are also not so flexible to change of use, and cannot easily benefit from heat recovery. However, they may be appropriate for hybrid solutions, or for use in transitional spaces. The glazed façade can also be thought of as a modern approach to passive design, providing good daylight, high levels of thermal insulation, and solar control through glazing treatment and blinds. Chilled ceiling cooling in offices has become

an increasingly favoured option, decoupling ventilation from the cooling and heating supply. This is less energy-intensive and takes up less space for services, and generally provides a more comfortable solution.

Sustainable Design

Sustainable design expands the environmental perspective, with more focus on embodied energy, building integrated renewable energy generation, and water efficiency. It also considers the impact on the economic and social aspects of the community, covering the triple bottom line of environmental, economic and social factors. Sustainable design builds on low energy and passive design, but with a greater emphasis on the following:

i. Renewable energy systems: An increase in the use of building integrated renewable energy. The main renewable energy systems are based on solar energy, including solar thermal and solar photo-voltaic (PV) electricity generation. Other sources of renewables include biomass heating, using sustainable sources of timber fuel. Local wind power generation is an option, but probably best at community scale rather than integrated into the building design, although, as discussed in chapter 8, some large buildings have significant amounts of building integrated wind energy generation.

ii. Environmentally friendly materials with low embodied energy: Sustainable construction uses environmental-friendly materials that are low embodied energy, non-toxic and ethical. Materials should be used efficiently, incorporating reclaimed materials and waste minimization during construction, operation and eventual disposal.

iii. Water use: Water efficiency can be achieved through reducing flows and using efficient water appliances. Rainwater harvesting and greywater recycling can reduce the demand from the water mains. In the UK, around 60 per cent of drinking water is used for applications that do not require drinking water quality, such as toilet flushing. Reducing mains water use will also reduce the energy used to provide potable water and treat waste. In the UK, around 3 per cent of electricity is used for pumping, water treatment and waste management, generating around 1 per cent of the UK's carbon dioxide emissions.

iv. Transport: Sustainable transport systems can reduce fossil fuel emissions, improve air quality, reduce traffic congestion, and reduce traffic-related accidents. A sustainable building development should reduce the need to travel through a flexible live/work mix of buildings and local access to amenities, as well as providing efficient mobility, and encourage cycling, walking and the use of public transport. Good quality broadband can reduce the need to travel, although broadband itself has an energy cost. The use of electric vehicles for public and private mobility reduces local emissions, and electric charging can be linked with renewable energy generation. Car sharing schemes can discourage private car ownership.

v. Green areas: The integration of nature-based systems, including green space and water features, will provide a range of environmental and amenity benefits, including improving air quality; mitigating urban heat island (UHI) effects; carbon capture and sequestration; increasing biodiversity, urban agriculture and local food supply; reducing external noise pollution; and improving social cohesion and pride. Storm-water management can use natural drainage through rain gardens and other sustainable urban drainage systems (SUDS), where water is dispersed through the ground slowly into the watercourse. Green roofs can retain storm water and minimize run-off[9.14].

vi. Health and wellbeing impacts: The built environment should provide a good quality of life for its occupants, and provide internal and external conditions that promote health, comfort and a general feeling of wellbeing. Indoor conditions should provide warmth in winter, minimize overheating in summer, and good indoor air quality all year round. The external environment should encourage exercise and social interactions, and be pollution free. Housing should be easy and economic to maintain, and to adapt as a 'lifetime home'. A building should enhance the local built environment in terms of its aesthetic appearance, and contribute to, and be part of, a safe and supporting neighbourhood.

Fig. 9.48 BedZED (a) natural ventilation chimneys incorporating heat recovery; (b) integrated Solar PV (Photos:Wikimedia Commons).

Sustainable design extends beyond the building and is best done at a community scale. Beddington Zero Energy Development (BedZED), by the architect Bill Dunster, consists of 100 homes, community facilities and workspaces, based on a holistic approach to sustainable housing. Completed in 2002, this high-density urban redevelopment promotes community involvement and a zero energy lifestyle (*see* Fig. 9.48). The workspaces are north-lit for good daylighting, without solar overheating, while the houses are south-facing, making use of passive solar heat gain and solar PV. Sustainable design features include thermal mass, passive ventilation stacks with heat recovery, water-saving devices, and the use of reclaimed materials. The sustainability concept was extended into the community, addressing issues of food supply, green travel planning, and community facilities.

The Sun Ship project in Freiburg, Germany, designed by architect Rolf Disch, was a sustainable urban development completed in 2004, comprising fifty-nine housing units that range in size from 75 to 162m^2, with integrated retail and commercial buildings (*see* Fig. 9.49). The houses were termed PlusEnergy, indicating high levels of energy efficiency, combined with renewable energy systems, and providing more energy than it needs for operational needs[9.15]. The income earned from the excess renewable energy generation offsets the relatively low additional capital costs to produce the PlusEnergy performance. The aim was to create a community, by combining sustainable mobility, with walkways, bike routes, car sharing, and connections to public transportation. Biomass co-generation provided additional heating to the PlusEnergy homes.

Community scale projects that cover a wide range of sustainability design features have been slow to develop and need a committed champion, with a skilled design team, such as the above two projects. The wide range of features requires more design time, which is often a problem with today's fast-track approach to development. Having multiple technical and social targets is also difficult to balance, and perhaps it is easier to have a main target, such as zero energy, and the other targets are then incorporated as appropriate.

Fig. 9.49 Sun Ship development, Freiburg, Germany. (Photo: Shutterstock)

Towards Zero Energy Design

In recent years the pace has quickened towards achieving zero energy buildings, as concern has risen over climate change and the security of energy supply. The focus is now changing from sustainable design to zero energy and zero carbon design. Industry may find it easier to deal with a single target of 'zero energy', rather than the multi-parameter nature of 'sustainable design'. In Europe we are seeing clear signals for achieving nearly zero energy buildings, and how this will be achieved through the ramping up of standards, through future building regulations.

Definitions can be confusing. A low energy building will have a reduced energy demand for thermal loads associated with heating, ventilation, cooling, together with more efficient lighting and appliances. A zero energy building will have further reductions in energy demand, with the energy being supplied from zero carbon generation (*see* Fig. 9.50). An energy-positive building will generate more energy from zero carbon sources than it needs to operate, averaged over a year. A zero energy and energy-positive building will generally generate renewable energy

at the building, and they are usually grid connected. Carbon neutral is a term generally used when the energy imported from the grid is totally offset by renewable energy generated at the building and exported to the grid, typically over a year. Such a building will also be zero energy. A building can be defined as truly zero carbon when there are no carbon emissions associated with the building's operation, and there is no fossil fuel energy supply used at all, not even if it is offset by exporting renewable energy to the grid. Such a building will essentially be off-grid. Off-grid zero carbon autonomous buildings are more challenging, and total autonomy is not really necessary unless the building cannot be connected to the grid; the combination of renewable energy supply and energy storage to provide total autonomy will generally be expensive and impractical in relation to the size of systems needed. In future the grid itself will become increasingly decarbonized, with a higher proportion of large-scale renewable energy generation connected to it, from wind farms and large-scale solar. The term nearly zero energy is used by the EU to describe a performance that approaches zero energy, and includes reduced energy demand and renewable energy supply. The energy refers to primary energy, so it includes any losses and generation system inefficiencies if fossil fuels are used. This plethora of terms can be confusing, and we often interchange them when describing a building's performance. Up to now we have mainly used the terms low and zero energy when related to a building, and zero carbon when we refer to future aspirations, when we will have a zero carbon energy grid and a zero carbon society as a whole.

For domestic and stretched domestic scale buildings, a zero energy and carbon neutral performance should be possible in most places, using building integrated renewable energy and energy storage. However, for larger buildings, especially in dense urban areas, and energy retrofits, we may need to rely also on decarbonizing the electricity grid, and possibly the gas grid, to support what we can achieve on the building.

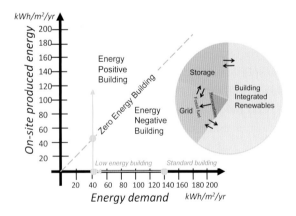

Fig. 9.50 Illustration of low energy, zero energy and energy-positive performance. The graph relates energy demand and a building integrated renewable energy supply. The pie chart illustrates the energy exchange between the building, storage, and the grid, with the grid being decarbonized with an increasing amount of renewable energy generation.

A zero energy building has the following design features:

i. Reduced energy demand: A zero energy building has a very low energy demand for heating, cooling, and ventilation. Heating applies to both space heating, and domestic hot water, which, for housing, now has a similar if not greater energy demand than space heating. Lighting and appliance energy loads also need to be reduced, as they contribute to overall electricity use. The demand will be similar to Passive hHaus standards of 15kWh/m^2 per year for heating or cooling, and a total primary energy use of less than 120kWh/m^2 per year for all applications (including heating, cooling, hot water and electricity).

ii. Renewable energy supply: A zero energy building will generally have renewable energy integrated into its design, and will be carbon neutral over a year. A building may import energy from the grid when there is no renewable energy available, but it will export back to the grid when there is excess renewable energy generated. The energy imported from the grid has an increasing proportion of 'green energy' from wind farms or other sources of grid-based renewables.

iii. Energy storage: Renewable energy is not always available, so energy can be stored, from when it is available to when it is needed. This applies to thermal and electrical energy. Thermal energy can be stored in the building fabric, surrounding ground, or in specific fluids, sometimes incorporating phase change or chemical-based technologies. Electrical storage may use batteries. Timescales for storage range from daily to seasonal. Storage may be at building or community scale, or the grid itself can be used as a form of storage. In future, electrical vehicles may be linked to a building's renewables and battery storage needs.

iv. Embodied energy: The embodied energy in the building construction also has associated energy use and carbon dioxide emissions, although this is not generally included in the definitions of zero energy and carbon neutral. This could also be offset by the renewable energy systems over the life of the building.

Fig. 9.51 presents a typical annual energy breakdown for a zero energy house.

We will now consider some case studies of buildings from the past twenty years that aim towards a low and zero energy performance.

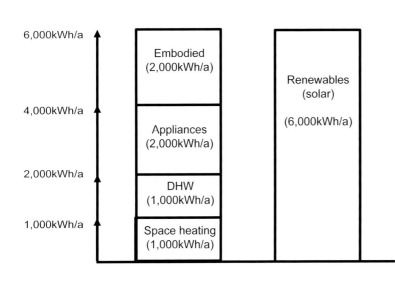

Fig. 9.51 Projected annual energy breakdown for a zero energy house (floor area 100m^2) located in the UK, which includes space heating and DHW loads, and appliance loads. The estimated embodied energy is based on around 4GJ/m^2 over a sixty-year lifetime.

Case Study 9.13 Gateway Building, Baglan Energy Park

Fig. 9.52 Gateway factory, Baglan Energy Park, South Wales, with solar PV also used as shading.

The Gateway factory at Baglan Energy Park, Neath Port Talbot, South Wales, was designed by the Welsh School of Architecture's Design Research Unit (DRU) in collaboration with Neath Port Talbot Council, and was completed in 2000[9.16]. The building is comprised of a large production area with south-facing offices (*see* Fig. 9.52). The office location presented an overheating risk, which was reduced using solar shading in the form of solar PV panels, allowing the offices to be naturally ventilated. A 1.5m wide panel of crystalline solar PV was located at a 45 degree angle above the office windows. In addition, two flat panels of amorphous thin-film solar PV were located above the entrances either side of the front façade. The total area of 100m^2 of solar PV was estimated to generate some 9,600kWh per year. Windows can be opened along the south-facing façade allowing fresh air into the office space, with ceiling extract ducts to the rear of the office high-bay glazed 'pop-up' zone, using a passive stack design (*see* Fig. 9.53).

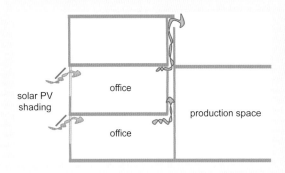

Fig. 9.53 Natural ventilation strategy for the offices.

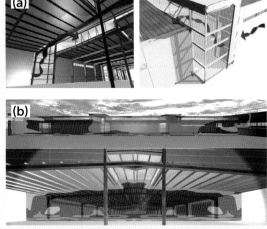

Fig. 9.54 Ventilation design: (a) for the production space, (b) CFD simulation of space temperature distribution.

The production area ventilation design included louvres at low and high level located within the pop-up areas, which had glazing to the north, and vertical strips on the east and west elevations (*see* Fig. 9.54). CFD airflow modelling was carried out as part of the ventilation design to ensure adequate ventilation and to assess indoor summertime temperatures. A 1:150 scale model of the building was made to test the daylighting performance in the Welsh School of Architecture's SkyDome (*see* Fig. 9.55), which resulted in adding additional ridge glazing to improve daylight distribution.

The building was the first factory in the UK to receive the BREEAM excellent rating, winning a regional RIBA design award, and was shortlisted for the Stirling sustainability award.

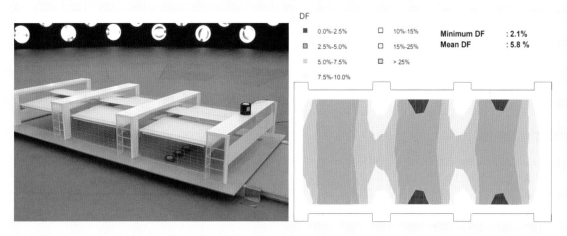

DF

■ 0.0%-2.5% □ 10%-15% **Minimum DF** : 2.1%
▣ 2.5%-5.0% □ 15%-25% **Mean DF** : 5.8 %
▦ 5.0%-7.5% □ > 25%
7.5%-10.0%

Fig. 9.55 Daylight analysis using the Cardiff University SkyDome.

Case Study 9.14 Sustainable Building Envelope Centre, Tata, Shotton

Fig. 9.56 Sustainable Building Envelope Centre (SBEC), Shotton: (a) front south-facing elevation; (b) internal view of the research/exhibition space.

The Sustainable Building Envelope Centre (SBEC) at Tata in Shotton, North Wales, was designed by the Welsh School of Architecture's DRU and was completed in 2010 (*see* Fig. 9.56). It formed part of a research programme to investigate building integrated renewable energy systems. The building was a retrofit of four bays of an old 300m long steelmaking shed. It incorporated offices and a large space for research and exhibitions.

Transpired solar (air) collectors (TSCs) were integrated into the south-facing façade to collect solar energy, for preheating the ventilation air (*see* Fig. 9.57). Frameless, lightweight solar PV panels were integrated into the roof design. The forty-two high-performance SOLON SOLbond crystalline panels cover an area of 84m^2, and weigh less than 10kg/m^2.

Fig. 9.57 The installation and operation of the TSC ventilation system and section through the TSC. The green cladding areas were TSCs, each linked to the adjacent office spaces. The larger dark façade to the right in Fig. 9.56 was also a TSC used to heat the large volume research and exhibition space.

An underfloor wet heating system was installed in the offices, with a temperature supply of 30°C to 35°C, using a heat pump to supply the warm water. The system also provides cooling in summer. The downstairs meeting room has a phase change ceiling to reduce overheating. The ceiling incorporates a paraffin wax that melts at 24°C, absorbing heat when the air temperature reaches 24°C. This heat is released back into the space when the space cools down, providing a pleasant, cool environment in warm weather.

Case Study 9.15 SOLCER House

Fig. 9.58 View of the south-facing elevation of the SOLCER House and roof integrated solar PV array.

The SOLCER (Smart Operation for a Low Carbon Energy Region) House was designed at the Welsh School of Architecture and was completed in 2015 (*see* Fig. 9.58)[9.17]. The three-bedroom detached house of 100m² floor area is targeted at the social housing market. The aim was to develop an energy-positive house, integrating a range of technologies using a whole system design approach, combining reduced energy demand, renewable energy supply and energy storage, based on outcomes from the Low Carbon Research Institute's (LCRI) Low Carbon Buildings Programme[9.18].

The energy demand of the house was reduced to a near 'Passivhaus' level. However, the design did not follow the Passivhaus standard rigorously, in order to allow greater freedom to use technologies and local suppliers that may not be compliant with Passivhaus requirements. The house had high levels of thermal insulation and a low air leakage. It used a modular SIPs (structural insulated panels) system construction, comprising 172mm of climate EPS insulation contained between two layers of OSB (oriented strand board) with an external insulated render, achieving an overall U-value of 0.12W/m².K. Double-glazed timber-frame windows, with an aluminium external finish, had U-values of 1.12 to 1.51W/m².K, depending on their dimensions and the influence of the frame. The ceiling and floor U-values were 0.1 and 0.15W/m².K respectively. The south-facing roof comprises an array of solar PV panels. The north-facing roof is constructed from a SIPs system with a standing seam metal cladding external finish.

The energy supply is all-electric, providing space and domestic hot water heating, and powering electrical appliances. The electrical and thermal technologies (*see* Fig. 9.59) combine solar PV (34m² area, capacity 4.3kWp) and a lithium-ion-phosphate Victron 6.9kW battery storage, which power an exhaust air heat pump (55W input with a COP – coefficient of performance – of 2.31), which together with a 14m² transpired solar (thermal air) collector (TSC) and mechanical ventilation with heat recovery system (MVHR) provide space heating and domestic hot water (DHW). Electricity is drawn from the grid when there is not enough power available from the PV and battery system. The solar PV and battery storage also provide power for lighting and electrical appliances. The aim was to maximize the use of the renewable energy in the house, and only export to the grid when all the house's energy needs are fulfilled. The energy systems were integrated into the design of the building, with the PV panels providing the south-facing roof, and the TSC providing the external south-facing first floor external wall finish. This approach provides a different aesthetic, and reduces costs, compared to a solar PV system 'bolted on' to a standard roof.

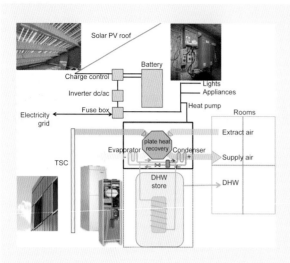

Fig. 9.59 Combined electrical and thermal technologies.

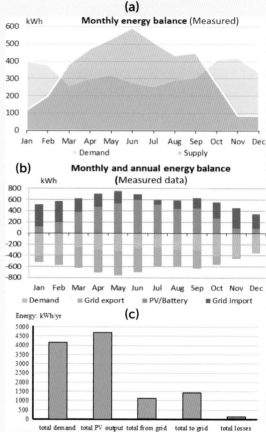

Fig. 9.60 (a) Monthly energy (renewable) supply and demand; (b) breakdown of monthly energy; and (c) annual energy breakdown.

The building has a very low heat demand and can therefore be heated through the mechanical ventilation system. External air enters the TSC and is preheated from incident solar radiation, when available. It then passes through the MVHR heat exchanger and, if needed, topped up with heat from the heat pump. Exhaust air exchanges heat with the incoming supply air through the MVHR, and then passes over the evaporator of the heat pump, which extracts further heat before the air is finally exhausted to outside. The exhaust air heat pump heats both supply air and the thermal water store.

The heat pump is able to maintain a relatively high COP throughout the heating season, by extracting heat from the exhaust air. The MVHR, heat pump, and thermal store are all contained within the single Genvex Combi 185LS EC unit.

Measurement data shows the house can achieve an energy-positive performance (see Fig. 9.60). The house was designed based on available technology and by using local supply chains. A major design criterion was affordability, and the estimated cost of replication at the time of construction was around £1,300 per m², which was considered acceptable for the then current social housing costs (2015).

Following the success of the SOLCER House, other projects have been initiated in South Wales, including fourteen SOLCER-type houses in Bridgend, for Wales and the West Housing Association (*see* Fig. 9.61), occupied in January 2021.

Fig. 9.61 Image of new houses based on the SOLCER design, constructed in Bryn Bragl, South Wales. (Zenergy Design)

CASE STUDY 9.16 SOLCER Retrofit Housing

Five whole house 'deep' retrofit housing case studies (*see* Fig. 9.62) were carried out to investigate an affordable and replicable 'whole house systems' approach, integrating a number of measures tailored to the specific property[9.19]. The measures used were similar to those applied to the SOLCER new build case, but appropriate to the construction and age of the house (*see* Table 9.1). The houses are all in the social housing sector and owned by registered social landlords (RSLs).

Fig. 9.62 Five retrofit houses: (a) before, and (b) after retrofit.

Table 9.1: Information summary of the retrofits.

	Retrofit 1	Retrofit 2	Retrofit 3	Retrofit 4	Retrofit 5
Basic information	Pre-1919, 2-bed, solid wall, end-terrace of 67m², gas boiler.	1960s, 3-bed cavity wall, semi-detached, 70m², gas combi boiler.	2000s, 3-bed filled cavity wall, semi-detached, 86m², gas boiler.	Pre-1919, 2-bed solid wall, mid-terrace, 74m², gas combi boiler.	1950s, 3-bed filled cavity wall, semi-detached, 80m², gas combi boiler.
Energy-efficient strategies	a. solid external wall insulation b. loft insulation and flat roof insulation to rear extension c. low-e double glazing d. MVHR e. LED lighting f. new system boiler with hot water tank	a. gable cavity wall insulation and front external wall insulation b. loft insulation c. MVHR d. LED lighting e. new energy-efficient fridge f. new combi boiler g. new radical radiators plus flush	a. loft insulation b. new positive pressure unit added on landing, new extractors added in kitchen, bathroom and shower room for sufficient ventilation c. LED lighting d. new gas boiler and hot water tank e. new radical radiators plus flush	a. rear external wall insulation, front internal wall insulation b. loft insulation c. floor and roof insulation of the rear extension d. LED lighting e. new radical radiators plus flush	a. external wall insulation b. loft insulation c. LED lighting
PV	2.5kWp PV roof	2.7kWp PV roof	4.5kWp PV roof	2.6kWp PV roof	3.97kWp PV roof
Energy storage*	Lead acid battery: 4.8kWh to feed LEDs and hot water.	Lead acid battery: 8.5kWh to feed LEDs and fridge.	Lead acid battery: 18kWh to feed all electrical appliances.	Lithium battery: 2.0kWh to feed all electrical appliances.	Lithium battery: 10kWh to feed all electrical appliances.
Retrofit cost	£30,452	£27,438	£30,446	£23,852	£30,510

* *The lead acid batteries were later replaced by lithium batteries.*

The whole house retrofit process included the following stages;

1. At the start of each retrofit, a survey was carried out to identify what retrofit measures might be appropriate, and any building owner and resident constraints. The surveys were based on a 'fabric first' approach, including external wall insulation, loft insulation, glazing and airtightness. This was followed by a consideration of LED lighting, improvements in HVAC systems, and the installation of renewable energy and energy storage systems.

2. A range of strategies was simulated using a dynamic building energy model (HTB2), to explore the impact of combinations of measures on energy consumption, carbon dioxide emissions, and operating cost savings.

3. The optimum package for each house was confirmed and agreed, considering budget limits and work timetables, and the installation took place.

The five SOLCER retrofit case studies were monitored over a two-year period, showing significant savings (see Table 9.2).

Table 9.2 A summary of performance optimization through domestic retrofit.

	Retrofit 1	Retrofit 2	Retrofit 3	Retrofit 4	Retrofit 5
Reduction ratio of electricity import	−37%	−41%	−79%	−72%	−84%
Gas reduction ratio	−56%	−23%	+1%	−35%	−6%
CO_2 reduction ratio	−64%	−49%	−54%	−74%	−61%
Cost savings	−62%	−52%	−85%	−81%	−84%

The benefits of installing a 10kWh lithium battery system to all five retrofits was evaluated to be around £100 to £200 per year. Although the cost of batteries is decreasing, it is still not a cost-effective investment on its own. This is where a whole house systems approach is needed, where not every measure is cost-effective now, but will still bring benefits. Instead of optimizing at component level, the system as a whole is optimized. More recent retrofit studies have demonstrated that the combination of PV generation and battery storage can reduce energy demand considerably (see Fig. 9.63), such that the import of electricity from the grid in summer is very low.

The last four decades or so have witnessed a range of developments towards sustainable zero energy design, some emphasizing a passive architectural approach, while others have been developed from a more engineering technological approach. Some have borne the test of time more than others, but all have contributed to our greater understanding of how to design and construct a zero energy and zero carbon built environment.

Annual electricity cost before : £522 **Annual electricity cost after : £155**

Fig. 9.63 Solar PV and battery storage installed as part of a whole house retrofit, showing the drop in electricity imported from the grid and cost savings.

Chapter Ten

Transition

THE MAIN FOCUS OF THIS BOOK HAS BEEN on technical solutions for thermal design. However, these can only be effective if they are implemented correctly, and at scale. They require people's acceptance, as users, builders and legislators, all within the context of the wider socio-economic aspects of future sustainability, including developing green jobs, skills, supply chains and financial models. Much has been achieved in developing our understanding of sustainable design. If we are to transition to a zero carbon built environment in the small window of time that we have left to avoid catastrophic climate change, it is urgent that we now put this understanding into practice. In this final chapter we shall summarize the issues relating to the transition of zero carbon thermal design technology into practice.

Technical Solutions

We have a range of technical solutions to hand, and more will be developed over time, their costs will come down, and the low carbon industry and skills base will expand. Throughout this book we have concentrated on building physics in relation to architectural and engineering solutions, which can be used to underpin thermal design and its integration into a whole building systems approach.

Whole Systems Approach

A whole systems approach integrates architecture and engineering solutions, to provide affordable comfort and health, rather than bolting on technology to an existing design.

- Through a whole system approach we can learn how the passive and active elements of design interact, and we should optimize our designs as whole systems. It may be that some elements are not yet cost-effective, such as battery storage, but costs will come down. If we wait until all elements are optimized before incorporating them into the system, we will never get there.
- We are relatively good at dealing with the building fabric, and reducing demand through a 'fabric first' approach is generally an accepted approach. However, there is still a 'performance gap' issue, in particular relating to integrity of insulation and air leakage, which needs to be addressed at the design, construction and operational stages.
- We need HVAC solutions that link heating and cooling to ventilation design, and to maximize the use of efficient ways of generating heating and cooling. Heat pump technology is well matched to low and zero carbon buildings, and is readily linked to a building integrated renewable energy supply.
- With reduced thermal energy demand, ventilation systems can provide heating and cooling within their fresh air delivery rates. Additional heating and cooling may be provided by surface systems. This provides an efficient way of heating and cooling, utilizing heat recovery options, which are also suited to heat pump technology.
- Building integrated renewable energy and energy storage are main features of zero energy design. Zero energy usually means some exchange with the supply grid. Zero carbon will only be achieved at scale when the supply grid itself becomes decarbonized.

- We need technical solutions that are people-friendly, legible and easy to use. They should be robust against a range of behaviours, and not require major behaviour changes. They should be attractive and not based on constraint. They should provide thermal delight, and not just designed to avoid problems.
- The retrofit of existing buildings will form a major activity in our drive to zero carbon. Many of the new technologies developed for new build will be applicable to retrofit, albeit at an increased cost and degree of difficulty. It may be appropriate to combine new build and retrofit programmes, such as downsizing for elderly people living in substandard housing, and providing healthy, comfortable, zero energy new housing, and freeing up and retrofitting older houses for larger families.
- We need to consider standardized solutions, not necessarily all looking alike but using standard technical systems. Off-site modular construction can lead to an improvement in quality, reducing the performance gap between design and operation, and reducing waste and embodied energy.
- We need to consider the embodied energy of materials and components, such as developing environmentally friendly insulation materials, and nature-based solutions that are both sustainable and pleasant and healthy for people.
- Our focus to date has been at building scale, and mainly housing. We need to expand to all building types and to urban scale, with opportunities to share solutions across buildings. We must ensure that buildings to not have a detrimental effect on each other or on the outside environment.
- New buildings are likely to be all-electric. However, existing buildings will be likely to use gas for some time. Both the electricity and gas grids have ambitions to decarbonize.

Future Energy Systems

The whole system approach can expand from individual buildings, to groups of buildings, and to the whole energy system. The question arises on how much renewable energy do we provide on the building and how much from the grid (*see* Fig. 10.1). As we strive for zero energy or zero carbon performance, the cost goes up, and there will be an optimum level for different building types.

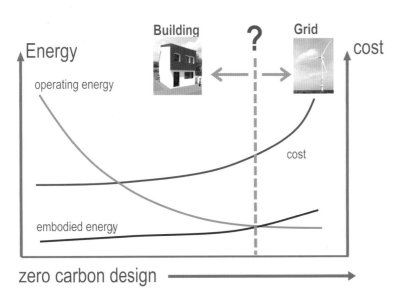

Fig. 10.1 Building versus grid energy supply.

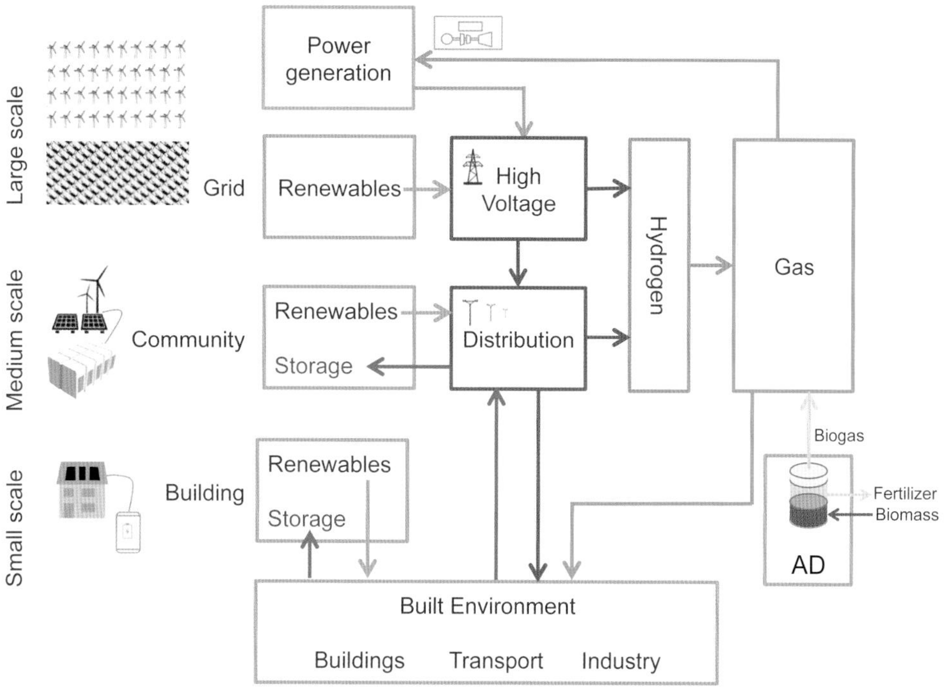

Fig. 10.2 Future energy system projection, with renewable energy and energy storage at all levels, and the interaction between the electricity and gas grid.

- As the grid is increasingly becoming decarbonized, our future energy system will be likely to look much different from the current one (*see* Fig. 10.2). There will be energy generation and storage at all levels, from building to community to central grid.

- With a greater proportion of grid renewable energy generation, carbon emission factors are reducing, making grid-based electricity a more sustainable option. However, the 'green' capacity of the grid will be limited for some time, and demand reduction, together with building and local renewable energy generation, is fundamental to achieving a greener grid.

- The level of renewable energy and energy storage at building scale will vary, depending on building form and density of development. A building can maximize its autonomy from the grid, becoming zero energy or even energy positive. This is attractive for new build. Another option would be to optimize the capacity of generation and storage over large numbers of buildings through an aggregation scheme,

where a company will control the exchange of energy between the buildings and the grid, in a cost-optimum way. This may be particular attractive for existing buildings, such as social housing estates, where not all houses will be optimally orientated for solar panels.

- Gas may still play a major role in this future energy system, not just in the transition stage to zero carbon, but also as a future energy provider. There are plans to decarbonize the gas grid. Excess renewable electricity can be converted to hydrogen, together with methane generation from waste, and can be stored and distributed through the existing gas system. Hybrid heating systems may use a combination of green gas and green electricity, with gas being used in colder weather and electric heat pumps in milder weather, when their COPs are higher.

- The building itself will become far more integrated with this 'smarter' future energy system, and users will become 'prosumers', both energy users and energy generators. Links between buildings and transport may use electric vehicle batteries as part of an overall energy storage system. Decision-making, using smart technology, will be required at the building scale, exchanging energy across the system in relation to the dynamics of supply, storage and demand.

Multiple Benefits

We need to look holistically at the benefits of zero energy buildings. It is not enough to simply equate energy saved with the cost of measures. There are many benefits to sustainable zero energy design, some quantifiable, and others more qualitative in nature. Benefits are realized at different scales, from building, to community, to national and global levels (*see* Table 10.1).

- The implementation of low and zero energy technologies comes with added-value 'multiple benefits'. Improved thermal design and reducing a building's energy demand can lead to affordable warmth, alleviate fuel poverty, improve health, improve productivity, and reduce local air pollution.
- Such buildings will have a higher asset value, attract higher rents, and be future-proofed against changes in regulations and standards, especially relating to climate change mitigation and adaptation.
- New industries associated with energy-efficient buildings, building retrofit programmes and new energy systems, bring socio-economic benefits, creating jobs, and generating local industries and supply chains.
- There will be societal and cost benefits from improving health and wellbeing and productivity at work.
- The cost of greener buildings is often lower than perceived if an integrative approach is taken when combining architectural aspects with engineering aspects; cost increases can be offset by cost reductions, for example, increased costs for a better thermally insulated building can be offset by reduced costs for heating and cooling systems.

Table 10.1 Scales of multiple benefits.

Building	Community	National/Global
• Healthy indoor and outdoor environment • Increased occupant wellbeing and productivity • Lower operating and maintenance costs • Reduced absenteeism in businesses • Longer tenancies and higher lease rates • Increased asset value and marketability • Future-proofed and reduced risk of obsolescence • Satisfying corporate social responsibilities	• Jobs and new supply chains • Local economic growth • Less pollution	• Carbon emission reductions • Reduced use of resources • Public health and social benefit savings • Security of energy supply • Reduced environmental damage • Reduced fossil fuel-induced global tension (wars and refugees)

- Any increase in capital costs need to be weighed up against the combined benefits. New cost models are needed for both new build and retrofit projects that place a cost value on all the benefits, recognizing the total societal value of multiple benefits, and not just relate energy savings to the cost of measures.

Policy to Practice

Although governments are declaring a climate emergency, there appears to be an increasing gap between policy and practice when it comes to energy use and meeting carbon dioxide emission targets for the built environment. Policy-driven emission reduction targets will not be achieved unless there is a clear transition route through to practice. In recent years, prioritizing on a top-down policy-driven approach to emission reduction has failed to deliver. There is a great need for a balance with bottom-up solutions (*see* Fig. 10.3).

Top-Down, Bottom-Up

Most of our energy policy has been driven by a central 'top-down' supply-led approach. From a built environment perspective, a top-down approach represents the actions and interests of big government and big industry, for example, in relation to grid-based energy supply, building regulations, and national and international carbon emission reduction targets.

- Top-down solutions often rely on regional implementation, which may not have the necessary resources, and there may be confusion where responsibilities lie.
- From a policy level, top-down might represent international policy on carbon emission reduction, and rely largely on building regulations for their implementation. On the other hand, bottom-up might relate more to the implementation of innovative low carbon technologies on specific projects.
- A demand-led 'bottom-up' approach represents the interests of the end user, whether individuals, organizations or communities, in relation to their specific building and built environment needs. There is currently a growing interest in bottom-up solutions to reduce energy demand and create better environmental conditions in the built environment, countering the slow delivery of top-down-driven initiatives.

Fig. 10.3 Top-down and bottom-up approaches.

- Adopting a bottom-up approach may be less prescriptive, encouraging improvements above minimum standards and regulations, and deal with problems at the lowest possible level of decision-making.
- Bottom-up follows the up-cycling concept of 'more good', whereas top-down approaches generally follow the 'less bad' concept. Bottom-up is potentially more engaged and comprehensive in relation to the needs of the inhabitants of the built environment.
- From a bottom-up building user perspective, comfort, health and wellbeing are fundamental to enjoying a good quality of life, as well as maximizing productivity and satisfaction. Affordable heating and cooling is of prime importance to householders and businesses. Efficient and clean energy use, with the eventual elimination of fossil fuels, leads to improved indoor and outdoor air quality. End users may be driven to take action if they can expect such bottom-up tangible benefits, rather than contributing to national and global targets, such as reduction in greenhouse gas emissions.
- The more bottom-up achieves, in reducing energy demand, the less pressure is on top-down to meet increasing demand by expanding supply. In that sense, both approaches are mutually reinforcing and inherently complimentary with each other and need to co-exist to achieve the needed transformations.
- Although bottom-up has potential advantages in moving the low carbon agenda forward from a people perspective, bottom-up alone lacks the holistic vision to deal with major national issues at hand, and it is generally dispirit in nature and sometimes short term. Whereas, top-down alone lacks penetration and its motives are bound up in maintaining the status quo. No matter how hard the top-down pushes unless there is a bottom-up acceptance and demand, delivery will be slow.
- This link between top-down and bottom-up may be best achieved through middle-out agents, who do not have vested interests in maintaining the status quo, possibly through non-profit organizations, or maybe the construction industries professions, if they have the appetite for it!
- For the transition to a sustainable zero carbon society to happen, there needs to be a greater emphasis on a bottom-up 'whole systems' approach. Roles and responsibilities need to be reviewed at all levels. New roles may emerge, and role of the building physicist will increase in importance, as a profession that deals specifically with the environmental and energy elements of future building design.

Procurement

Sustainability is as much about process as technical solutions, which includes, how we plan, design, construct and commission our buildings, as well as how we operate them over time and eventually dispose of them.

- Top-down solutions, especially on larger projects, are often implemented through generalized procurement arrangements and framework contracts, which tend to adhere to minimum standards and regulations, and are inherently resistant to change.
- Technology 'lock-in' is often associated with top-down approaches, where government incentives and various assessment schemes require accreditation of new technologies before they can be recognized. This can prove expensive, introduce time delays and may exclude small local more innovative players from the supply chains.
- Large construction companies and volume house-builders generally pay only lip service to energy and sustainable design, and they have a huge influence on government policy,

for example, in delaying the development of energy-related building regulations.

- The architectural profession in general has lacked the ambition to take responsibility for a more sustainable approach to building design.
- Targets, regulation, compliance, performance in use, all lag behind policy advancement (*see* Fig. 10.4). Although long-term targets for carbon dioxide emission reduction are ambitious, shorter-term targets are often put back due to uncertainties in their implementation, and lobbying from sectors of industry that are opposed to change.
- Regulations lag behind for similar reasons, and not all aspects of energy use are regulated.
- Compliance lags behind the introduction of new regulations, either intentionally through periods of grace, advanced planning applications, or due to a lack of understanding within the industry.
- At the end of the 'pipeline', performance in use is often compromised by poor design and workmanship, and a general lack of understanding of how to integrate low carbon technologies into the existing planning, design and construction, processes and practices. The performance gap persists!
- Low carbon technologies and innovative solutions are being developed, especially at building and community scale, but they are slow to feed up into policy and down into general practice.

The Way Forward

Our generation has the singular opportunity to keep the world's climate stable. There is an urgent need to speed up the transition of zero carbon design and technology into practice in the built environment. The evidence relating to global warming, polluted air and security of supply is overwhelming. There is no excuse to wait. Solutions are available.

Every project should strive to be zero energy, setting targets that are adhered to throughout the design and construction process, with proper commissioning and monitoring of in-use performance.

- Government response is often to set up committees and demonstration projects, the results of which sometimes never emerge, or are forgotten; this pushes the problem into the future, and we carry on as normal. We need to change our approach and use real everyday projects to demonstrate what is possible, to feedback information and be prepared to fail; the continuing performance gap issue shows that buildings often fail anyway!
- We must challenge current procurement practices and vested interests that are protected by

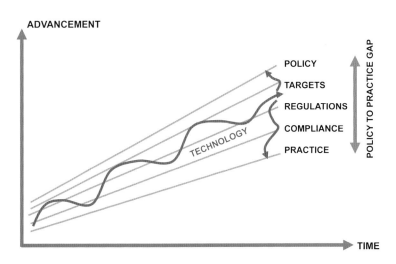

Fig. 10.4 Policy to practice.

standards, regulations, framework agreements, and hidden subsidies. The delays in progressing towards a zero carbon built environment are more related to the culture and processes of the construction industry rather than a lack of technology.

- We must challenge the status quo, to remove the obstacles that inhibit the transition to a zero carbon built environment, and redesign our procurement methods such that they can help push forward the zero carbon agenda and facilitate the rapid changes needed.

- All sectors of the construction industry need to engage with zero carbon goals. Government needs to provide greater support to those who want change, rather than propping up those that do not want change. The low carbon industry is a major future growth area and will contribute to a vibrant clean future economy, with products that benefit both people and the environment. However, some industries seem to want to control any change to their financial benefit, leading to a conflict between environmental policy and industry uptake, and between business interests and ethical values.

- Industry cannot continue to make the excuse that it is unprepared for change, and that people do not want change. It can no longer make the excuse that because it is archaic and cannot deliver on performance, it should be allowed to continue to produce substandard buildings that do not meet the needs of society and the environment.

- Industries that resist change generally have greater lobbying powers with governments. They often receive subsidies and preferential taxation. On the other hand, some industries welcome change as a means to produce new innovative high-value products that support the transition to zero carbon. These industries need greater support from government, including a fairer distribution of subsidies and tax incentives.

- We need to activate 'middle-out agents' that are able to effect change, who can make informed decisions, and who are properly equipped to implement systematic change, through best practice and operational excellence, and through a cycle of continuous improvement. An opportunity to rebalance bottom-up and top-down approaches, and enhance community ownership, lies in recognizing the potential attributes of a 'middle-out' approach.

- There should be clear transition routes and government forward planning from policy to practice, to which industry and the public can respond. Communication is often weak, both between different government departments, between central and local government, and between government and industry. Policy change is often erratic in relation to industry timescales for developing new products, and the skills required to apply them effectively. Government decisions must be unbiased and research-based evidence-led, with clear transition paths identified to enable industry to forward plan, and develop new skills, finance models and stable supply chains. The knowledge triangle of government, industry and research should be used to spin out innovative solutions quickly into practice.

- We need to create a bottom-up demand for zero carbon solutions, which is underpinned and safeguarded by regulations. The rate of replication of exemplar demonstration projects into standard practice is too slow. Reasons may include the lack of understanding of what is possible and the fear of taking a risk, at both policy level and from an end user's perspective. The research sector has a crucial role in dissemination and demonstration of zero carbon solutions, to tangibly influence decision makers in both government and industry.

- We need to change our 'sales pitch' for a zero carbon built environment, from the negative bad news terms of zero, reduce, minimize, and constrain, to the positive good news terms of healthy, productive, clean, feel good, economically vibrant and socially supporting. When the awareness of what is possible is effectively demonstrated to both government policymakers and end users, there is a high level of interest, which stimulates a demand for change.

- A zero carbon built environment will only be achieved in the short timescale left, through a wide-scale bottom-up demand from organizations, communities and the public. The challenge now is to create this demand.

This transition is taking place at a time of chaotic change: the climate is changing; society is changing; our energy systems are changing; our security and health is more at risk than ever from global events. Thermal design of buildings and an understanding of heating, cooling and decarbonization is central to these global and people related issues. We are told there is a climate emergency, and the future environment is one of the most serious issues that humanity has ever faced. It is an enormously exciting time for those of us involved in the built environment to be at the forefront of this challenge.

Chapter 2

2.1 Jones, H., (2007). 'Exploring the Creative Possibilities of Awkward Space in the City', Landscape and Urban Planning An International Journal of Landscape Ecology, Planning and Design Editor-in-Chief: J.E. Rodiek. 12th November 2007. Volume 83, Issue 1. ISSN: 0169-2046. Pages 70–76.

2.2 UN Environment and International Energy Agency (2017): Towards a zero-emission, efficient and resilient buildings and construction sector. Global status report 2017, page 8.

2.3 UN Environment and International Energy Agency (2017): Towards a zero-emission, efficient and resilient buildings and construction sector. Global status report 2017, page 32.

2.4 CLOSING THE GAP BETWEEN DESIGN & AS-BUILT PERFORMANCE Evidence Review Report, March 2014, Zero Carbon Hub.

2.5 World Green Building Council (2013), The Business Case for Green Building, A review of Costs and Cost Benefits for Developers, Investors and Occupants.

2.6 Comprehensive study of building energy renovation activities and the uptake of nearly zero-energy buildings in the EU, Final Report, ISBN 978-92-76-14632-2, European Union, November, 2019.

2.7 Jones, P. J., Lannon, S. C. and Patterson, J. L. (2013). Retrofitting existing housing: how far, how much?. Building Research and Information 41(5), pp. 532–550.

2.8 Jones, P. et al. (2017). Five energy retrofit houses in South Wales. Energy and Buildings 154, pp. 335–342.

2.9 Directive 2010/31/EU of the European Parliament and Council on the energy performance of buildings, Official journal of the European Union, 18.6.2010, L153/13 – L153/35, Article 7.

2.10 Hot Cities: battle-ground for climate change, Cities and Climate Change: Global Report on Human Settlement, UN HABITAT (2011).

2.11 Maria Avgerinou, Paolo Bertoldi and Luca Castellazzi Trends in Data Centre Energy Consumption under the European Code of Conduct for Data Centre Energy Efficiency, Energies 2017, 10(10), 1470.

2.12 Jones, P. (2017). A 'smart' bottom-up whole systems approach to a zero carbon built environment. Building Research & Information 46(5), pp. 566–577.

2.13 Mcdonough W and Braungart M (2013), The Upcycle: Beyond Sustainability—Designing for Abundance 2013.

2.14 Robinson J and Cole R J (2015), Theoretical underpinnings of regenerative sustainability, Building Research & Information, 43:2, 133–143.

2.15 UN Environment and International Energy Agency (2017): Towards a zero-emission, efficient and resilient buildings and construction sector. Global status report 2017, page 14.

2.16 Berardi B, A cross-country comparison of the building energy consumptions and their trends, Resources, Conservation and Recycling, RECYCL-3232, p 12, (2016).

2.17 Energy use in offices, Energy consumption guide 19, Best Practice Programme, 2000

2.18 European Commission: Evaluation of Directive 2010/31/EU on the energy performance of buildings. Commission staff working document. 30.11.2016. SWD(2016) 408 final.

2.19 I A Grant Wilson, *et al.*, Historical daily gas and electrical energy flows through Great Britain's transmission networks and the decarbonisation of domestic heat, Energy Policy 61 (2013) 301–305.

2.20 Wilson, G, Taylor, R and Rowley P, Challenges for the decarbonisation of heat: local gas demand vs electricity supply Winter 2017/2018, UKRERC, https://d2e1qxpsswcpgz.cloudfront.net/uploads/2020/03/ukerc_bn_decarbonisation_heat_local_gas_demand_vs_electical_supply_web.pdf

2.21 UK HOUSING: Fit for the future, COMMITTEE ON CLIMATE CHANGE, FEBRUARY, 2019.

2.22 DIGEST OF UNITED KINGDOM ENERGY STATISTICS 2018, Department for Business, Energy and Industrial Strategy, July 2018.

2.23 Barton, J., Emmanuel-Yusuf, D., Hall, S., Johnson, V., Longhurst, N., O'Grady, A., & Robertson, E. (2015). Distributing power: A transition to a civic energy future. Report of the Realising Transition Pathways, Research Consortium 'Engine Room'.

2.24 Farrow, A., Miller, K.A. & Myllyvirta, L. Toxic air: The price of fossil fuels. Seoul: Greenpeace Southeast Asia. 44 pp. February 2020.

2.25 Sarah Payne and Tony Dutzik, The High Cost of Fossil Fuels Why America Can't Afford to Depend on Dirty Energy, Frontier Group, Emily Figdor Environment America Research & Policy Center, 2009.

2.26 Hidden Costs of Energy: Unpriced Consequences of Energy Production and Use US National Academy of Sciences (2010).

2.27 World Health Organization (WHO). Global Status Report on Road Safety 2018. December 2018. [cited 2019 April 8]. Available from URL: https://www.who.int/violence_injury_prevention/road_safety_status/2018/en/ external icon

2.28 Kovats, R.S., and Osborn, D., (2016) UK Climate Change Risk Assessment Evidence Report: Chapter 5, People and the Built Environment. Contributing authors: Humphrey, K., Thompson, D., Johns, D., Ayres, J., Bates, P., Baylis, M., Bell, S., Church, A., Curtis, S., Davies, M., Depledge, M., Houston, D., Vardoulakis, S., Reynard, N., Watson, J., Mavrogianni, A., Shrubsole, C., Taylor, J., and Whitman, G. Report prepared for the Adaptation Sub-Committee of the Committee on Climate Change, London.

2.29 Gasparrini, A *et al*. Mortality risk attributable to high and low ambient temperature: a multicountry observational study, Lancet, VOLUME 386, ISSUE 9991, P369–375, JULY 25, 2015.

Chapter 3

3.1 Lewis, P T and Alexander D K, 1990. HTB2: A flexible model for dynamic building simulation, Build Environment, 25 (1) 7–16.

3.2 Lomas K J, Martin C, Eppel H, Watson M, and Bloomfield D. Empirical validation of detailed thermal programs using test room data, Final report, vol. 1International Energy Agency (1994).

3.3 Oscar Faber and Partners IEA annex 1 computer modelling of building performance: results and analyses of Avonbank simulation Faber O. and Partner, St Albans (1980).

3.4 Neymark J, Judkoff R, Alexander D, Felsmann C, Strachan P, and Wijsman A IEA BESTEST multi-zone non-airflow in-depth diagnostic cases 12th IBPSA. Sydney, 14–16 November, 2011 (2011).

Chapter 4

4.1   ASHRAE. ANSI/ASHRAE Standard 55-2013, Thermal environmental conditions for human occupancy, American Society of Heating, Refrigeration and Air-conditioning Engineers, Inc., Atlanta, GA, USA, 2013.

4.2   Lisa Heschong, *Thermal Delight in Architecture*, published December 5th 1979 by MIT Press.

4.3   Busch J F. Tale of two populations: thermal comfort in air- conditioned and naturally ventilated offices in Thailand. Energy and Buildings, 1992, 18(3–4): 235–249.

4.4   Ealiwa M A, Taki A H, Howarth A T, *et al.* An investigation into thermal comfort in the summer season of Ghadames, Libya. Building and Environment, 2001, 36 (2): 231–237.

4.5   Fanger, P. (1970). Thermal comfort: Analysis and applications in environmental engineering. Copenhagen: Danish Technical Press.

4.6   ANSI/ASHRAE Standard 55-2017, Thermal Environmental Conditions for Human Occupancy, 2017.

4.7   Jianxiang Huang, Jose GuillermoCedeño-Laurent, John D Spengler, CityComfort+: A simulation-based method for predicting mean radiant temperature in dense urban areas, Building and Environment, Volume 80, October 2014, Pages 84–95.

4.8   Huang, Jianxiang, Chen, Yang, Jones, Phil and Hao, Tongping (2020). Heat stress and outdoor activities in open spaces of public housing estates in Hong Kong: a perspective of the elderly community. Indoor and Built Environment, https://doi.org/10.1177/1420326X20950448

4.9   de Dear, R., & Brager, G. S. (2002). Thermal comfort in naturally ventilated buildings: revisions to ASHRAE Standard 55. Energy and Buildings, 34, 549–561.

4.10   Humphreys, M. and Nicol, J.F., (2000). Outdoor temperature and indoor thermal comfort – raising the precision of the relationship for the 1998 ASHRAE database of field. ASHRAE Transactions 206, 2, 485–492.

4.11   Kenney, W. L. and Munce, T. A. (2003) 'Invited Review: Aging and human temperature regulation', Journal of Applied Physiology.

4.12   Kenny, G. P. *et al.* (2010) 'Heat stress in older individuals and patients with common chronic diseases', CMAJ. doi: 10.1503/cmaj.081050

4.13   J van Hoof *et al.*, (2017) Ten questions concerning thermal comfort and ageing, Building and Environment, volume 120, pages 123–133.

4.14   Kinma, Energy consumption in buildings and female thermal demand Gender differences in thermal comfort and use of thermostats in everyday thermal environments Sami Karjalainen Building and Environment Volume 42, Issue 4, April 2007, Pages 1594–1603.

4.15   Jessica Kuntz Maykot, Ricardo Forgiarini Rupp and Enedir Ghisi, A fields study about gender and temperatures in office buildings, Energy and Buildings 178 (2018) 254–264.

4.16   The World Health Organization defines health, not as the absence of ill-health, but as "a state of complete physical, mental and social well-being"

4.17   https://www.who.int/en/news-room/detail/27-09-2016-who-releases-country-estimates-on-air-pollution-exposure-and-health-impact

4.18   S Wilson, P O'Sullivan, P Jones and A Hedge, Sick Building Syndrome and Environmental Conditions: Case Studies of Nine Offices, published by Building Use Studies Ltd, 1987.

4.19   http://ergo.human.cornell.edu/student-downloads/DEA3500notes/Thermal/thperf-notes.html

4.20   P. Wargocki, D.P. Wyon Providing better thermal and air quality conditions in school classrooms would be cost-effective. Build. Environ., 59 (2013), pp. 581–589.

4.21 Temperature and Office Work Performance, Berkeley Laboratory, https://iaqscience.lbl.gov/performance-temp-office

4.22 Assessing the Value of Green Buildings, Institute for Building Efficiency, Johnson Controls factsheet (2012).

4.23 Davis Langdon, The cost & benefit of achieving Green buildings 2007.

4.24 Loftness, V, Hartkopf, V, Gurtekin, B, Hansen, D, Hitchcock, R. (2003) Linking energy to health and productivity in the built environment. Evaluating the cost-benefits of high performance building and community design for sustainability, health and productivity. Greenbuild Conference.

4.25 Kats G, Leon A, & Adam B (2003) The costs and financial benefits of green buildings, Sustainable Building Task Force.

4.26 Fisk WJ (2000) Health and productivity gains from better indoor environments and their relationship with building energy efficiency, Annu. Rev. Energy Environ., 25 pp. 537–566.

Chapter 5

5.1 Nicola Jones Redrawing the Map: How the World's Climate Zones Are Shifting, Yale Environment 360, published at Yale School of Environment, Yale OCTOBER 23, 2018.

5.2 Mahlstein, Irina, John S. Daniel, and Susan Solomon. "Pace of Shifts in Climate Regions Increases with Global Temperature." Nature Climate Change 3, no. 8 (April 21, 2013): 739–743.

5.3 Bernard Rudofsky, Architecture without Architects.

5.4 Buhagiar, V.M. (2001), *The Refurbishment of historic buildings for re-use: an energy efficient and heritage sensitive approach: generic guidelines with applications for Malta.* Cardiff University, Wales.

5.5 Nan Zhou, Masaru Nishida & Hiroki Kitayama (2002) Study on the Thermal Environment of the YaoDong Dwelling in the Loess Plateau of China, Journal of Asian Architecture and Building Engineering, 1:1, 81–86, DOI: 10.3130/jaabe.1.81

5.6 Usama A. R Al-Bakri, Natural ventilation in traditional courtyard houses in the central region of Saudi Arabia, UWC 1997, PhD, Cardiff University,

5.7 David King Architecture and Astronomy: The ventilators of Medieval Cairo and their Sectrets, Journal of the American Oriental Society 104.1 (1984).

5.8 Jones,P.J. and Yeang,K., The Use of the Wind Wing-Wall as a device for Low-Energy Passive Comfort Cooling in a high-rise Tower in the Warm- Humid Tropics, accepted for presentation at the Conference on Passive Low Energy Architecture (PLEA'99), Brisbane 1999.

5.9 Alexander, D. K., Burnett, J. and Jones, P. J. (2004). Pedestrian wind environment around high-rise residential buildings in Hong Kong. Indoor and Built Environment 4(13), pp. 259–269.

5.10 Huang, J. *et al.* (2020). Urban Building Energy and Climate (UrBEC) simulation: example application and field evaluation in Sai Ying Pun, Hong Kong. Energy and Buildings 207, pp. -., article number: 109580. (10.1016/j.enbuild.2019.109580)

5.11 Weihui Liang, Jianxiang Huang, Phil Jones, Qun Wang, Jian Hang Building and Environment Vol 132, 15 March 2018, Pages 160–169

Chapter 6

6.1 Eshrar Latif, et al, Thermal Insulation Materials for Building Applications, ICE Publishing, 2019.

6.2 Greenspec,Thermal insulation properties Green book? Insulation materials and their thermal properties, https://www.greenspec.co.uk/building-design/insulation-materials-thermal-properties/

6.3 Pavel, C.C., Blagoeva, D.T. (2018) Competitive landscape of the EU's insulation materials industry for energy-efficient buildings, JCR Technical Report, D.T.2018 EUR 28816 EN

6.4 Xing, Ying, Brewer, M., El-Gharabawy, H., Griffith, G. and Jones, P., (2018). Growing and testing mycelium bricks as building insulation materials. IOP Conference Series: Earth and Environmental Science 121, pp. 22032.

6.5 Thermal Bridging Guide, Zero Carbon Hub, http://www.nhbc.co.uk/zmedia/filedownload,65040,en.pdf

6.6 Andew Heath, Greenspec, Unfired clay bricks, https://www.greenspec.co.uk/building-design/unfired-clay-bricks/

6.7 Environmental Advisory Service, Thermal transmission of windows, (3rd edition), Supplement to IHVE Guide (Book A) March 1973.

6.8 Alexandri, E. and Jones, P. J. (2008). Temperature decreases in an urban canyon due to green walls and green roofs in diverse climates. Building and Environment 43(4), pp. 480–493. (10.1016/j.buildenv.2006.10.055)

6.9 Hammond G. P. and Jones C. I. (2006) Embodied energy and carbon footprint database, Department of Mechanical Engineering, University of Bath, United Kingdom.

6.10 Hammond G. P. and Jones C. I., Embodied energy and carbon in construction materials, Proceedings of the Institute of Civol Engineers, Energy 161 May 2008, p 87–98.

6.11 Ding G Development of a multi-criteria approach for the measurement of sustainable performance for the measurement of sustainable performance for built performance (2004) PhD thesis University of Technology, Sydney Australia .

6.12 Aktas and Bilec (2012) Impact of lifetime on US residential building LCA results, The International Journal of Life Cycle Assessment volume 17, pages337–349(2012)

6.13 Koezjakov, A., Urge-Vorsatz, D., Crijns-Graus, W., and van den Broek, M. Energy and Buildings Volume 165, 15 April 2018, Pages 233–245 The relationship between operational energy demand and embodied energy in Dutch residential buildings.

6.14 Ramesh, T., Prakash, R., and Shukla, K.K. Life cycle energy analysis of buildings: An overview, Energy and Buildings, 42 (2010) 1592–1600.

6.15 I. Sartori *, A.G. Hestnes , Energy use in the life cycle of conventional and low-energy buildings: A review article, Energy and Buildings 39 (2007) 249–257.

6.16 Panagiotis Chastas Theodoros Theodosiou, Dimitrios Bikas, Embodied energy in residential buildings - towards the nearly zero energy building: A literature review, Building and Environment, Volume 105, 15 August 2016, Pages 267–282.

Chapter 7

7.1 Environmental design, CIBSE Guide A (2006) Section 4.6.

7.2 Environmental design, CIBSE Guide A (2006) Section 4.7.

Chapter 8

8.1 BEIS Energy Consumption in the UK (2018UK), National Statistics, Table 3.08, July 2018.

8.2 Zimmermann, J. *et al.*, 2012. Household Electricity Survey: A study of domestic electrical product usage. Milton Keynes: Intertek.

8.3 How much electricity does a home use?, OVO Energy, https://www.ovoenergy.com/guides/energy-guides/how-much-electricity-does-a-home-use.html

8.4 Solar Building Study: Spinney Gardens, EPA technical Report (1990) ETSU 1163 /7

8.5 Oliver Ruhnau, Lion Hirth and Aaron Praktiknjo, Times series of heat demand and heat pump efficiency for energy system modelling, Scientific Data, (2019) 6:189.

8.6 Markusson C, Efficiency of building related pump and fan operation: Application and system solutions, PhD, Chalmers University of Technology, Sweden, 2011.

8.7 Education and Skills Funding Agency, Building Bulletin 101, Guidelines on ventilation, thermal comfort and indoor air quality in school, Version 1, August 2018.

8.8 Richard F. Smith and Shaun Killa, Bahrain World Trade Center: The first large-scale integration of wind turbines in a building, the structural design of tall and special buildings, *Struct. Design Tall Spec. Build.* **16**, 429–439 (2007).

Chapter 9

9.1 Office of Energy Efficiency and Renewable Energy, US Department of Energy

9.2 Stern, N. H. (2006). The Economics of Climate Change: The Stern Review. London: HM Treasury.

9.3 RIBA Journal September 1972 The President introduces his long life / loose fit / low energy study. 1972 the Welsh architect and president of the Royal Institute of British Architects (RIBA), Sir Alex Gordon, described good architecture as buildings that exhibit long life, loose fit and low energy.

9.4 Solar Building Study: Spinney Gardens, EPA technical Report (1990) ETSU 1163 /7

9.5 Solar Building Study: Copper Beech House, EPA technical Report (1990) ETSU 1163 /2

9.6 Solar Building Study: St Michael's Close, EPA technical Report (1990) ETSU 1163 /9

9.7 Solar Building Study: Solar Cottage, EPA technical Report (1990) ETSU 1163 /5

9.8 Jones, P.J., and Whittle, G.E., Air Flow Modelling of the Gateway II Atrium Building, ETSU S 1323 (1992)

9.9 Thomas Herzog Design Centre Linz, published by Gerd Hatje 1994, ISBN 3-7757-0524-4.

9.10 Eteghad A.N., *et al.*, Reinterpretation of Energy Efficiency in Thomas Herzog's Architecture, January 2014, DOI: 10.15640/jea.v2n2a8, Project: Enviromental History of the Architecture.

9.11 Thiomas Herzog, Architecture and Technology, Prestel Verlag, 2001, ISBN 3-7913-2577-9.

9.12 Thomas Herzog Sustainable Height, Deutche Messe AG Hannover, Administration Building, EXPO 2000.

9.13 Jones P. J. and Kopitsis K., The building physics design of the EMPA "Forum Chriesbach" low carbon office, CLIMA2005 Congress, pages 258–264 (Switzerland), (2005).

9.14 Yangang Xing, Phil Jones and Iain Donnison, Characterisation of Nature-Based Solutions for the Built Environment, Sustainability 2017, 9, 149

9.15 The Sun Ship: An ecological model for the future, Brochure_The_Sun_Ship, www.solarsiedlung.de

9.16 Forster, Wayne Peter and Jones, Phillip John 2000. Studies in the design of the low energy speculative factory. Presented at: TIA 2000: Third International Conference, Oxford, UK, 9–12 July 2000. Published in: Roaf, Susan, Sala, Marco and Bairstow, Andrew eds.

9.17 Jones, P. *et al.* (2020). Energy-positive house: performance assessment through simulation and measurement. Energies13 (18), article number: 4705. (10.3390/en13184705)

9.18 Jones P (ed), LCRI 2015, an overview of LCRI research 2008 to 2015, 57 pages, published by LCRI.

9.19 Jones, P. *et al.* (2017). Five energy retrofit houses in South Wales. Energy and Buildings 154, pp. 335–342.

THIS BOOK IS LARGELY BASED ON SOME FOUR decades of my own experiences as a building physicist, teacher and researcher at the Welsh School of Architecture; as well as my input into a range of real design projects, and my activities on professional and government bodies.

The book is well illustrated, and I thank the publishers, Crowood, for the opportunity to addresses the topic with an abundance of photographs and graphic images. I am also grateful to those who have supplied images that were not my own.

Throughout my career I have had the privilege to work with, and learn from, some of the best people in the subject area. At the Welsh School of Architecture, Cardiff University, I thank colleagues from over the years, including: Don Alexander, Ester Comas Bassas, Dave Bull, Phil Bowen, Hu Du, Wayne Forster, Shan Shan Hou, Huw Jenkins, Simon Lanon, Xiaojun Li, Phil McGeevor, Pat O'Sullivan, Malcolm Parry, Jo Patterson, Emmanouil Perisoglou, Greg Powell, Chris Tweed, Nigel Vaughan, and all my past and present PhD students. I am also grateful to have worked on a number of large projects and networks, within the UK and abroad, which have provided me with a global perspective on the subject area. I recently served as Distinguished Visiting Professor at Hong Kong University, and give thanks to Dean Chris Webster and Jianxiang Huang for the opportunity to participate in their High Density Cities Laboratory research. Thanks also for similar experiences, over the years, working with staff and students at the universities in Beijing, Tianjin, Shanghai, Chongqing, Xi'an, Malaysia, and the British University in Dubai.

I am grateful for the many opportunities I have had to apply my research and teaching in practice. This includes working with Keith Clark and Richard Smith (Atkins), Wayne Forster (Design Research Unit, Welsh School of Architecture), Thomas Herzog (Herzog and Partner, Munich), Denis Kopitsis (Kopitsis Bauphysik, Switzerland), Phil Roberts (Design Consultant), Alan Short (Architect), Ken Yeang (T.R. Hamzah and Yeang, Kuala Lumpur) and all my colleagues at Warm Wales Ltd. Also, thanks to the Welsh Government for the opportunity to chair the devolved Building Regulation Advisory Committee for Wales (BRACW).

Of course, I could not have indulged myself in my work and in writing this book without the support of my family, my wife, Jane, my children, Hannah and William, and my mother, Marjory.